Disaster Security

This book is for a broad audience of practitioners, policy makers, scholars, and anyone interested in scenarios, simulations, and disaster planning. Readers are led through various planning scenarios that have been developed over several years under the auspices of the US Department of Energy and the US Air Force, and through continued work at GlobalInt LLC. These scenarios present different security challenges and their potential cascading impacts on global systems – from the melting of glaciers in the Andes to hurricanes in New York and Hawaii and on to hybrid disasters, cyberoperations, and geoengineering. The book provides a concise and up-to-date overview of the lessons learned, with a focus on innovative solutions to the world's pressing energy and environmental security challenges.

CHAD M. BRIGGS is Strategy Director at GlobalInt LLC and global security lecturer at Johns Hopkins University. He has been a Fulbright professor in Budapest and Berlin; a senior advisor to the US Department of Energy; and Minerva Chair and Professor of Energy and Environmental Security at the Air University of the US Air Force at Maxwell Air Force Base. Dr. Briggs specializes in the use of scientific information in environmental and security policy. In recent years, he has been a defense and security consultant in Kosovo, and he cooperates with the Ukrainian Army on hybrid war strategies.

MIRIAM MATEJOVA is an economic advisor at Canada's Ministry of Environment. She holds a PhD in Political Science from the University of British Columbia. She is a Vanier Scholar, Killam Laureate, Liu Scholar, and previously Kovler Fellow at the John F. Kennedy Presidential Library. She is a recipient of numerous awards for research and leadership and the editor of *Wherever I Find Myself*, an anthology that was long-listed for the 2018 George Ryga Award. Matejova has worked in academia, policy making, and the nonprofit sector. She has published articles on foreign intelligence, international conflict management, energy and environmental security, and global environmental activism.

"Briggs and Matejova clearly demonstrate that complex scenario planning and simulations, familiar tools for the security community, provide real value for better understanding and preparing for environment and energy disasters. In *Disaster Security*, the authors draw upon their extensive experience in this field to make clear the utility, and one might even say necessity, for both security and environment communities to pursue these tools jointly to reap mutual benefits."

— *Geoff Dabelko, Ohio University*

"The nature of the emerging security risks from climate change and environment is complex. The authors paint a clear picture of how grave and vulnerable the situation is and also show how best to use some of the existing planning tools of the military to perform strategic foresight planning to meet the challenge. Drawing on their experience of leading energy and environmental security teams in US government, they explain how correct advance forecasting can mitigate disaster risk."

— *Major General Muniruzzaman, Bangladesh Institute of Peace and Security Studies*

"Simply put, there is no security without climate security. We all need to prepare for future climate disasters—from deadly heat waves and raging wildfires to violent storms. In this fascinating study, Chad Briggs and Miriam Matejova reveal how military and intelligence communities have pioneered catastrophic risk assessment. *Disaster Security* is a must read for anyone interested in finding ways to prepare for the growing security risks posed by climate change."

— *Alice Hill, Stanford University*

"Briggs and Matejova provide a concise and accessible guide to how disaster scenarios and wargaming can improve management of climate risks and other large-scale environmental risks, as well as some of the common pitfalls of these approaches."

— *Robert Kopp, Rutgers University*

"This book is essential reading for all disaster planning, and climate and energy security practitioners who should be integrating wargaming and scenario development into their work. The authors share their real-world experience helping the inner sanctum of government decision makers make better decisions about preparing for today's most pressing security challenges, from cyber to climate risks."

— *Sherri Goodman, Woodrow Wilson International Center for Scholars*

Disaster Security

Using Intelligence and Military Planning for Energy and Environmental Risks

CHAD M. BRIGGS
Johns Hopkins University
MIRIAM MATEJOVA
University of British Columbia, Vancouver

CAMBRIDGE
UNIVERSITY PRESS

CAMBRIDGE
UNIVERSITY PRESS

University Printing House, Cambridge CB2 8BS, United Kingdom

One Liberty Plaza, 20th Floor, New York, NY 10006, USA

477 Williamstown Road, Port Melbourne, VIC 3207, Australia

314–321, 3rd Floor, Plot 3, Splendor Forum, Jasola District Centre,
New Delhi – 110025, India

79 Anson Road, #06–04/06, Singapore 079906

Cambridge University Press is part of the University of Cambridge.

It furthers the University's mission by disseminating knowledge in the pursuit of
education, learning, and research at the highest international levels of excellence.

www.cambridge.org
Information on this title: www.cambridge.org/9781108472357
DOI: 10.1017/9781108560023

First published 2019

Printed and bound in Great Britain by Clays Ltd, Elcograf S.p.A.

A catalogue record for this publication is available from the British Library.

Library of Congress Cataloging-in-Publication Data
Names: Briggs, Chad M., 1972– author. | Matejova, Miriam, author.
Title: Disaster security : using intelligence and military planning for energy and
environmental risks / Chad M. Briggs, Johns Hopkins University; Miriam Matejova,
University of British Columbia, Vancouver.
Description: Cambridge, United Kingdom ; New York, NY, USA : Cambridge University
Press, 2019. | Includes bibliographical references.
Identifiers: LCCN 2018049864| ISBN 9781108472357 (hardback : alk. paper) | ISBN
9781108459372 (paperback)
Subjects: LCSH: Emergency management – Planning. | Energy security – Planning. |
Environmental management – Planning. | Risk management.
Classification: LCC HV551.2 .B75 2019 | DDC 363.34/6–dc23
LC record available at https://lccn.loc.gov/2018049864

ISBN 978-1-108-47235-7 Hardback
ISBN 978-1-108-45937-2 Paperback

To the many unnamed victims of disasters and conflict
around the world

Contents

Preface

In November 2016, the Netherlands Foreign Ministry sponsored a Planetary Security Conference in The Hague. It brought together a relatively small collection of environmental security experts to help assess the increasing risks from climate change. One session, organized by the Skoll Global Threats Fund and located in a back room, discussed intelligence methods to deal with uncertain futures. Although the topic is often only of niche interest even within environmental security, this time the room was packed to overflowing with people from across North America and Europe. Many were motivated in the wake of the US presidential election to learn how to deal with uncertain futures and how to grapple with what could seem like overwhelming risks. With the USA poised to step back from the UN Paris Accords on climate change, what would happen in the future? How could governments plan when, not only were hazards worsening, but the world was becoming more fragmented, more conflictual, and the former key player in climate security was now about to shift policies drastically?

This book was partly motivated by colleagues who asked for a more complete story about the approaches to climate security, learned over the past ten years inside certain agencies that are often opaque. While numerous media stories over the years had commented on the US military's and intelligence agencies' interest in climate change and increasing risks from disasters, often these stories only described the summary conclusions. Offices and programs dedicated to assessing climate change, energy security, and environmental security had grown since the mid-2000s (notably, this began before the 2008 US election), but beginning in 2017, the programs and their data began to disappear. The environmental pressures did not. A wave of migrants and refugees was entering southern Europe, the Lake Chad region of Africa was torn by drought and terrorism, record wildfires burned from California to

British Columbia and Alaska, and Hurricanes Harvey, Irma, and Maria hit the USA. By August 2018, the death toll from Hurricane Maria alone stood at just under three thousand, making it one of the worst disasters in US history.

The work described in this book only covers a small selection of the military and intelligence efforts to assess energy and environmental security (EES) and disaster risks in recent years. Much of that work will likely remain classified. Certain projects, however, were intentionally kept unclassified in order to involve outside experts and the public and to ensure that research could be quickly disseminated. One of those projects, which began in the US Department of Energy in 2008, was tasked with determining the security risks of abrupt climate change. The project was transferred to the US Department of Defense under the Minerva Initiative in 2010. While only part of a larger picture, the lessons from the climate security research may provide some guidance on how to deal with an increasingly uncertain and hazardous world.

On a personal level, this work began in the 1990s with the earlier wave of environmental security research. In 1995, during my master's program, I wrote a paper that called for more attention to complexity and working across disciplines. I argued that political experts had failed to predict the fall of the Berlin Wall in large part because they simplified too much. Yet, it is far easier to complain about simplification than to tackle complexity. I spent most of my grad school and early faculty years researching risk and the use and communication of scientific data, struggling with how to rework security policies. I was greatly assisted by geographers (especially my wife, Tracy) and the experts in the field of public health. It was the work of conducting postconflict vulnerability assessments in Bosnia-Herzegovina and Serbia that led me to the US Department of Energy and later to the US Air Force.

I am in the debt of the many who taught and influenced me along the way, and those who then worked collaboratively on these EES and disaster security assessments. From Mark Bassin's course on environmental risks in the former Soviet Union while I was an undergraduate student at UW-Madison to my current colleagues in Kosovo and Ukraine, it has been difficult at times not to be overwhelmed with all the information and knowledge available.

While spouses are usually referred to last in acknowledgments, in this case, Tracy Briggs was central to all the work described in this book. We met in an environmental security seminar taught at Carleton University in 1996, and we have influenced each other's work ever since. Although Tracy was not formally involved with the Department of Energy between 2008 and 2010, her work with the Swedish Defence Research Agency (FOI) starting in 2009 was the basis for what became Global Interconnections LLC (GlobalInt) the following year, when she was picked up by the Air Force to be the deputy Minerva chair. We worked together 24/7 for two and a half years, which is a testament to her expertise – and says many positive things about our marriage.

The work described here was a large, collective effort, and the editorial "we" used throughout is meant to refer to the efforts of team members, directors, and the various experts who helped throughout the years. For early influence on risk, complexity, and environmental security, I thank Luke Ashworth, Simon Dalby, Joan DeBardeleben, David Tarr, Kristin Shrader-Frechette, Geoff Dabelko, Betsy Hartmann, and Sharon Sutherland. The US Fulbright program and its commissions in Hungary, Germany, and Belgium helped spark some of this work, and the Regional Environmental Center (REC) in Hungary, and Stephen Stec in particular, helped lead me to my introduction to the US Department of Energy. My colleagues at the Institute for Environmental Security in The Hague were also instrumental, particularly Ron Kingham.

At the Department of Energy, my thanks go most to Carol Dumaine but also to the formal team, including Anita Street, Dan Milstein, Larry Lanes, and others, and the wider network with Cleo Paskal, Jennifer Gonzalez, David Robson, Sean Costigan, and those who continued to support us even after the program was disbanded in spring 2010. I owe a great deal to my coauthors during that time, who, besides Tracy Briggs and Miriam Matejova, include Inka Weissbecker, Stacy VanDeveer, Jennifer Bath, Lucy Anderson, Moneeza Walji, Shannon O'Lear, and COL (ret) Mike Denning.

At the Air Force, the program would not have been possible without COL (ret) Dan Henk, with Robert Sands and the rest of the Air War College and Spaatz Center. From General Dynamics IT (GDIT), we thank LTC (ret) Blair Ellis, LTC (ret) Katie Veazie, and COL (ret) Robyn Read, who provided the bulk of support for the USAF Minerva work at Air University. At the Department of Defense was Erin Fitzgerald, CDR (ret) Esther McClure, Dan Chiu, Sharon Burke, Amanda Dory, and Rachel Posner-Ross. From the wider defense field, we owe thanks to Sherri Goodman, RADM (ret) Neil Morisetti, MGEN (ret) A. G. Muniruzzaman, BGEN (ret) Chris King, COL Michaelle Munger, Cheryl Rosenblum, and RADM (ret) David Titley. We also remember LTC (ret) Kent Butts and MAJ Shannon Beebe, both of whom are no longer with us and who left a critical gap in US military expertise in environmental security and Africa.

Many thanks must also go to the various people who volunteered to work as facilitators during the various scenario creation workshops from 2011 to 2014, including Miriam Matejova, Laura Deutsch, Lauren Herzer-Risi, Louise Shaxson, Alun Rhydderch, Chiara de Franco, Andrew Holland, Jennifer McKee, Rebecca Ng, COL Mark Read, Kevin Kelly, Robert Weiss, and Kate

Diamond. And although we cannot list everyone, many thanks as well to the dozens of people who participated in the workshops and follow-up activities and to the hosts of the various events (NATO Headquarters, University College London, International Polar Year, Woodrow Wilson Center, Johns Hopkins University, the University of Hawaii, Air University, Virginia Tech University, National Council for Science and Environment, and International Institute for Strategic Studies).

In Ukraine, our thanks to Tatyana Malyarenko, whose Jean Monnet project helped fund earlier meetings and cooperation, and thanks to my coauthors MGEN Yuri Danyk and Tamara Maliarchuk, as well as others who helped instruct me on the Ukrainian security environment and Russian language, such as Alexander Benz, David Galbreath, Olga Danchenko, and Stefan Wolff. Other countries deserving thanks include Sweden (FOI, and particularly Annica Waleji and Birgitta Liljedahl), Australia (David Connery and Sarah Logan), Singapore, Iraq, Canada (Conference of Defence Associations), and the UK.

A special note should be made for Victoria Herrmann, whom I first knew as a first-year undergraduate but who then became an expert herself in climate security, including as a Fulbright scholar at Carleton University, a Gates scholar at Cambridge, and president of the Arctic Institute in Washington, DC.

Miriam Matejova I met early during the Air Force project, and she has remained a valuable and extremely intelligent colleague and coauthor. Her research at the University of British Columbia and Oxford University contributed greatly to the book, and I was very fortunate to have her as a coauthor.

We must also thank Matt Lloyd and Zoë Pruce at Cambridge University Press for their professionalism and encouragement as well as the reviewers of the original proposal.

A final thanks to our parents, who often didn't know where Tracy and I were or what we were doing – and maybe still aren't completely sure.

Chad Briggs
August 2018
Prishtina, Kosovo

I met Chad at an intelligence conference in Wales, UK, more than seven years ago. I was a graduate student at Carleton University in Ottawa, researching issues in international peacebuilding and foreign intelligence. Shortly after the conference, I became involved in the energy and environmental security work, first as a volunteer with the USAF Minerva Project and later as a doctoral student at the University of British Columbia. Over the years, Chad and I have collaborated on several papers and facilitated workshops across the world. For a short while, we both called Ottawa home. There we would meet at an obscure café called Mad Hatter, where I drank oversized lattes after work (at the time, I was an economist at Canada's Ministry of Environment) and where we talked about anything from travel plans to disaster hotspots to apocalyptic futures. My academic career would eventually lead me to the University of Oxford, where I wrote parts of this book, pondering the nature of risk, disasters, and resilience. Chad and Tracy Briggs have introduced me to ideas that have fundamentally shaped my view of the world. Our work is not about predicting the future. It is about adapting, learning to think about where we want to go, acknowledging that we cannot have a perfect view of any path, and accepting that we may end up somewhere else. Knowing how to walk that path nonetheless is what our work – and this book – calls for.

Miriam Matejova
August 2018
Vancouver, BC, Canada

1

Toward Disaster Security

August 2005 began with news headlines of continued violence in the Middle East, US casualties mounting in Iraq, and the dramatic rescue of Russian sailors from the stricken submarine in the Pacific Ocean. The summer had been fixated on violent conflict, from the July bombings in London and Cairo to nuclear arms talks with North Korea. What most Americans remember about that summer, however, were the images from late August of Hurricane Katrina and its aftermath in New Orleans and nearby regions. The news reports on CNN International showed a United States where flooding had destroyed a large part of an iconic city, where thousands of people were trapped in a large sports stadium, and where bodies were floating in the muddy floodwaters.[1] The contrasts with the news reports coming from Iraq could not be more striking, and it soon became evident that there was a connection between the domestic disaster in the United States and the country's overseas military involvement. Many of the National Guard troops and their helicopters were not available for rescue and disaster relief, as they had been deployed to Iraq and Afghanistan.

The US invasion of Afghanistan in 2001 was widely supported both domestically and internationally. While the 2003 invasion of Iraq was far less popular, it was Hurricane Katrina that most severely undercut confidence in the administration of President George W. Bush. Whose security was being protected? Were the Americans prepared for more such disasters, and would those worsen in the future? Warnings concerning climate change and global warming had been officially discussed since the 1980s, but there was a growing sense in

---

[1] I (Briggs) was in Budapest, Hungary, that year with my wife, Tracy, while Miriam Matejova was living a short distance away in Bratislava, Slovakia. We would not actually meet until six years later, in Wales and then Ottawa. The images of Hurricane Katrina that Tracy and I saw in 2005 were pivotal in motivating a shift in our work from risk governance and management to environmental security.

some communities that climate-related hazards would grow worse. It was also not only the human suffering in cities like New Orleans that was noticeable. In the first days of Hurricane Katrina, gasoline prices in the United States skyrocketed as oil production and processing operations in the Gulf Coast region were interrupted or shut down.[2] In the aftermath of the storm, it became evident that the disaster risks had been known. The US Army Corps of Engineers had warned about possible flooding in the lower wards of New Orleans, climate scientists had warned about potential strengthening of tropical storms from warmer waters, and ecologists and geologists had warned about the impacts of human development on potential tidal surge in the Mississippi Gulf region. Yet, much like what was noted in the conclusions of the 9/11 Commission Report (released in 2004), the US government had failed to "connect the dots" – it had not tied together disparate (and sometimes weak) signals, it had relied on historical data that ignored both environmental and human changes, and it had failed to plan for the necessary disaster mitigation and response.[3] Environmental changes had been accelerating, and we seemed to be unprepared for what the future would look like.

Concerns over environmental changes have been growing in both scholarly and policy circles. Severe consequences of environmental problems have been "depicted as comparable to or even greater than those of military conflict."[4] An increasing number of natural disasters are transboundary issues, affecting more than one country simultaneously and transcending the boundaries of administrative levels. Many of them have been becoming more frequent and more severe due to climate change, which is expected to exacerbate heat waves, droughts, floods, cyclones, and tropical as well as polar storms. Negative health impacts, food insecurity, loss of assets, and human casualties are all likely consequences of these environmental events that are now increasingly regarded as existential risks.

Historically, human societies have been dependent on their ability to predict when certain environmental conditions occur, from the timing of food harvests and ice fishing to choosing the location and type of dwellings. However, now that extreme weather and climate are becoming more of the norm, our latent

---

[2] Gene Laverty, "Oil, Gas May Soar as Storm Shuts US Gulf Production," *Bloomberg*, August 28, 2005.

[3] Tom Davis, "Select Bipartisan Committee to Investigate the Preparation for and Response to Hurricane Katrina," Final Report, US House of Representatives, February 15, 2006; Robert R. M. Verchick, "Risk, Fairness, and the Geography of Disaster," *Issues in Legal Scholarship* 6, No. 3 (2007): 1–33.

[4] Mutiah Alagappa, "Rethinking Security: A Critical Review and Appraisal of the Debate," in *Asian Security Practice: Material and Ideational Influences*, ed. Mutiah Alagappa (Palo Alto, CA: Stanford University Press, 1998), 44.

predictive abilities are unable to cope with new and changing risks. The predominant approaches in disaster risk assessment force planners to rely heavily on available data and historical precedence. Yet, some combinations of factors are impossible to calculate probabilistically.[5] Because planners tend to avoid venturing into the realm of uncertainty caused by lack of historical precedence, they limit disaster planning to simplified models and thus consideration of fewer hazards. The resulting uncertainty can lead to paralysis in adapting to new conditions. In this book, we present some practical solutions to this and other problems in disaster risk assessment.

Our intention is not to provide a template for predicting disasters but to explain how lessons from the intelligence and military communities can help in preparing for them. Of course, many lessons have already been learned from the past, such as in contingency planning and disaster response, but today many countries face ever-increasing and accelerating pressures due to shifts in demographics, resource use, and technology as well as climate change. In light of these new challenges, the purpose of this book is threefold: (1) to identify weaknesses of traditional risk assessment approaches as they apply to extreme environmental events and complex disasters, (2) to explain one of the new approaches – complex scenario planning – in order to illuminate new energy and environmental security risks and improve our understanding of disasters and security, and (3) to discuss the lessons learned from several years of developing and applying scenario planning in order to inform and improve current disaster planning practices.

In the following chapters, we explain the entire process of developing and applying planning scenarios for energy and environmental risks, from open-source collection of emerging scientific data and construction of new scenarios to their application in policy and military planning (both strategic and operational) and use in military training. As the breadth of potential topics for energy and environment is exceedingly vast, a central focus of the book is on climate change–related risks as a background driver of change, with water as the other defining focus to tie together disparate issues related to disaster risks. Drawing on the experiences of the US military and intelligence sectors, this book is intended to provide a solid overview of the lessons learned on energy and environmental security (EES) from 2007 to the present. Major disasters can be assessed using relatively modest means, allowing planners and policy makers to prepare for highly uncertain future events. The book addresses concepts such

---

[5] See, e.g., US Department of Homeland Security (DHS), "The Strategic National Risk Assessment in Support of PPD 8: A Comprehensive Risk-Based Approach toward a Secure and Resilient Nation," December 2011, www.dhs.gov/xlibrary/assets/rma-strategic-national-risk-assessment-ppd8.pdf.

as scenario planning, integrating scientific data into risk assessments as well as ways to deal with uncertainty and risk.

This chapter provides some necessary background to EES literature and concepts. Through historical examples, we discuss long-standing practical understandings of energy and environmental security (linked predominantly to military considerations) as well as the prevailing academic research and assumptions behind military and intelligence programs in the same field. Specifically, we focus on the US military perspective and recent programs developed in response to changing environmental conditions.

Approaches to Energy and Environmental Security

Our work originates in the academic fields of geography and political science, particularly the translation of scientific data into policy decisions. We draw on critical geography and the work of scholars, such as Simon Dalby, who recognize the limitations in using traditional international relations concepts to describe the nature of environmental security risks. Our focus on science-policy interactions has been inspired by scholars, such as Kristin Shrader-Frechette, who call attention to the nature of scientific uncertainty and the related challenges faced by policy makers.

Some of our approaches have been addressed in different publications. For example, Ron Suskind's *The Way of the World* (2008) described the new post-9/11 security challenges faced in Washington, DC, noting that the Director of Intelligence and Counterintelligence at the US Department of Energy, Rolf Mowatt-Larssen, directed some funding toward nontraditional risks in the second half of the 2000s.[6] In 2007, despite political opposition, the CNA Corporation (namely, Sherri Goodman) published a national security report that emphasized the multidimensional impacts of climate change.[7] More recently, groups such as the Center for Climate and Security have emphasized the military's interest in climate-related security risks.[8] None of these publications, however, has gone into detail into how and why the military and intelligence communities have created planning scenarios for issues like abrupt climate change. The media portrayal of these efforts (as well as much of academic research) have focused on climate change sparking conflict. Yet,

---

[6] Ron Suskind, *The Way of the World: A Story of Truth and Hope in an Age of Extremism* (New York: HarperCollins, 2008).

[7] The CNA Corporation, *National Security and the Threat of Climate Change* (Alexandria, VA: The CNA Corporation, 2007).

[8] See their reports at https://climateandsecurity.org/reports/.

the real motivations and planning scenarios are much more nuanced and, in many cases, focus on risks other than military conflict.

The broader academic literature on risk assessment approaches is substantial, particularly with respect to environmental issues.[9] However, complex risks, such as those stemming from environmental disasters, are seldom addressed in relation to security, international affairs, and energy politics. A general shortcoming of the prevailing literature is the reliance on established methodologies for assessing disasters (e.g., extrapolation of probability from historic events), which is often an obstacle to envisioning unique events and risks. Few publications deal with both energy and environment comprehensively, with, perhaps, the exception of Michael Klare's book on resource wars.[10] Yet, Klare's work falls into a larger literature of environmental security that dates to Homer-Dixon's work in the 1990s, premised on showing how resource scarcities lead to conflict. Similar work has been done by Andrew Price-Smith on disease in Africa, the University of Texas consortium on climate change in Africa, and the Strauss Center at the University of Texas.[11] Our approach is quite different, both in specifically not focusing on conflict as an end point[12] and in sidestepping the academic science pressure to show causal links between variables. We also shift emphasis from the world's developing regions to industrialized areas and their vulnerabilities to energy and environmental security risks.

Our backgrounds draw from the lessons of the academic study of environmental security, mixed with energy security, intelligence studies, and military planning. Traditionally, these have not been easy mixes. While in the post–World War II period, energy and environmental security have been viewed by both scholars and practitioners as more or less separate concepts, we maintain not only that the energy and environmental systems are inherently linked but also that the security risks associated with them cannot be adequately addressed without seeing them as such.

---

[9] See the Routledge and Earthscan series, including authors and editors such as Ragnar Lofstedt and Paul Slovic.

[10] Michael Klare, *Resource Wars: The New Landscape of Global Conflict* (New York: Henry Holt, 2002).

[11] Andrew Price-Smith, *Contagion and Chaos: Disease, Ecology, and National Security in the Era of Globalization* (Cambridge, MA: MIT Press, 2009); Idean Salehyana and Cullen S. Hendrix, "Climate Shocks and Political Violence," *Global Environmental Change* 28 (2014): 239–50. See also Strauss Center's research on Climate Change and African Political Stability available at www.strausscenter.org/ccaps/.

[12] There is an environmental peacemaking literature, developed partly in opposition to the scarcity-conflict theses, which also addresses topics such as disaster diplomacy (Ilan Kelman, Michael Renner), peace parks (Geoffrey Dabelko), and international cooperation (Ken Conca).

Energy and Environmental Security: The Past, the Present, and the Future

Security, in its simplest meaning, refers to the basic need of human societies for protection from danger. On the international stage, the term has long been understood as security for states, principally in military terms.[13] However, since the 1970s, the concept has undergone dramatic redefinitions, moved away from a narrow military focus, and eventually split into two distinct understandings of security: security for states and security for people (i.e., human security).[14] Different forms of security have thus revolved around claims about referent objects (i.e., an object that is viewed as existentially threatened and has legitimate claim to survival). While state security focuses on the concept of sovereignty, human security is organized around the concept of human life and dignity.[15] The shift from the traditional military dimension of security to nontraditional risks is most prominently captured in the theory of securitization developed by the Copenhagen School and its critics.[16] These scholars consider environmental security as one of the five general areas of nontraditional security where the focus changes from state sovereignty as the referent object to human dimensions, and specifically as they relate to the environment and environmental risks.[17]

Energy security has been viewed differently – originally in terms of disruptions to oil supply – due either to political decisions or to uncontrollable events affecting oil production or transport facilities.[18] Recently, the concept has moved away from a single interpretation and became somewhat blurred, including anything from attempts for energy independence to protection of energy infrastructure to energy efficiency and conservation.[19] Europe, for

---

[13] See Charles Tilly, "War Making and State Making as Organized Crime," in *Bringing the State Back In*, ed. Peter Evans, Dietrich Rueschemeyer, and Theda Skocpol (Cambridge, UK: Cambridge University Press, 1985), 169–91; Stephen M. Walt, "The Renaissance of Security Studies," *International Studies Quarterly* 35, No. 2 (1991): 211–39.

[14] Barry Buzan, "Rethinking Security after the Cold War," *Cooperation and Conflict* 32, No. 1 (1997): 5–28; Richard Ullman, "Redefining Security," *International Security* 8, No. 1 (Summer 1983): 129–53. See also Astri Suhrke, "Human Security and the Interests of States," *Security Dialogue* 30, No. 3 (1999): 265–76; Roland Paris, "Human Security: Paradigm Shift or Hot Air?," *International Security* 26, No. 2 (2001): 87–102.

[15] Scott Watson, "The 'Human' as Referent Object? Humanitarianism as Securitization," *Security Dialogue* 42, No. 1 (2011): 5.

[16] See Shahar Hameiri and Lee Jones, "The Politics and Governance of Non-Traditional Security," *International Studies Quarterly*, No. 1 (2012): 3.

[17] Mely Caballero-Anthony and Ralf Emmers, "The Dynamics of Securitization in Asia," in *Studying Non-Traditional Security in Asia: Issues and Trends*, ed. R. Emmers, M. Caballero-Anthony, and A. Acharya (Singapore: Marshall-Cavendish Academic, 2006).

[18] David Robinson, "Energy Security Revisited," *Oxford Energy Forum*, No. 100 (May 2015): 39–42.

[19] Christian Winzer, "Conceptualizing Energy Security," *Energy Policy* 46 (2012): 36–48.

example, is facing energy security risks due to its dependence on Russia's natural gas, while Russia (as well as other energy-exporting countries) views energy security in terms of security of demand.[20] Taking these differences into consideration, Christian Winzer offers a workable definition of energy security, viewing it as "the absence of, protection from or adaptability to threats that are caused by or have an impact on the energy supply chain."[21] Such risks, of course, may stem from environmental hazards. As seen in the historical examples below, environmental and energy security considerations are closely linked, and the recent separation of the two concepts is rather artificial.

Energy and Environmental Security in the Nineteenth and Early Twentieth Centuries

Prior to the oil shocks of the 1970s, energy considerations were inextricably linked to the natural environment in military and security planning, in large part because of the role of food. For example, during the Napoleonic wars of the early nineteenth century, all transport of cargo, food, artillery, and ammunition relied on animals, which themselves required an extensive food train. Depending on distance, for example, if six oxen were needed to transport one artillery piece, they would need food that itself required eight horses to transport, while the horses themselves would require an additional four horses to transport their own food, and so on. In many ways, the same logistical trains still exist today, and transporting either a liter of water or a gallon of aviation fuel to a forward operating base in Afghanistan can be both enormously expensive and complex. These modern logistical challenges are still often seen as removed from most environmental conditions. In earlier times, armies had to be acutely aware of the availability of food and water as they operated on campaigns.

During the Peninsular Wars between France and Britain in Spain and Portugal in the early 1800s, attention to logistics in the natural environment may have been decisive in the outcome of the conflict. The British, investing in complex and expensive logistical support under General Arthur Wellesley (later known as the Duke of Wellington), were careful to import necessary equipment and materiel, while reimbursing locals for any food bought or used. This helped engender support among locals both in the areas in which conflict was occurring and in the rear areas along the coasts. The French, in contrast, directed their troops largely to live off the land, taking whatever food and

---

[20] Daniel Yergin, "Ensuring Energy Security," *Foreign Affairs* 85, No. 2 (2006): 71.
[21] Winzer, 41.

materiel they deemed useful or necessary. This practice was dangerous during times when food was not readily available, and it quickly bred resentment among locals whose livelihoods or savings were destroyed. The modern term *guerilla*, referring to an insurgent or freedom fighter, was derived from Spanish partisans fighting against the French forces. These rearguard actions were highly detrimental to French operations.

Other examples are perhaps even more obvious, such as Napoleon's ill-fated invasion of Russia during the winter of 1812–13. Like the German Wehrmacht more than a century later, severe cold in the winter conditions of Russia left armies ill prepared and unable to operate. Some argue that an outbreak of the disease typhus was also instrumental in ravaging Napoleonic forces.

Whatever the specific causes, these campaigns are well remembered as being enormously harmed by adverse environmental conditions. Although cold weather is perhaps more easily remembered and better depicted in visualizations of the conflict, for armies, diseases have always been a constant concern factor – from the effects of malaria on earlier Crusaders in the Middle East and later colonial armies in Africa and Asia to the ravaging effects of yellow fever on British forces in the Caribbean. It is little coincidence that some of the most preeminent institutes for researching tropical disease medicine are located in the former colonial capitals of London, Paris, Brussels, and Berlin. To some early geographers, the ability to overcome diseases like malaria was inextricably linked to the ability of the British Empire to maintain colonial power in far-flung areas of the world.

More recent understandings of environmental security lend at least some credit to other military concerns, namely, of the air forces and navies. Meteorology became a professional science during the Second World War, led by the US Army Air Forces, who desperately needed both accurate prediction of severe weather systems and increased knowledge of high-altitude winds for its new bombers. Weather was a constant factor for air forces, not only in operations but also in casualties. During the Solomon Islands Campaign in 1942–45, the US Army Air Forces lost nearly half its pilots due to severe weather, not enemy actions.[22] Military concerns over environmental risks to soldiers, sailors, and airmen formed the basis of a "force protection" tradition. Advancements in meteorology facilitated US research in oceanography, which was initially led by military requirements in understanding sonar and ocean thermal layers during Cold War submarine operations.

---

[22] Eric M. Bergerut, *Fire in the Sky: The Air War in the South Pacific* (Boulder, CO: Westview Press, 2000).

Energy and Environmental Security during the Cold War and the 1990s

The US lead in science during the Second World War and into the Sputnik era of the Cold War has a mixed history. On one hand, it prompted massive public investments in areas of science that would later become crucial for climate sciences. On the other hand, technological developments severely affected the natural environment and posed their own risks.

The development of nuclear technologies remains perhaps the most visible symbol of this human-made risk. The modern academic understanding of environmental security can be traced to the efforts of groups such as Physicians for Social Responsibility in the 1960s, who were concerned over atmospheric nuclear testing and the human health impacts from fallout and radiation. Carl Sagan later popularized the link between military action and climate change with his warnings of "nuclear winter," where dust and particulates from nuclear war would bring about a new ice age and kill far more people than the nuclear weapons themselves.[23] This tradition of environmental damage forms the basis for what we refer to as "reflexive risk," meaning those risks that derive from our own actions to secure other forms of security.

The 1960s also witnessed increased warnings over global environmental and demographic changes, popularized by Ehrlich's book *The Population Bomb*[24] but drawing on ideas from as early as Thomas Malthus in the late 1700s. Shaped both by local environmental damage in the 1960s and the energy shocks of the 1970s, a scarcity-conflict understanding of environmental security developed. In this view, as unavailability of natural resources and food become more common (from a combination of environmental degradation and population growth), the scarcity will drive many into violent conflict. The scarcity-conflict understanding of environmental security formed the basis for many academic debates in the 1990s, with scholars such as Thomas Homer-Dixon attempting to explain new forms of order or disorder in the world following the end of the Cold War.[25] Other scholars, such as Ken Conca and Geoff Dabelko, pointed out the lack of empirical evidence in environmental scarcity as a cause of violent conflict and focused instead on the "cooperative security" aspects of

---

[23] Matthew R. Francis, "When Carl Sagan Warned the World about Nuclear Winter," *Smithsonian Magazine*, November 15, 2017, www.smithsonianmag.com/science-nature/when-carl-sagan-warned-world-about-nuclear-winter-180967198/.

[24] Paul R. Ehrlich, *The Population Bomb* (New York: Sierra Club/Ballantine Books, 1968).

[25] Thomas Homer-Dixon, "On the Threshold: Environmental Changes as Causes of Acute Conflict," *International Security* 16 (1991): 76–116; Homer-Dixon, "Environmental Scarcities and Violent Conflict," *International Security* 19, No. 1 (1994): 5–40.

the environment.[26] Supporters of cooperative security, who also drew from the literature on effective disaster response, argued that environmental scarcity more often led to cooperation among different groups and could be the basis for positive political developments if framed properly following a disaster or conflict.[27]

Climate Change, Environmental Disasters, and Environmental Security

The academic debate over the scarcity-conflict thesis had largely exhausted itself by the late 1990s. In the early 2000s, following the September 11, 2001, terrorist attacks on the USA, the environmental security debate disappeared from view. Security debates reoriented around terrorism risks, and the US and coalition invasions of Afghanistan and Iraq overwhelmed discussions in North America and Europe. Conferences for international relations scholars had few panels on environmental security, and few articles appeared discussing the topic, especially with regard to climate change, despite its increasing security risks.[28]

Throughout the 1990s, climate change (or global warming) was little discussed in reference to environmental security and future environmental risks. This was not due to lack of understanding. The basic concepts of global warming were established in the 1800s, and scientists decades ago warned that sufficient increases in greenhouse gases could raise global atmospheric temperatures through the greenhouse effect.[29] The lack of severity in warnings in the 1990s was largely due to an overabundance of caution among scientists. The large uncertainties concerning global climate models led many to conclude, at least publicly, that climate change would be gradual, with its worst effects likely not visible until late in the twenty-first century. Furthermore, earlier discussions of climate change (and even the basis for the negotiations of the UN Framework Convention on Climate Change) were based largely on the understanding that climate change would not only be gradual but would also primarily impact less developed countries in Africa and parts of Asia.

---

[26] Ken Conca and Geoffrey D. Dabelko, eds., *Environmental Peacemaking* (Washington, DC: Woodrow Wilson Center Press, 2002); Geoffrey D. Dabelko and David D. Dabelko, "Environmental Security: Issues of Conflict and Redefinition," *ECSP Report 1* (1995): 3–13.

[27] See Adrian Martin, Andy Blowers, and Jan Boersema, "Is Environmental Scarcity a Cause of Civil Wars?," *Environmental Sciences* 3, No. 1 (2006): 1–4.

[28] John Barnett, "Security and Climate Change," *Global Environmental Change* 13, No. 1 (2003): 7–17.

[29] See, e.g., Rupert Darwall, *The Age of Global Warming: A History* (London: Quartet Books, 2013).

The first consideration of climate change as a security issue came around 2003, in the academic community from researchers such as Jon Barnett, and in the military community from the Pentagon's Office of Net Assessment. The 2003 Pentagon report, written by Peter Schwartz and Tony Randall, was a thought experiment on how climate change might affect societies on a larger scale.[30] Although the report was somewhat simplistic in terms of both the science and impacts, it was novel and interesting in that it discussed the potential for abrupt, nonlinear changes in global environmental systems. Through a discussion of the potential shutdown of the global thermohaline ocean circulation system (also the basis for the film *Day after Tomorrow*, which was released the following year), Schwartz and Randall argued that large-scale environmental changes could occur much sooner than the predictions from the Intergovernmental Panel on Climate Change (IPCC).

The 2003 was also the year of intensive catastrophic heat waves across Europe, which resulted in tens of thousands of deaths in France, highlighting that environmental disasters could significantly affect developed regions of Europe and North America. Scientifically speaking, the exact role of climate change in the 2003 heat wave was inconclusive, but the event played an important role in European understanding that climate change may occur much more quickly than previously thought. Another contributing factor to the growing sense of vulnerability was the 2004 Boxing Day earthquake and tsunami that devastated at least fourteen countries along the Indian Ocean.[31] The event resulted in almost two hundred and thirty thousand casualties, displacement of 1.6 million people, destruction of property, and a large-scale loss of employment.[32] While not a climate-related issue, tens of thousands of Europeans were affected by the disaster, meaning that media coverage of the event and its consequences was immediate and intense. There were, for example, some three thousand Swedes in the affected areas, with 543 deaths of Swedish citizens alone.[33] Although this is a relatively small number compared to the two hundred and thirty thousand people killed across the region, it again highlighted the vulnerability of northern, developed countries to natural forces.

---

[30] Peter Schwartz and Tony Randall, *An Abrupt Climate Change Scenario and Its Implications for United States National Security* (Pasadena, CA: California Institute of Technology/Pasadena Jet Propulsion Lab, 2003).

[31] Lynn Letukas, "Indian Ocean Tsunami (2004)," in *Encyclopedia of Disaster Relief* (Thousand Oaks, CA: Sage, 2011), 342–45; Hari Srinivas and Yuko Nakagawa, "Environmental Implications for Disaster Preparedness," *Journal of Environmental Management* 89 (2008): 7.

[32] Letukas, 342–43.

[33] Charlie Campbell, "The Tsunami's Wake," *Time*, December 25, 2014, http://time.com/tsuna mis-wake/; Glenn Frankel, "Tourists Bring Home Tales of Nature's Random Horror," *Washington Post*, December 31, 2004, www.washingtonpost.com/wp-dyn/articles/A36930-2004Dec30.html?nav=rss_world/europe/westerneurope/sweden.

If the Europeans had been ahead of North Americans in slowly realizing these vulnerabilities, events in the US Gulf Coast states brought these images home for the Americans as well as the rest of the world. Seven major storms, including hurricanes Katrina, Rita, and Wilma, hit the United States during the 2005 hurricane season, contributing to nearly four thousand deaths and some $160 billion in damages.[34] Hurricane Katrina is perhaps best remembered, as the flooding of New Orleans led to nightmarish TV images and the sense that the powerful United States was itself at the mercy of natural disasters. The disaster also had a different security dimension. While primary responsibility for disaster response lies with the National Guard, by 2005 many of the affected states' Guard and Air Guard assets (particularly helicopters) had been deployed to Iraq and Afghanistan. While this was not the only factor leading to images of stranded citizens in the flooded streets or the squalid Superdome, in subsequent years, security planners' discussions revolved around the preexisting knowledge of the risks to the city and surrounding states, and lack of prioritizing of the plans and capabilities for effective disaster response.

By 2006, the availability of scientific data on climate change grew. There was new evidence concerning melting of glaciers, and emerging risks that had been well understood by glaciologists but which, for various reasons, had not yet been included definitively in the latest IPCC report. Once massive melting of the Greenland ice sheet became obvious in the 2000s and deeper ocean waters exhibited significant warming, the abrupt climate change community's alarm over potential phase shifts in the stability of climate systems grew larger.[35] The nature of nonlinear risks began to percolate beyond the typically small group of climate scientists who specialized in abrupt changes. When combined with the extensive damage of the previous year's storm season, certain groups within the US government began to understand that advance planning for security implications of climate change may be necessary in a more concrete sense.

Energy and Environmental Security in US Intelligence and Military Planning

In 2006, the US military community had a renewed interest in potential climate change impacts and their security risks. Based at the CNA Corporation and led

---

[34] Doyle Rice, "Remembering the Catastrophic 2005 Hurricane Season," *USA Today*, August 24, 2015, www.usatoday.com/story/weather/2015/08/24/2005-hurricane-season-katrina/32269245/.

[35] Timothy M. Lenton, Hermann Held, Elmar Kriegler, Jim W. Hall, Wolfgang Lucht, Stefan Rahmstorf, and Hans Joachim Schellnhuber, "Tipping Elements in the Earth's Climate System," *Proceedings of the National Academy of Sciences* 105, No. 6 (2008): 1786–93; Paul Valdes, "Built for Stability," *Nature Geoscience* 4 (2011): 414–16.

by former Deputy Under Secretary of Defense Sherri Goodman, a military advisory group consisting of over a dozen retired three and four-star generals and admirals produced a report that significantly influenced the Washington, DC, security community. In this report, released the following year, senior military officers expressed concerns about climate change worsening existing security risks for the United States, and potentially sparking new crises.[36] The CNA report was released against the wishes of the White House; it presented a new angle to our understanding of climate change – not merely as a left-leaning, environmental issue, but rather as a common security issue that cut across typical party and political lines. The authors of the report described climate security as a potential "threat multiplier," in military terms meaning that potential security threats such as insurgency and civil war could increase as environmental conditions deteriorate.[37] Crucially, the CNA report also addressed concerns over uncertainty of climate change, and explained that, in military terms, waiting for full information and full certainty meant waiting until it was too late.

The CNA report was crucial for establishing climate change as a legitimate military security issue, but in 2007, the concept still did not translate well into practical security planning. Where would security risks increase? What were the mechanisms between environmental change and potential conflict? Even if one should not wait for full certainty, how could the scientific data be translated in ways that were useful for decision makers? It was here that the US Department of Energy (DOE) became an important player, a development that grew from two relevant factors. The first was concern from the international security community (i.e., various national, regional and international government and academic bodies working on global security issues) about the emerging link between energy and environmental security. These concerns, expressed in networks such as the Global Futures Forum, had brought together military and intelligence experts who were asking many of the same questions about translation of complex data into decision-making. The other factor, more immediate to DOE, was the fact that hurricanes Katrina, Rita, and Wilma effectively shut down much of the Gulf Coast oil production and refinery infrastructure, with enormous impacts that for the first time strongly suggested a link between traditional definitions of energy security and environmental change. In cooperation with international partners, such as the Scottish government Foresight Office, DOE set up a division to address energy and

---

[36] CNA Corporation, *National Security and the Threat of Climate Change* (CNA Corporation, 2007).
[37] CNA Corporation, 6.

environment security, based on the idea of unclassified networks, and leveraging the knowledge of outside experts.

From a certain DOE perspective, the IPCC had been overly conservative in its estimations of environmental change. This was partly due to the inherent conservatism of scientific research (i.e., needing 95 percent confidence before passing peer review), the added conservatism of the IPCC process, and the fact that by 2009 some of the most recent climate data included in the IPCC reports had been collected no later than 2003.[38] From a security standpoint, this was unacceptable. Rules of evidence for responding to terrorist threats, for example, would never wait for full certainty before reporting, and using information that was many years old would be unconscionable. The DOE climate team engaged with scientists to collect data as they emerged and, more importantly, worked to map out the boundaries of uncertainty. It was crucial to understand, for example, why the Greenland ice sheets were melting so quickly, when almost no mention of such risks existed in the IPCC's Fourth Assessment only one year earlier. For the first time, the intelligence community was trying to conduct a capabilities analysis on environmental systems, a sort of net assessment for risks and response.

Among the newly established intelligence teams was one specific to abrupt climate change and security impacts. Much of that team's effort was directed to establish baseline methodologies for assessing the effects of climate change on energy and environmental systems as well as the security implications of those impacts for the United States and its allies. Potentially abrupt climate change was the wildcard that could easily undermine previous assumptions concerning stability of complex systems. The concern was that maintaining steady-state assumptions on all other relevant factors may no longer have been possible, and that important security impacts would be felt if we were blinded by our assumptions of the past.

Military motivations were likewise pragmatic, and insofar as climate change was seen as a highly charged political issue in the United States, officers' inclinations were to shy away from discussion of politics. Certain key figures in the US military, such as Chief of Naval Operations Admiral Roughead, asked whether energy and environmental trends would pose new challenges to military operations and strategy. Naval officers such as Rear Admiral

---

[38] James E. Hansen, "Scientific Reticence and Sea Level Rise," *Environmental Research Letters* 2, No. 2 (2007); Chad M. Briggs, "Risk and Scenario Planning for Climate Security," *Environmental Change and Security Program Report* 14, No. 2 (2013): 49; Susan Solomon, Dahe Qin, Martin Manning, Zhenlin Chen, Melinda Marquis, K. B. Averyt, Melinda Tignor, and H. L. Miller, eds., *IPCC, 2007: Climate Change 2007: The Physical Science Basis. Contribution of Working Group I to the Fourth Assessment Report of the Intergovernmental Panel on Climate Change* (Cambridge: Cambridge University Press, 2007).

David Titley (Oceanographer of the Navy before his retirement) explained that to sailors, the appearance of an entirely new sea in the Arctic, the result of melting sea ice, could hardly be ignored, and demanded questions concerning expanded responsibilities for operations such as search and rescue. Naval bases, could also be at risk to rising sea levels, and expanding duties from humanitarian assistance and disaster response risked placing heavier burdens on existing duties of the Navy and Marine Corps. Admiral Roughead therefore created new task forces for climate change and energy to help identify emerging risks and potential solutions (both strategic and technological) to address them.

The US Army was also, perhaps more quietly than the Navy, coming to terms with the existence of emerging risks that affected their operations and strategies. Army motivations may have been grounded more in operational experiences of continued conflicts in Iraq and Afghanistan, where soldiers were encountering energy and environmental risks reminiscent of nineteenth-century military planning concerns. The logistics trains for operations in Iraq and Afghanistan were both massive and complex, requiring not only substantial monetary investments, but exposing military personnel to risks that had not been part of the original campaign plans. Even seemingly simple issues like garbage disposal rose to become serious health concerns, as evidenced by US Department of Defense (DOD) efforts to stop the standard practice of open-pit burning of garbage in Iraq, a practice that posed significant health risks to its own troops. On a larger scale, shipments of water and fuel to the front lines became exceedingly expensive, with the total transport and security cost of a gallon of fuel rising to over $300 by the time it was delivered to a forward operating base in Afghanistan. In Iraq, Afghanistan, and the Persian Gulf region, DOD was spending $20 billion per year just on air-conditioning, while theater operations had to commit between $15 and $30 per gallon for transportation of drinking water.[39] The energy and environmental concerns were not limited to logistics and supply. The army also identified that conflict was highly damaging to energy and environmental infrastructure, which was often targeted by insurgents. Those areas that lacked clean water, electricity, and sewers were much more likely to support the insurgents (as

---

[39] *Week*, "The Military's $20 Billion Air Conditioning Bill: By the Numbers," June 18, 2011, http://theweek.com/articles/483608/militarys-20-billion-air-conditioning-bill-by-numbers; American Physiological Society, "Army Study Improves Ability to Predict Drinking Water Needs," *ScienceDaily*, July 11, 2009, www.sciencedaily.com/releases/2009/07/090708073849 .htm; James S. Moore, *The US Military's Reliance on Bottled Water during Military Operations* (Norfolk, VA: National Defense University/Joint Advanced Warfighting School, 2011).

occurred in the Sadr City region of Baghdad), as residents held US occupation forces responsible for any inability to provide basic human security needs to the civilian population.

Climate change and disaster risks formed only part of what the military took into consideration under the larger spectrum of energy and environmental security (EES). While EES itself affected the background to military planning and operations, it has never been considered central to the core mission in the United States. The US military, in contrast to the training and operations focus of other militaries around the world, consider themselves "war fighters" and did not see operations such as disaster response as primary to their mission. However, some very real operational and strategic considerations led to broader discussions of how military and intelligence organizations could help identify emerging risks, and either mitigate or adapt to them. In a strange way, this focus allowed the military to understand potential impacts of energy and environmental security more clearly than other organizations. Although this may seem counterintuitive, it is an important lesson to keep in mind when discussing how institutions and organizations can best approach assessing risks for climate security.

Conclusion and Book Structure

Climate change is so broad that it cannot be identified as a discrete hazard. Likewise, climate security-related disasters are diffuse and seemingly abstract in their origins, and finding appropriate responses may seem difficult. Since most disaster and environmental risk planning has been based on assumptions that the future will look very much like the present (see Chapter 2), we have not been forced to examine our underlying systems. Instead, the focus has remained on surface changes. Like the end of the Cold War, climate change and increasing disaster risks threaten to pull the rug out from our assumptions on how we plan and respond to security risks, by shifting the "environment" within which we both think and operate. We will not be able to isolate changes into discreet hazards the way that we have often been able to in the past, nor can we look to historical records of events as guidance for what happens next. We need to examine systems as a whole, in addition to understanding how we fit into them, and what sort of world we wish to live in thirty or forty years from now. Moving forward, we need advance planning that requires new techniques and tools.

The international security community had been addressing growing complex risks, updating older approaches, and integrating early warning techniques into both strategic and operational planning. The new programs in the US military and intelligence communities, starting in the mid-2000s, diverged from the traditional approaches to environmental security or energy security first by combining the two topics of energy and environment, which until that time had remained relatively distinct. The military and intelligence agencies and programs then merged some of their methods for early warning and risk assessment with emerging knowledge from the scientific and academic communities. By shifting the emphasis away from hard proof and prediction, the military/ intelligence approach was not one supported by traditional university research and publication norms. In several programs, such as the DOD's Minerva Initiative, the new energy and environmental security assessments were successful, and demonstrated that highly complex and uncertain risks could be assessed well in advance.

In the following chapters, we present several planning scenarios that have been developed over the years under the US DOE, US Air Force, and continued work at GlobalInt LLC. Each cluster of scenarios represents different approaches depending on the type of information available, the scale of risks being assessed (global, regional, local), and mix of assumptions used (e.g., mixing insurgency with cyberwarfare against energy infrastructure). Since several of these scenarios were used in planning or were prepared before related events occurred, we are able to offer a critical view of what went right and what went wrong, whether in terms of describing events or communicating the risk. A general purpose of this critical reflection is to improve future assessments and methods.

The book is not intended for scholars who are deeply involved in methodological concerns of disaster risk or environmental security. Our intention has been to reach out to a larger audience, and as such, we may state what is to others fairly obvious – that historical records can hardly be used to effectively plan for climate change, and that risks are complex and cannot be isolated into single variables. We are also not claiming that this work at DOE or US Air Force (USAF) follows true intelligence and military planning tradecraft. In many cases, we were working against the grain, whether in keeping all the work unclassified, or in taking outside factors to influence operational and strategic planning risks. The GlobalInt team took lessons from the intelligence and military world, and imported them into risk assessments that had seemed incomplete when trying to follow traditional academic rules. In many ways, the assessments described here belonged neither in academia nor in the military/ intelligence world. While the DOE and USAF project teams kept hoping that such efforts were already under way in government agencies, too often we were surprised at being told that these ideas were new. Not wanting to take anything for granted, the book therefore describes these risk concepts from the beginning.

Chapter 2 explains some of the traditional theories of disaster risk assessments, where we discuss in more depth definitions and applications of the prevailing risk assessments along with their purpose, benefits, and shortcomings. The chapter provides definitions of the concepts of hazard, risk, threat, and vulnerability, and discusses some key developments in risk assessment such as environmental impact assessments and multiple-risk assessments. We explore some methodological, cognitive, and organizational limitations of the prevailing risk assessment practices, emphasizing the difficulties with using the past for predicting the future. The chapter also outlines the characteristics and workings of complex systems, providing the rationale for the need for new risk assessment methods and tools.

Chapter 3 focuses on one such approach – the use of scenarios, in assessing emerging EES risks in complex systems. We provide background on the origins and significance of scenarios, and discuss the beginnings and basic ingredients of the complex risk scenario approach. The chapter outlines the process of developing complex scenarios – from foresight workshops to scenario validation to addressing cascading impacts and creating regional assessments. We also include a brief discussion of the role of uncertainty in scenario building, arguing for more engagement with uncertainty when identifying potential disaster risks in complex systems.

Chapters 4 and 5 present specific scenarios developed and used by DOE along with lessons learned from these exercises. Communicating these lessons is one of the crucial objectives of our work. The chapters are organized according to specific ways in which to address uncertainty: how to prepare for environmental changes and cascading risks from abrupt climate change (Chapter 4), and how to identify weak signals and translate them into workable scenarios for energy and environment security (Chapter 5). Each of these chapters contains a set of scenarios applied to specific geographic areas: Peru, New York, Japan, and Hawaii.

We show in Chapter 6 how to use scenarios, once developed, for training decision makers to respond to new risks. Specifically, we argue that it is not enough to identify potential futures – we need to know how to make recommendations on which future is desirable and achievable, given preexisting conditions. Wargames and simulations are an effective way of doing so. This chapter presents the main ingredients of wargaming – from objectives and the underlying scenarios to rules, roles, and the wargaming environment. We maintain that wargames and simulations are an effective approach to learning how to make decisions under uncertainty. To illustrate our points, we discuss a set of three wargames run between 2008 and 2018 for West Africa, the Mediterranean, and the Middle East. We also show how wargames have been institutionalized by the US military in the Pacific, discussing their application and future potential in disaster planning. We specifically highlight the usefulness of applying the concept of net assessment on complex energy and environmental security risks.

Building on some lessons from the wargames presented in Chapter 6, Chapter 7 emphasizes the increasingly pressing problem of the environment as a weapon. We discuss the concepts of hybrid disasters, resilience targeting, and hybrid warfare, including cyberoperations and their links to energy and environmental security risks. We present two forms of hybrid disasters: the deliberate use of energy and environmental systems for destabilization of countries and regions, and the development and use of geoengineering technologies (and particularly solar radiation management). In both cases, we argue that scenario planning is one of the few techniques available for assessing potential risks associated with these forms of hybrid disasters. Like in the previous chapters, we rely on lessons from sets of scenarios.

Chapter 8 addresses the obstacles for translating and communicating complex risks, from climate denial efforts and bureaucratic stovepiping to psychological barriers to risk acceptance and dealing with uncertainty. We conclude the book with Chapter 9, where we discuss two pressing energy and environmental security challenges for the future: abrupt climatic changes and their effects on the water, energy, and food production systems. We also suggest areas for future scenario development, and specifically Canada, the Arctic region, and Antarctica. The underlying concepts and background to energy and environmental security in disaster risk assessment are presented in the following chapter.

2

Environmental Disasters and Risk Assessment

We often find ourselves in situations in which the most obvious reaction to environmental factors may in fact be worsening the very issue that concerns us. In response to the 2003 heat wave in Europe, for example, sales of air-conditioning units rose considerably across the continent, including in places where people have lived for hundreds of years without climate control of their houses and businesses.[1] Since such extreme events were likely to become more common in the future, from an individual perspective, buying an air conditioner was a logical decision. Yet, from a more systemic point of view, widespread use of air conditioners put a much greater demand on European energy suppliers, particularly in developing economies of eastern and southeastern Europe, necessitating the construction of new power plants. Without carefully linking changes in energy demand to renewable sources, a reaction to increasing heat waves could increase greenhouse gas emissions, which in turn increases the risks of such heat waves occurring. In complex systems like energy and environmental networks, a systemic perspective is necessary to assess risks more accurately.

Heavily influenced by the impacts of large-scale natural disasters, current energy and environmental security assessments have evolved to include analytical tools for discerning potentially significant disruptions of critical systems that impact national security. EES risk assessment tools can be used to explain how complex energy and environmental systems are interconnected and how vulnerabilities and disruptions in one area can cascade into others. Yet, contingency planners do not typically look at systems in this way, in large part because of the complexity and uncertainty involved. There are also several, largely cognitive obstacles to effective disaster risk assessment: a tendency to

---

[1] John Tagliabue, "Europe Decides Air-Conditioning Is Not So Evil," *New York Times*, August 13, 2003, www.nytimes.com/2003/08/13/business/europe-decides-air-conditioning-is-not-so-evil.html.

learn from past events only after they occur, lack of ability to imagine future events that would be significantly different from the present (or past) environment, and a tendency to value the present over the future. Planners are often drawn to the wealth rather than dearth of data, which leaves many possibilities unaccounted for. We see the world in linear terms, assuming the future will look much like the past did. Such linear vision can hardly anticipate sudden shocks and cascading effects of complex disasters.

Making risk decisions within complex systems is difficult, particularly when scientific evidence is still emerging, uncertainty is high, and establishing easily recognized cause-and-effect mechanisms is unfeasible. This chapter begins to outline the ways in which we can make better decisions when assessing risks in complex EES systems. We first provide definitions of the basic concepts of risk, hazards, threats, and vulnerability, which we follow by an overview of the prevailing risk assessment approaches that integrate these concepts in their frameworks. We then discuss why contingency planners keep failing to "predict the predictable" and explain the need for new tools for risk assessments in complex systems.

Hazards, Risks, Threats, and Vulnerability

Environmental disasters[2] are "extraordinary, calamitous situations in the vital activity of population caused by essential unfavourable changes in the environment."[3] These changes are known as *triggering agents*.[4] Triggering agents are not, in and of themselves, risks or security concerns. Floods in Pakistan are a disaster only when they overwhelm human response. They become a security concern, for example, when that lack of response provides an avenue for Taliban to extend control over populations. Meanwhile, living in a flood zone is merely a hazard.

Hazards – whether natural or human caused – are existing conditions or potential events that can generate disasters. Natural hazards include natural phenomena – geological, hydrological, weather related, or others. Human-

---

[2] Environmental disasters can be human induced (e.g., factory or transportation accidents, such as oil spills), natural phenomena (e.g., earthquakes and tsunamis), or a combination of natural and human-made events (e.g., the 2011 Fukushima nuclear disaster) that can be either abrupt (e.g., a tsunami) or slow moving (e.g., desertification). See Kirill Ya. Kondratyev, Alexei A. Grigoryev, and Costas A. Varotsos, *Environmental Disasters: Anthropogenic and Natural* (Chichester, UK: Springer-Praxis, 2002), 20.

[3] Kondratyev et al., 20.

[4] David A. McEntire, "Triggering Agents, Vulnerabilities and Disaster Reduction: Towards a Holistic Paradigm," *Disaster Prevention and Management: An International Journal* 10, No. 3 (2001): 189–96.

caused hazards stem from human activity such as infrastructure, transportation, or other human alterations of natural environment as well as social events such as wars. Risk then captures the probabilities that specific hazards will cause harm; it is a combination of the impact of a hazard and the probability of its occurrence.[5] The impact depends in part on preventive measures the government and the affected stakeholders (i.e., population, businesses, and others) take as well as on unintended consequence of other actions and failures to act.[6]

The distinction between risk and threat is a key component in energy and environmental security. In contrast to risk, threat refers to a potential action or intent to cause harm to others. Within the context of EES, the focus of analysis is generally on risks rather than threats. Yet, despite the absence of overt intent to harm others in addressing EES vulnerabilities, ultimately, these actions can create security risks for others. In a larger political sense, it is therefore critical to understand how EES vulnerabilities can motivate the actions of state actors, whether in securing access to oil fields in the South China Sea or leasing farmland in Congo. Risk reduction efforts by one side may appear to be hostile acts to another state. For example, actions undertaken by China to dam the Brahmaputra River and divert its water inside China could be interpreted by India and other neighbors as a hostile act. The domestic Chinese logic of responding to serious internal energy and water shortfalls may thus result in deflecting disproportionate security risks elsewhere. The awareness and anticipation of China's actions in response to critical EES vulnerabilities exposes the potential for an increase of cross border tensions between China and its neighbors over riparian water rights. In other cases, such as India, vulnerabilities to disasters could easily dislocate its economic trajectory and hamper its ability to respond to domestic security concerns.

The damage from energy and environmental security impacts can be disproportionately severe if the event comes as a surprise and hits critically vulnerable systems. For example, the impacts from the 2011 Japanese tsunami were both surprising (despite warnings from some scientists) and disproportionately damaging due to both vulnerable infrastructure and energy policies.[7] Given the sudden and irreversible nature of many environmental events and the

---

[5] Disaster impacts can be human (e.g., deaths, injuries, and permanently displaced people), economic and environmental (e.g., the cost of emergency measures, health care, restoration, and environmental damage), and political/social (e.g., public anxiety, psychological impacts, and violations of public order and safety). See, e.g., European Commission, "Risk Assessment and Mapping Guidelines for Disaster Management," Commission Staff Working Paper SEC (2010) 1626 (2010): 10.

[6] European Commission, 10.

[7] Phillip Y. Lipscy, Kenji E. Kushida, and Trevor Incerti, "The Fukushima Disaster and Japan's Nuclear Plant Vulnerability in Comparative Perspective," *Environmental Science and Technology* 47, No. 12 (2013): 6082–88.

static nature of critical infrastructure, advance warning of potential EES risks can help prevent or mitigate their impacts. Even for uncontrollable events, such as hurricanes and tsunamis, human decisions on siting infrastructure or housing directly affect how vulnerable those systems are.

Society's vulnerability to hazards determines disaster impacts (and therefore the risk they pose). Vulnerability is a characteristic of a system in which changes result in disproportionate impacts or dislocations and where the system (be it political, ecological, or economic) is unable to adapt to these changes. While some vulnerabilities are obvious, many are exposed only after significant damage has already been done. Vulnerability has four components: exposure, resilience, sensitivity, and fragility. *Exposure* captures the probability of physical exposure to hazards. Disruptive events occur in certain places and in certain frequencies more than others, which means that the risk of exposure varies according to regional geographical, social, political, and economic structures. Less visible is the component of resilience, or how well a system or society can recover following a major event. Resilient systems are those where resources and backups exist if certain parts of the system fail. In technical terms, these are scale-free networks where random removal of any node rarely risks instability of the whole. In societal terms, *resilience* consists both of available resources to rebuild and healthy relationships between people in the society so that rebuilding efforts are possible. Vulnerable systems may also exhibit *sensitivity*, or the distance from which a system is pushed during a given event. Sensitive ecosystems, for example, are those that are damaged more easily by a smaller rise in temperature.[8] There is finally the component of *fragility*, or the amount of stress a system can endure before it ceases to act as the same society, ecosystem, or economy. The system may fall to a lower level of stability, where its essential character has changed permanently.[9]

Risk assessment approaches rely on frameworks that, in some way, encompass these elements of vulnerability along with the concepts of hazard, risk, and threat. In general, these frameworks do not examine and engage with multiple risks and are therefore unable to provide comprehensive assessments of environmental, political, economic, and social risks.[10] We elaborate on these

[8] Piers Blaikie, Terry Cannon, Ian Davis, and Ben Wisner. *At Risk: Natural Hazards, People's Vulnerability and Disasters* (New York: Routledge, 2004).

[9] While the first three components of vulnerability were taken from Blaikie et al., the concept of fragility used here originated at a NATO meeting in Budapest in November 2007, with due credit to James McQuaid.

[10] See Louise Bosetti, Alexandra Ivanovic, and Menaal Munshey, "Fragility, Risk, and Resilience: A Review of Existing Frameworks," United Nations University Centre for Policy Research Background Paper (October 2016).

prevailing approaches below, focusing especially on their limitations in assessing complex systems.

The Nature of Risk Assessment

Both natural and technological disasters are planned for through a risk management system, which consists of two main components: (1) risk assessment (data gathering for evaluating risk) and (2) risk control (application of risk assessment evaluations).[11] The goal of risk assessment is to minimize the source of danger through identification of potential hazards and their risk levels. Good risk assessment should reduce the losses from future disasters – principally through early warning.[12] Several tools exist to accomplish this task. Some of the most prevalent ones are preliminary hazards analysis, failure mode and effect analysis, event trees, human reliability analysis, and probabilistic risk assessment.[13] These tools serve to determine potential hazards; failure modes in the system; consequences of events; human factors; and risks in complex systems, processes, or operations.

Most risk assessments base their methodologies on a tradition set out in toxicology, most notably the assumption of single-agent monotonic dose-response (or in layman's terms, "the dose makes the poison").[14] Accordingly, there are three assumptions embedded in most risk assessment approaches. First, hazards operate singly (single agent). Second, the more one is exposed to hazard, the greater is the risk (dose-response). Third, there is a more or less linear relationship between exposure and risk (monotonic). These assumptions underlie (and limit) many common risk assessment practices. For example, in establishing a causal relationship between exposure and risk, it is generally necessary to isolate a single agent. In some cases, however, this is complicated. For example, a human body reacts more adversely to a lower (rather than higher) dose of some endocrine-disrupting chemicals, such as perchlorate.[15] The dose-response assumption also leads to judgments over threshold effects: how much of a chemical or how much radiation can one be exposed to before it becomes dangerous? Scientists and risk assessors must first identify what they consider to be adverse effects and then determine a point under which no such

---

[11] Lee T. Ostrom and Cheryl A. Wilhemsen, *Risk Assessment: Tools, Techniques and Their Application* (Hoboken, NJ: John Wiley, 2012), 7.

[12] Ronald J. Daniels, Donald F. Kettl, and Howard Kunreuther, "Introduction," in *On Risk and Disaster: Lessons from Hurricane Katrina*, ed. Ronald J. Daniels, Donald F. Kettl, and Howard Kunreuther (Philadelphia: University of Pennsylvania Press, 2006), 5.

[13] Ostrom and Wilhemsen, 9.

[14] Dan Fagin, "Toxicology: The Learning Curve," *Nature* 490 (2012): 4624–65. [15] Fagin.

effects are observed (i.e., the no-observed-adverse-effect-level, or NOAEL). There can be acute and chronic effects (e.g., a certain amount of arsenic will kill a person, while chronic exposure can cause skin cancer), aggregate effects on population, or ecological effects where human health is not directly harmed. Some adverse effects, such as health impacts from smoking or alcohol, are more commonly accepted, while risks of cancer from radiation exposure are publicly (and politically) considered unacceptable.[16]

The single-agent assumption is perhaps more of a methodological limitation than a belief, as it is well understood that chemicals and other environmental hazards can act synergistically (i.e., adding ingredients together is far more dangerous than having one agent alone). Yet, the limitations of toxicology – and the use of its assumptions in risk assessment – serve to emphasize the difficulties of translating from hazards to risks even under controlled laboratory conditions. In trying to make risk assessments on larger, more complex systems, we cannot rely on concrete probabilities, known threshold effects, and well-identified causal relationships. Simplification is especially common in risk aggregation (i.e., combining of individual risks into one, applicable to a larger population); it is a problematic yet well-established practice in risk assessment, whether in environmental security research or its applications.[17]

In international security studies, many of the categories of thought have been "blocky," meaning that the traditional focus on nation-states has been ill-suited for making usable assessments of EES risks. Most countries are essentially large and fairly random collections of individuals and communities, and while national militaries remain undoubtedly important for security discussions and planning, country-level analyses may tell us little about what is actually happening inside the borders. Critical security studies researchers have understood this for years and have often pointed out the inherent contradictions between the maintenance of state security and the impacts such actions can have on the country's own citizens.[18] So while, for example, development of nuclear weapons was considered important for US national security, concerns over the environmental and health effects of nuclear weapons production and testing suggested that aggregating security at the national level can blind us to impacts on humans at the community level. These dynamics were even more forceful in the former Soviet Union, where radiation poisoning from nuclear

---

[16] Carole A. Kimmel, "Quantitative Approaches to Human Risk Assessment for Noncancer Health Effects," *Neurotoxicology* 11, No. 2 (1990): 189–98.

[17] Kristin S. Shrader-Frechette, "The Conceptual Risks of Risk Assessment," *IEEE Technology and Society Magazine* 5, No. 2 (1986): 4–11.

[18] Keith Krause and Michael C. Williams, *Critical Security Studies: Concepts and Strategies* (New York: Routledge, 2002); Simon Dalby, *Environmental Security, Vol. 20* (Minneapolis: University of Minnesota Press, 2002).

weapons development and testing affected large populations in places such as the southern Urals around Chelyabinsk, northern Arctic regions, and nuclear weapons testing sites in Kazakhstan.[19]

At an organizational level, many risks are assessed in an aggregate fashion, leaving the impression that all members of the group or system under study share the same risks. This blending of parts with the whole is what Shrader-Frechette refers to as the *naturalistic fallacy*, which can blind decision makers to the nature and topography of the risk landscape.[20] When faced with the enormous complexity of the world, we naturally place people, things, and places into artificial categories. While we might understand that individuals within a group are different, we still tend to stereotype them. Decisions are often made based on broader categories – a practice that can blind us to particular risks or their impacts on specific groups of people. For example, most toxicological studies rely on small groups of people or animals to demonstrate potential impacts of chemicals, with results extrapolated to the population at large. However, the test subjects may not be representative of groups that are harmed or at risk. In perchlorate studies, for example, initial human studies focused on groups that were composed largely of white males. It took several years for researchers to notice that women were disproportionately affected by perchlorate intake, and that among ethnic groups, Native Americans were far more sensitive than others.[21]

One of the most prominent areas in which naturalistic fallacies can pose problems for decision makers is climate change. As the politics around climate change are also highly charged, the natural tendency for many is to retreat to more conservative positions of potential risk and to look at averages of only particular categories. At the international level, we see the United Nations Framework Convention on Climate Change climate negotiations focused on targets such as the 2°C warming limit beyond which the warming is believed to be catastrophic. But what does this mean? The 2° limit refers to average global air temperature, and therefore simplifies not only the variations within those 2°, but also warming experience within the atmosphere as well as the hydrosphere and the cryosphere. As we have seen in recent years, it is precisely the warming

---

[19] Hansruedi Volkle, "A Brief History of Nuclear Disasters: Prevention, Consequences and Re-coverage," *Planet@Risk* 2, No. 3 (2015): 1–4.

[20] E.g., Kristin S. Shrader-Frechette, "Comparative Risk Assessment and the Naturalistic Fallacy," *Trends in Ecology and Evolution* 10, No. 1 (1995): 50; Shrader-Frechette, *Nuclear Power and Public Policy: The Social and Ethical Problems of Fission Technology* (Dordrecht, Netherlands: D. Reidel, 1980).

[21] Chad M. Briggs, "Science and Environmental Risk: The Case of Perchlorate Contamination in California," *Environmental Politics* 15, No. 4 (2006): 532–49; Chad M. Briggs, "Risk Assessment: Perchlorate as a National Security Threat," *IEEE Technology and Society Magazine* 27, No. 3 (2008).

of the oceans and the ice that has often been the most dramatic. Yet, since people's everyday experiences are limited to atmospheric temperatures, these become the focus of many discussions, even though at times winter air temperatures in highly populated areas of Europe and North America have decreased. Complex risk decisions require tools and methods that can help identify vulnerable populations and points in systems. This is not simply an environmental justice argument. Decisions based on simplistic information and categories can have unintended consequences that spread far from the original risk or hazard.

One approach to handling the uncertainty stemming from complex systems is the reliance on environmental impact assessments (EIAs), first mandated to use by the US government under the 1969 National Environmental Policy Act (NEPA). EIAs assess both positive and negative environmental consequences of proposed projects, policies, or programs. They are intended to provide a systematic treatment of environmental risks associated with certain actions and over the years have evolved to include considerations such as social impacts. The idea for EIAs grew out of common law traditions where preventing a project is much easier than dealing with environmental consequences later. Legislation like NEPA mandated EIAs for large government projects that would have severe environmental consequences, meaning the original idea centered on point-sources of pollution like factories, airports, and hydroelectric dams. EIAs have been crucial for environmental policies in the United States as well as Canada, Australia, the European Union, and elsewhere, but, as risk assessment approaches, they also have limitations.[22]

Perhaps because of their origins in dealing with large projects, EIAs tend to focus on singular actions or geographical locations. Collective actions, such as the environmental risks associated with building houses in a floodplain over forty years, fall outside EIAs' scope because of diffuse responsibility and long time horizons. EIAs can be also used by more powerful political or economic groups to impose "unacceptable risks" on others, often minority populations. This not-in-my-backyard (NIMBY) assertion of risk poses environmental justice concerns, as a factory rejected in a wealthier neighborhood may instead be built and pollute a poorer neighborhood (or country) farther away.[23] The environmental risks may therefore merely be transferred from one group to another, and the links between cause and effect can be lost in the process. If it is an environmental risk to dispose of electronic waste in a landfill, then ship the

---

[22] Judith Petts, ed., *Handbook of Environmental Impact Assessment: Vol. 2. Impact and Limitations* (London: John Wiley, 2009).

[23] Eileen Maura McGurty, "From NIMBY to Civil Rights: The Origins of the Environmental Justice Movement," *Environmental History* 2, No. 3 (1997): 301–23.

waste overseas.[24] If the city of Toronto does not want to dispose of its own waste nearby, it pays for it to be shipped to Detroit (with environmental impacts from road transport).[25]

Crucially, EIAs assess potential environmental risks from *known* and *intended* actions. Disaster risks, although sometimes covered in EIAs as part of industrial accidents, cover a broader and more complex set of hazards and probabilities. In cases where both the hazards and the impacts are surrounded by large amounts of uncertainty, development of scenarios is often used to describe and assess future risks. Scenarios "condense the realm of possibilities to a limited number of identified situations."[26] They are "plausible descriptions of how the future may develop" and are generally based on past experiences.[27] Scenarios may involve single- or multiple-risk assessments. The former type focuses on the singular risk from a specific hazard in one area in a given period of time. The latter type strives to determine the aggregate risk from several hazards, given specific vulnerabilities and other possible hazards. Due to the complexity of environmental, social, political, and other systems, the multirisk approach seems better suited for capturing a wide range of potential environmental hazards to prepare for.

Multiple-risk assessments focus on two types of hazards: (1) those that occur at the same time or shortly follow each other (i.e., cascading impacts) and (2) those that threaten the same elements at risk without chronological coincidence.[28] Cascading impacts are a prominent feature of compound disasters, which are "very large, progressive or cascading disasters," such as the 2011 earthquake in Japan. They are "multiple sequential disaster events that produce 'more serious damage than individual disasters occurring independently.'"[29] For example, some volcanoes, such as Mount Tambora in Sumbawa Island, emit millions of tons of ash and volcanic materials that remain in the atmosphere for months, blocking the sunlight. A year after Indonesia's Mount Tambora erupted in 1815, a subsequent cold wave damaged crops and led to famine in many parts of the world.[30] More than thirty years

[24] Charles W. Schmidt, "Unfair Trade e-Waste in Africa," *Environmental Health Perspectives* 114, No. 4 (2006): A232–35.

[25] Keith Matheny, "Canadian Trash Again Filling Michigan Landfills," *Detroit Free Press,* February 19, 2018, www.freep.com/story/news/local/michigan/2018/02/19/canadian-garbage-michigan-landfills-solid-waste/337837002/.

[26] European Commission, 21; Crisis and Risk Network, *Focal Report 2: Risk Analysis – Integrated Risk Management and Societal Security* (Zurich: Center for Security Studies, 2009), 7.

[27] European Commission, 21. [28] European Commission, 23.

[29] Asian Development Bank and Asian Development Bank Institute, *Disaster Risk Management in Asia and the Pacific* (Tokyo: Asian Development Bank Institute, 2013), 5–6.

[30] Clive Oppenheimer, "Climatic, Environmental and Human Consequences of the Largest Known Historic Eruption: Tambora Volcano (Indonesia) 1815," *Progress in Physical Geography* 27, No. 2 (2003): 230–59; State Ministry for National Development Planning,

later, the eruption of Mount Krakatau in the Sunda Strait collapsed part of the mountain, which triggered a massive tsunami with over thirty-five thousand casualties.[31]

Since any hazard may trigger a number of subsequent hazards, planners tend to focus on the correlation between the likelihood of each event and the other (or prior) triggering event.[32] Yet, consequences of events with cascading impacts are cumulative, and several hazards and risks are often interdependent. Due to complexity and considerable uncertainty associated with such events, the effects of compound disasters are not yet fully accounted for in contingency planning. Planners tend to stop short of bringing together dissimilar hazards (e.g., combinations of different natural hazards or human-made hazards or both).[33] They tackle uncertainty merely by acknowledging it exists in both data and models. For example, a sensitivity analysis may be employed to determine the size and significance of the magnitude of risks to changes in specific input parameters. The use of precautionary principle is also emphasized when the scientific evidence is weak. Often, however, lack of data leads to lack of preparedness. Because planners seek as precise information about a specific disaster as possible, they tend to wait until such information becomes available.[34] They thus either fail to plan for certain events (especially compound disasters that require a lot of information) or, once confronted with a crisis, their action is crippled by lack of data.[35] This problem is amplified due to a mixture of cognitive and institutional biases in risk assessment.

Why Do We Fail to Predict the Predictable?

In 2005, Hurricane Katrina was recorded as the most expensive natural disaster in US history, causing vast destruction in the southeastern United States.[36] Prior to Katrina's arrival, preparedness procedures and training exercises were in place, and there were plenty of warnings of the looming catastrophe. Why then did a predictable hazard cause so much damage? The existing literature on disaster risk management draws answers mainly from psychology, focusing on

"National Action Plan for Disaster Risk Reduction 2010–2012," www.bnpb.go.id/uploads/pubs/451.pdf.

[31] See Research Center for Disaster Reduction Systems, "Tsunamis in Indonesia," www.drs.dpri.kyoto-u.ac.jp/eqtap/report/indonesia/tsunamis_in_indonesia/tsunamis_in_indonesia.htm; State Ministry for National Development Planning.

[32] European Commission, 23.   [33] European Commission, 28.   [34] Daniels et al., 6.

[35] Chad M. Briggs, "Abrupt Environmental Changes: Scenario Planning for Catastrophic Security Risks," in *Governing Disasters: The Challenge of Emergency Regulation – Beyond the European Volcanic Ash Crisis*, ed. Alberto Alemanno (London: Edward Elgar, 2011), 167.

[36] Daniels et al., 1.

both residents and planners. For example, Robert J. Meyer offers a comprehensive list of cognitive biases that prevent effective preparedness for low-probability, high-consequence events. Among the most prominent ones are (1) the learning bias, (2) the tendency to forecast the future based on the present conditions, and (3) the preference for present versus future benefits. These biases stem from a human tendency to learn by focusing on short-term feedback, to see the future as a simple extrapolation of the present, and to overly discount the value of ambiguous future rewards compared to short-term costs.[37]

The learning bias has several dimensions. We are much better at learning from the mistakes we make than those we almost make.[38] Warning systems' propensity to generate false alarms (because warning zones are much larger than impact zones) lowers residents' belief in reliability of warnings. Also, more investment in mitigation may result in better results and, in turn, lower preparedness for surprising events. In case of Katrina, a multi-billion-dollar investment into additional flood protection in New Orleans was difficult to justify given a long-term absence of severe flooding.[39] In temporal terms, residents make their decisions based on perceived likelihood of costs and benefits of an action. The problem is that people often make decisions based on recent events, underweighting long-term hazard trends.[40] Thus, as Meyer argues, we tend to think that if "a region goes without a hurricane hit for a few years, it must be because the odds of getting hit have gone down (or were previously overestimated), not that such a run should be expected under a constant base probability."[41]

The second challenge in dealing with unknown-probability, high-consequence events stems from biases in forecast and impact. Since people find it difficult to imagine an environment vastly different from the one they are currently facing, both residents and planners base their decisions on the current settings, largely ignoring the unknown.[42] This projection bias then forces many decision makers to stray away from costly mitigation. A similar problem stems from a tendency of both residents and planners to engage in *hyperbolic discounting*, a process in which we value immediate action much more than future action, which hampers our ability to plan for future events.[43] This bias is especially evident in policy circles.

---

[37] Robert J. Meyer, "Why We Under-prepare for Hazards," in *On Risk and Disaster: Lessons from Hurricane Katrina*, ed. Ronald J. Daniels, Donald F. Kettl, and Howard Kunreuther (Philadelphia: University of Pennsylvania Press, 2006), 154.

[38] Meyer, 154–55. [39] Meyer, 157. [40] Meyer, 158. [41] Meyer, 160. [42] Meyer, 162.

[43] Meyer, 165.

Some scholars argue that a failure of risk assessment to predict adequately the likelihood and consequences of a disaster is not as much in the inability of planners to do so as in certain areas receiving disproportionate risk after a systematic cost-benefit analysis.[44] Governments conduct cost-benefit analyses to estimate the expected costs and benefits of specific policies. Given their limited budgets, governments allocate resources and make decisions according to the results of these cost-benefit analyses. The problem is, as Daniels et al. argue, that "just as individuals tend to ignore disasters until the costs are all too clear – and then to overact, there are powerful incentives for government to postpone action until crises hit and then to respond with strong, but often not more than symbolic action."[45] A common argument is that governments have limited budgets and catastrophic events have low probability of occurrence. The future risk is thus disproportional to the present cost of policy. But when such events occur, the cost of impacts (economic, political, social, psychological, and other) vastly outweighs the cost of mitigation.

It is also increasingly misleading to refer to certain disaster risks as low probability. Probabilities of the future risks are based on known data sets over time. As we discuss below, the assumed certainty over occurrences of disasters is overshadowed by several concerns stemming from our understanding of the past.

Dwelling on the Past, Misunderstanding the Future?

An analysis of the past events (Have they occurred before? In what frequency? With what severity?) underlines almost all current risk assessment approaches.[46] Yet, relying on the past to predict the future is inherently flawed. In the words of John Ratcliffe, "however good our research methods may become, we shall never be able to escape from the ultimate dilemma that all our knowledge is about the past, while all our decisions are about the future."[47] Risk assessment approaches are constrained by data availability. The human records of certain disasters, and particularly from geological hazards, is limited and often incomplete. Accurate records of many environmental conditions are perhaps no more than one hundred years old (much less in some cases such as ocean temperatures). Relying heavily on available data and historical precedence may lead to lack of consideration of risks and impacts that are not immediately obvious. For example, the impacts of volcanic eruptions on human activities include human life loss and property damage, mostly from

[44] Daniels et al., 8. [45] Daniels et al., 8. [46] Ostrom and Wilhemsen, 24.
[47] John Ratcliffe, "Scenario Building: A Suitable Method for Strategic Property Planning?" *Property Management* 18, No. 2 (2000): 129.

debris avalanches, lateral blasts, ash flows, and mudflows. But pyroclastic flows also damage vegetation and contaminate water bodies over a large area in a short period of time, affecting both food and water security of people living in the vicinity. Ash from eruptions is often kept aloft for prolonged periods of time; it may disrupt flight routes (including patrol or search-and-rescue flights), damage the stratospheric ozone layer, and even lower global temperatures. Ash can move thousands of kilometers from its source. For example, ash from the 1991 eruption of the Mount Pinatubo in the Philippines traveled more than eight thousand kilometers eastward, damaging aircraft along the way until it reached the east coast of Africa. Forecasting volcanic eruptions is problematic, because some of the most destructive ones have occurred at volcanoes that had been dormant for thousands of years. The 2010 eruption of Mount Sinabung in North Sumatra, Indonesia was the first in four hundred years, catching the scientists off guard, largely because volcanoes in Indonesia are classified and observed based on their past activity.

In other regions, assessments are based on far fewer data points. The Colorado River Compact of 1922, for example, was an agreement between riparian states in the United States and Mexico over allotment of the river water, but it was based on rainfall and streamflow data from only 1905–22, which subsequent studies found to be unusually wet years. Legal obligations to downstream states and Mexico then have been almost impossible to fulfill, since the "average" data were not representative of long-term trends, let alone long-term drought.[48] The Colorado River case highlights the sensitivity of assessments to increasingly severe climatic changes.

While disaster risk assessments increasingly attempt to take climate change into account, doing so is extremely difficult, precisely because there are no historical analogs to what might change in the future. Compared to most prior geological periods, the Holocene, which covers all modern human history, has been remarkably stable with respect to long-term air temperature trends. Yet, within the Holocene, even small changes to the climate have immense impacts. The Tambora volcanic eruption changed global climate for several years following 1815. Changes occurring now due to greenhouse gas emissions are even more significant and long term, and we have little guidance as to how global systems will adapt or what new disaster-related risks will emerge.

Historically, we have not been that good at heeding warnings about potential impacts of human activity on environmental systems. In the early 1900s, advances in mechanized agriculture in the United States allowed for massive

---

[48] Bradley Udall and Jonathan Overpeck, "The Twenty-First Century Colorado River Hot Drought and Implications for the Future," *Water Resources Research* 53, No. 3 (2017): 2404–18.

expansion of food production in the Central Plains, requiring plowing of the prairie grasses that had held soil in place for millennia. Hugh Hammond Bennett, who helped found the US Soil Conservation Service, warned Congress that "Americans have been the greatest destroyers of land of any race or people, barbaric or civilized."[49] Despite his warnings of the mechanized practice of farming, lands continued to be plowed until successive droughts (starting in 1934) desiccated the soil and left it open to windstorms that blew millions of tons of topsoil as far as Washington, DC. The cascading impacts on societies led to massive migration of people from the central United States to the west (the "Okies"), subsequently altering farming and settlement of the Central Valley of California. Even today, central US farming relies heavily on groundwater reserves from the Ogallala Aquifer, a source that may run dry in future years without concerted sustainability efforts.[50] Similar groundwater withdrawal concerns are echoed in California, India, China, and many parts of the world, leaving communities more vulnerable to shifts in other environmental conditions. As environmental changes accelerate with climate change, traditional warnings and planning methods will prove inadequate for the challenge.

Complex Systems, Interconnectivity, and the Need for New Risk Assessment Approaches

Energy and environmental risk policies are full of inherent contradictions, with the behavior of individuals within a system not necessarily corresponding to the behavior of the system at large – much like the example of the 2003 European heat wave. Complex systems have emergent properties that are more than the sum of their parts. Therefore, we must be careful with both the unit and level of analysis in order to avoid focusing on insignificant risks or wrong pathways for response. For example, one may look at a countrywide level for evidence of instability, while in fact the most relevant information may come from knowledge of communities within that country. Conversely, in an attempt to determine how people might respond to a particular natural disaster, one may focus on individuals. Yet, the more relevant focus might be on sets of relationships – for example, how these individuals relate to their families, communities, and

---

[49] PBS, "The Father of Soil Conservation," www.pbs.org/wgbh/americanexperience/features/surviving-the-dust-bowl-biography-hugh-hammond-bennett/.

[50] Richard Hornbeck and Pinar Keskin, "The Historically Evolving Impact of the Ogallala Aquifer: Agricultural Adaptation to Groundwater and Drought," *American Economic Journal: Applied Economics* 6, no. 1 (2014): 190–219.

natural environment. In short, context always matters. For historians trying to explain the origins of World War I, saying that the war was sparked by the assassination of Archduke Franz Ferdinand in Sarajevo is meaningless outside of the context of early twentieth-century European nationalism, military structures, treaty arrangements, social and economic conditions, and political geography. While the killing of the Austro-Hungarian emperor's nephew and wife was tragic, it would hardly explain why Canadians would soon find themselves fighting Germans in the trenches of Belgium. The challenges are similar in explaining energy and environmental systems, and in trying to provide adequate foresight to help guide decisions.

Complex systems – whether environmental or others – are characterized by networks of relationships known as complex adaptive systems. Their stability and functioning depend on how relationships are formed and maintained. The clearest example of these relationships is the internet, a scale-free network reliant upon redundant communication pathways where random failure of most computer servers or routers generally causes only local disruption. Yet, critical nodes within this system (e.g., Google) are so central to the network that their loss would be felt globally. Highly connected systems can also spread risks quickly and widely – whether due to a computer virus or an influenza virus. Other networks are more sensitive, where loss of even peripheral nodes can create cascading impacts capable of disrupting the entire network. At-capacity systems, such as commercial air travel, are often sensitive to minor disruptions, while larger events (e.g., temporary closure of a major hub due to weather or terror threats) can create global instability in the transportation matrix.

In energy terms, electrical grids rely on large, central nodes of electrical generation, and often operate at peak capacity. This means that even the loss of one power line or substation can overload connecting lines, which in turn cascades throughout the system. The 2003 Northeast United States/Canada blackout affected 55 million people and was caused by a twelve-second power surge that cascaded outward and forced the shutdown of more than one hundred generating plants in the United States and Canada.[51] Recent power outages in India affected even more people. The Monday, July 30, 2012, blackout hit some 350 million people in seven states in northern India. It was followed the next day by an even larger loss affecting approximately 600 million, or roughly half of India's population.[52] Similar dynamics can be seen in economic systems (e.g., bank runs) and ecosystems (e.g., invasive species). It is also not

---

[51] CBC, "2003: The Great North America Blackout," August 14, 2003, www.cbc.ca/archives/entry/2003-the-great-north-america-blackout.

[52] Helen Pidd, "India Blackouts Leave 700 Million without Power," *Guardian,* July 31, 2012, www.theguardian.com/world/2012/jul/31/india-blackout-electricity-power-cuts.

uncommon for disruption in one system to spark cascades in another seemingly unrelated system. The 2011 Japanese tsunami is a telling example.

The Fukushima incident in 2011 was an example of a complex disaster that affected economic and geopolitical systems from Japan to Europe. On March 11, 2011, a magnitude 9.0 earthquake occurred off the eastern shore of Japan, generating a tsunami that inundated the Japanese coastline exceeding thirty meters above the sea level.[53] Near Fukushima, the Fukushima Nuclear Power Station was flooded, sparking a nuclear crisis not only at the Daiichi plant but across Japan. This nuclear crisis cast long shadows not only due to the radiation concerns it caused in the Pacific Ocean[54] but also because it illustrated how complex disasters contribute to cascading national security risks on a global level. The Japanese tsunami affected automobile manufacturing in Europe and the United States as sole-source parts from Japan became unavailable. Generally, the more efficient a system is and the more it runs at full capacity, the more vulnerable such a system can be to failure.

Like all complex systems, environmental systems can be nonlinear and change abruptly from one state to another – like a lake that absorbs too much nitrogen fertilizer and suddenly becomes choked with algae. When additional energy in a system reaches certain thresholds or tipping points, its behavior changes as well, much the same way that water can shift from ice to liquid to gas. Abrupt changes are also not limited in space or form and can "cascade" across systems to affect areas that might seem, at first glance, to be separate or distinct. Such impacts can be understood in terms of potential forcings rather than "most probable" outcomes; they can be assessed with tools such as scenario planning and network analysis to determine vulnerabilities in larger systems along with available response capacities. Considering that shifting environmental systems and demographics often combine to multiply risks (e.g., sea levels rise as more infrastructure is built along coastlines), historically "good enough" assessments must be updated with the latest available scientific data. It is this dynamic interplay between hazards, risks, and environmental changes that must be further studied.[55]

---

[53] 2011 Tohoku Earthquake Tsunami Joint Survey Group, "Nationwide Field Survey of the 2011 off the Pacific Coast of Tohoku Earthquake Tsunami," *Journal of Japan Society of Civil Engineers, Ser. B2* 67 (2011): 63–66.

[54] John N. Smith, Robin M. Brown, William J. Williams, Marie Robert, Richard Nelson, and S. Bradley Moran, "Arrival of the Fukushima Radioactivity Plume in North American Continental Waters," *Proceedings of the National Academy of Sciences* 112 No. 5 (2015): 1310–15.

[55] US Department of Defense, "National Security Implications of Climate-Related Risks and a Changing Climate," OSD report to the Senate Appropriations Committee, July 23, 2015, www.defense.gov/pubs/150724-Congressional-Report-on-National-Implications-of-Climate-Change.pdf.

Conclusion

The prevailing risk assessment approaches assume that environmental conditions are linear and predictable. Yet, emerging research on energy and environmental security suggests that environmental systems are complex and chaotic, and they resist easy prediction.[56] Often, complex systems are described in binary terms – the system is either stable or unstable, functional or nonfunctional. The truth is that complex systems may have multiple points of stability, many of them potentially shifting as conditions change. Triggering events can result in security risks far out of proportion to their initial impact. At the US homeland security level, for example, the 2001 anthrax mail attacks in Washington, DC, had significant though indirect security implications. These attacks forced the closure of post offices in the area, effectively disrupting cash flows from utility customers to Pepco, which provides electricity to the entire Beltway region. Because of this cash flow disruption, Pepco required immediate financial assistance to prevent widespread blackouts across DC and Virginia, the security consequences of which would have been profound. The ability to understand these relationships and to identify critical vulnerabilities can help prevent or mitigate disruptions to security.

We are flooded with so much information that it is difficult to sift through warnings and make sense of the "noise" and uncertainty. When confronted with large amounts of information, especially if highly uncertain and conflicting, humans use "cognitive shortcuts" to make decisions, falling back onto known patterns of thought and action. What has worked in the past – can't we just do more of that? Can't we wait until more (certain) information is available? Why take actions based only on incomplete pictures of the future? When we become overloaded with information and when the patterns of risk are unfamiliar, we tend to become indecisive and avoid taking action.

Overcoming this decision-making paralysis requires an ability to see new patterns and recognize warning signals in advance. This is the goal of much of professional military education, training that is meant to help prevent soldiers, sailors, airmen, coastguardsmen, and marines from freezing with indecision in the middle of risk situations. In military training, men and women must be able to act

---

[56] See, e.g., Chad M. Briggs, Moneeza Walji, and Lucy Anderson, "Environmental Health Risks and Vulnerability in Postconflict Regions," *Medicine, Conflict and Survival* 25, No. 2 (2009): 122–33; Briggs, "Developing Strategic and Operational Environmental Intelligence Capabilities," *Intelligence and National Security* 27, No. 5 (2012): 654; Briggs, "Environmental Change, Strategic Foresight and Impacts on Military Powers," *Parameters* 40, No. 3 (2010): 1–15; Briggs and H. Carlsen, "Environmental and Climate Security: Improving Scenario Methodologies for Science and Risk Assessment," *American Geophysical Union,* Fall Meeting (2010).

when information is uncertain, when time pressure is enormous, and when the consequences of wrong decisions are potentially fatal. On a broader scale, these same training and education approaches can be applied in climate and disaster security, where judgments and decisions must respond to novel constellations of hazards and risks. A different model of risk assessment for energy and environmental issues is therefore required – one that is based on foresight rather than forecast. While forecast is predominantly about gathering data and evaluating risks within the realm of probability, foresight focuses on broader (and extreme) possibilities. A complex scenario-based risk assessment with a general focus on abrupt changes in energy and environmental systems is an effective way of using foresight in disaster risk assessment.

3

Scenario Planning and Complex
Scenario Approach

In July 2011, the US Federal Emergency Management Agency (FEMA) held a multiple-day scenario planning workshop, intended to help chart the agency's potential futures by involving outside experts in emergency and disaster response and strategic planning. During the opening briefing, a senior FEMA official illustrated the potential shortcomings of planning for disaster response without considering all possible futures. He explained that in the United States, when a major disaster strikes, the first item on FEMA's checklist for how to respond is "call the National Guard." National Guard units of each state are routinely called upon to provide resources that go beyond what would normally be available to local and county police and fire departments – resources such as helicopters, cargo aircraft, and military-grade vehicles. Over decades, it became routine for FEMA (itself largely a coordinating agency) to expect to have these resources available.

In September 2005, as Hurricane Katrina made landfall, FEMA called the National Guard, but there was no one there to pick up the phone. A great many of the National Guard units from Louisiana and neighboring states had been called to active service in Iraq and Afghanistan, taking with them crucial assets, such as helicopters (which were needed for rescue operations following the hurricane).[1] Outside events can leave us more vulnerable to disasters if we do not have the imagination to plan for alternative futures. While there are different methods available for foresight planning, in this book, we focus largely on scenario planning, tracing its evolution from a military business tool to an asset in anticipating emerging climate change risks and disasters.

Much like in any strategic planning, contingency planners need to recognize that there is not one but many different plausible futures. Scenario building

---

[1] Margaret B. Takeda and Marilyn M. Helms, "'Bureaucracy, Meet Catastrophe': Analysis of Hurricane Katrina Relief Efforts and Their Implications for Emergency Response Governance," *International Journal of Public Sector Management* 19, No. 4 (2006): 397–411.

involves assumptions about what will and will not occur. Are the current trends likely to continue? What changes should we anticipate? What events are likely or unlikely to occur?[2] Scenarios allow planners to understand the whole range of possibilities and to take actions "to make a desirable future occur, quickly adapt to unfavorable environments, and efficiently implement strategies that will succeed in many different . . . conditions."[3] A scenario approach therefore minimizes "tunnel thinking" and provides common language for scientists, researchers, planners, and policy makers from diverging areas. In this chapter, we discuss the origins and significance of using scenarios in military planning as well as the need for complex scenarios and the ways to build them. Rather than providing a comprehensive guide for creating scenarios, we hope to draw attention to some of the challenges associated with departing from the expectations of hard predictions of a knowable future. We argue for the necessity of acknowledging and confronting the uncertainties and complexities of emerging hazards and risks.

Scenarios, as described in this chapter, are fundamentally about the process of learning about the present by discussing the future. There is no guarantee that the questions asked will resonate or provide accurate insights. For every scenario described in this book, at least six others were started and then abandoned as unworkable or not salient. The task of scenario planners is to recognize when processes are working and when they are not. In the absence of set formulas for conducting foresight studies of complex systems and disaster risks, our intention is to explain what worked well and to admit when we were wrong, and why.

Why Scenarios? The Origins and Significance of Scenario Planning

Historically, one of the first references to "conditional future contingents" or "futuribilia" came from the Spanish Jesuit theologist Luis de Molina in the sixteenth century.[4] Moving out of the Dark Ages (where fate was considered predetermined), the modern notion of liberty and free will had to grapple with the concept of a contingent future, meaning humans had choices and no single set destiny. The concept of free will has placed something of a burden on us. If we do not simply accept what happens to us as fate, then we are responsible

---

[2] See, e.g., James A. Dewar, "The Importance of 'Wild Card' Scenarios," Air University, 2003, www.au.af.mil/au/awc/awcgate/cia/nic2020/dewar_nov6.pdf.

[3] Ratcliffe, 129.

[4] Pentti Malaska and Ilkka Virtanen, "Theory of Futuribles," *Futura* 24 (2005): 2–3.

for understanding the consequences of our actions, and navigating through that world as best as we can. The concept of a contingent future was linked to scientific advances during the Renaissance, where prediction of events in the world became possible. The ability to predict, make calculations, and determine the state of future conditions from weather to human actions had been an underlying assumption behind many of the concepts of rationality in politics and policy. Throughout the twentieth century and into the twenty-first, we had become accustomed to both the accuracy of predictions and the ability to access that information. We may now ask our smartphones to give us predictions on everything from the weather to traffic. It can be a frustrating experience if that information is not available or if the forecasts are not accurate.

Scenarios are essentially discrete narratives of different contingent futures. In everyday life, this can be translated into "if I take action A, this is the story of how my life will change." One may, for example, dream about what one's life will be like if one pursues a particular course of education or begins different careers. We often dream up scenarios of what it will be like to fall in love with particular people, to live with them, or perhaps to be without them.[5] We try to imagine what our experiences will be like in a given vacation destination and perhaps plan contingencies for various minor disasters: missed flights, lost luggage, or stolen credit cards. For most of us, it is a difficult balance between being disappointed by creating scenarios with very high expectations and losing our ability to enjoy the present, because we spend so much time worrying about things that could go wrong. When teaching scenario planning to graduate students, some of them have remarked that their biggest and most stressful scenario planning challenge was preparing for their own wedding. An entire industry has been created around trying to anticipate and prevent wedding disasters.

Scenarios are created based on available information of what we think might happen given available choices and their consequences.[6] The more experience people have with a given risk and its associated uncertainties, the less surprised they may be once different events occur. The essence of anticipating disaster risks is not to give a solid prediction of what will happen but to be prepared

---

[5] On a personal note, my (Briggs) real introduction to scenario planning began when I was a Rotary exchange student in high school. Before leaving for my year in Norway, I tried imagining every possible scenario of what life would be like in Europe, what it would be like to study in a foreign language, and how I would react given several tragic events. My best friend, Erich, was killed one month after I arrived in Norway, and I realized it was a scenario I had refused to even contemplate. We can try to prepare ourselves, but some potential realities are too difficult or painful to think about. Part of my motivation in working in this field was attempting to overcome that very real obstacle.

[6] Antonio Martelli, *Models of Scenario Building and Planning: Facing Uncertainty and Complexity* (New York: Palgrave Macmillan, 2014).

should a given constellation of risks translate into particular impacts. The goal is to prevent paralysis from a novel and unique situation, where one cannot make decisions because of too much uncertainty and no obvious path on how to navigate out of the bad situation. When a pilot is credited with keeping her cool during an emergency, it is not because she was able to anticipate the engine explosion and subsequent cabin depressurization. She appears calm because, pilots have been trained at length on how to deal with different emergency situations, including how to project calm when communicating with passengers.[7]

Just because we use scenarios in our own lives, however, does not mean that we do it well. When we try to imagine scenarios about the future, we encounter three primary problems. First, we tend to become fixated on our past experiences and knowledge, believing that tomorrow will look more or less like today. Most scenarios have an assumption of this simple extrapolation embedded in them, although in most cases, past experience tends to be a reliable guide.[8] The second problem, however, is that if too many things begin to change, we lose track within all the complexity and "noise." Scenarios are easier to create when only one or two primary variables are at work and all other background environmental factors are held constant.[9] Finally, people tend to avoid scenarios describing futures they dislike. The more intensely harmful these are, the more one tends to build psychological barriers to disbelieve the incoming information.[10] Therefore, since the nineteenth century, organizations have employed formal models to develop and use future planning and risk scenarios in order to overcome the obstacles of complexity, anchoring, and disbelief. Most approaches have been sufficient to tackle one of the three challenges at a time, but as we will see throughout the rest of this book, climate-related risks have forced attempts at facing all three obstacles at the same time.

Formal Methods of Scenario Development and Use

The origin of more modern scenario concepts can be traced to the Prussian Army in Germany in the early nineteenth century, when Baron von Massenbach

---

[7] Eduardo Salas, Jennifer E. Fowlkes, Renee J. Stout, Dana M. Milanovich, and Carolyn Prince, "Does CRM Training Improve Teamwork Skills in the Cockpit? Two Evaluation Studies," *Human Factors* 41, No. 2 (1999): 326–43; Robert L. Helmreich, "Managing Human Error in Aviation," *Scientific American* 276, No. 5 (1997): 62–67.

[8] Daniel Kahneman and Amos Tversky, "On the Psychology of Prediction," *Psychological Review* 80, No. 4 (1973): 237.

[9] Paul J. H. Schoemaker, "Forecasting and Scenario Planning: The Challenges of Uncertainty and Complexity," in *Blackwell Handbook of Judgment and Decision Making*, ed. Derek J. Koehler and Nigel Harvey (Oxford: Blackwell, 2004), 274–96.

[10] Richard A. Clarke and R. P. Eddy, *Warnings: Finding Cassandras to Stop Catastrophes* (New York: HarperCollins, 2017).

proposed to King Frederick William III the creation of a military general staff, which would plan wartime scenarios during peacetime and have direct access as advisors to the king. The Prussians also developed the first modern use of wargaming (*Kriegsspiel*), first recorded in 1812, which provided officers with tactical and strategic training in decision-making.[11] The idea behind wargaming is to tackle complexity and associated uncertainty by providing repeated variations on an accepted (and largely unquestioned) background environment. We discuss wargaming in more detail in Chapter 6. For now, it is important to emphasize that wargames use background scenarios to provide the environment within which officers train for how to make decisions under stressful conditions.

The shortcomings of the Prussian/German version of *Kriegsspiel* became evident in the First World War. The German armed forces had become highly proficient at preparing war plans, but once these were put into motion, there was little possibility of "scaling down," and war was assumed from the outset to be a "total" conflict.[12] Historians have also criticized war planning in that era for not realizing how technology (specifically, the creation of new weapons such as machine guns and aircraft) would affect older tactics. Despite their skills at directing mass troop movements, general officers in World War I were rightly criticized for "fighting the last war," or anchoring their plans according to old information and past practices.[13]

The modern concepts of scenario planning are generally linked to the Second World War, where US Air Force efforts to use newly invented computing power for planning helped create what is now known as the RAND Corporation. The Army Air Forces (from 1947, the US Air Force) were confronted with radically new environmental conditions as a result of introducing new technology during the war (e.g., the B-29 bomber and nuclear weapons). With the constant nuclear readiness of the Cold War, the US Air Force and Navy had to be able to operate from the deep oceans to outer space, while keeping track of political-economic developments and threats around the world.[14] The United States, it was felt, could not afford to be reactive to events, when escalating conflicts would result in a nuclear war. In other words, the

---

[11] Some argue that wargames began earlier. See Jorit Wintjes, "Europe's Earliest Kriegsspiel? Book Seven of Reinhard Graf zu Solms' Kriegsregierung and the 'Prehistory' of Professional War Gaming," *British Journal for Military History* 2, No. 1 (2015).

[12] Barbara Wertheim Tuchman, *The Guns of August* (New York: Ballantine Books, 1962).

[13] David Stevenson, *Cataclysm: The First World War as Political Tragedy* (New York: Basic Books, 2004).

[14] The uneasy connection between the science and military/intelligence communities began in earnest in the early Cold War and still presents obstacles today. See Jacob Darwin Hamblin, "The Navy's 'Sophisticated' Pursuit of Science: Undersea Warfare, the Limits of Internationalism, and the Utility of Basic Research, 1945–1956," *Isis* 93, No. 1 (2002): 1–27.

United States had to tackle complexity in order to avoid the mistakes of the First World War.[15]

The RAND Corporation became central to many discussions of military planning during the Cold War, from infamous nuclear strike scenarios to the influence on Robert McNamara's staff during the Vietnam war in the 1960s. RAND was also the home of Herman Kahn, a prominent military strategist known for theorizing the consequences of nuclear warfare. Kahn was instrumental in the development of modern scenarios for wargames and security planning. His approach aimed to avoid the age-old mistake of "fighting the last war" by using advanced statistical techniques in computing power to identify future trends and describe the security environment within which officers and policy makers would be forced to make decisions.[16] With the development of nuclear weapons, the military could not afford to make mistakes or be paralyzed by indecision if a new and unique set of circumstances presented themselves to the officers on duty or the White House staff.[17]

The RAND Corporation and Herman Kahn therefore set out to take all available information on economic, political, military, and related trends, seeing how they interrelated and how conditions would change should the underlying variables be altered (much like a modern spreadsheet does). The result was a multivariate analysis that allowed the exploration of potential future worlds. What would be the future security environment, for example, should the Chinese population continue to grow while the Soviet Union's decreased? How would changes in demographics affect economic output, military expenditures, and foreign military assistance to allies? Rather than simply guessing, Kahn and his colleagues were intent on establishing data-driven analyses.[18]

This approach to scenarios was not only used by the RAND Corporation and the US Department of Defense but also became a standard for analyzing issues such as energy security at the International Energy Agency (IEA), where trend line analyses explored the interrelationships between available oil reserves, oil

---

[15] Historians like Weart note that US military investment in oceanography and meteorology contributed greatly to the development of climate sciences. See Spencer R. Weart, *The Discovery of Global Warming* (Cambridge, MA: Harvard University Press, 2008).

[16] Ron Bradfield, George Wright, George Burt, George Cairns, and Kees Van Der Heijden. "The Origins and Evolution of Scenario Techniques in Long Range Business Planning," *Futures* 37, no. 8 (2005): 795–812.

[17] Bruce G. Blair, *The Logic of Accidental Nuclear War* (Washington, DC: Brookings Institution Press, 2011).

[18] Philippe Durance and Michel Godet, "Scenario Building: Uses and Abuses," *Technological Forecasting and Social Change* 77, No. 9 (2010): 1488–92; Celeste Amorim Varum and Carla Melo, "Directions in Scenario Planning Literature – A Review of the Past Decades," *Futures* 42, No. 4 (2010): 355–69.

production, and market futures. Climate change scenarios were based on similar trend line analyses, illustrated by the so-called hockey stick increase in global air temperatures (attributed to Michael Mann).[19] The future temperature charts have been commonly included in IPCC assessments, and a combination of scenarios has been used to show future temperatures linked to high or low greenhouse gas emission policies. Such scenarios are useful – it is difficult to imagine formulating policy on anything from energy security to climate change mitigation without using these approaches that were first developed and formalized by RAND. Yet, there were potential problems with using historically based trends to determine potential futures. The underlying assumption behind such scenarios is that the future will look very much like the present, only more so. Disaster risk assessments, as discussed in Chapter 2, often follow such an assumption, not expecting or planning for environmental hazards that fall outside of historical averages or experience.

Underestimating or overestimating potential risks in scenarios posed problems with the traditional RAND approach to scenario creation. One could underestimate risk because of an inability to see abrupt changes in the future, or overestimate risk, because a scenario predicts inevitable conflict. In both cases, scenarios can become closed and formalized, leaving out essential variables that would allow divergent futures. In the case of historically based risk assessments, we tend to underestimate risks, because we are only including observable and measurable data and assuming that the boundary conditions of that scenario will change slowly over time. Even when risks are perceived, there can be a significant disconnect between perception and preparation.[20]

As shown through various examples in this book, climate change has rendered many historical assumptions about disaster risks and hazards obsolete. Yet, when a scenario gives us a dire warning, it is also worthwhile to consider whether the warning itself – the knowledge that such a future world exists – can lessen that risk when human choices are involved. Some scenarios have warned about abrupt and potentially catastrophic changes in the future, such as the predictions popularized by the Club of Rome in the 1970s that anticipated future food shortages as a result of human overpopulation.[21] These

---

[19] Michael E. Mann, *The Hockey Stick and the Climate Wars: Dispatches from the Front Lines* (New York: Columbia University Press, 2013).

[20] Eric J. Johnson and Amos Tversky, "Affect, Generalization, and the Perception of Risk," *Journal of Personality and Social Psychology* 45, No. 1 (1983): 20; Gisela Wachinger, Ortwin Renn, Chloe Begg, and Christian Kuhlicke, "The Risk Perception Paradox – Implications for Governance and Communication of Natural Hazards," *Risk Analysis* 33, No. 6 (2013): 1049–65.

[21] Donella H. Meadows, Dennis L. Meadows, Jorgen Randers, and William W. Behrens, *The Limits to Growth* (New York: Potomac Associates, 1972), 27; Graham M. Turner,

scenarios contained compelling internal logic but were incomplete, because they rested on many embedded assumptions about human behavior.[22] Demographic trends can change considerably, either through direct action (e.g., the Chinese "one child policy") or due to external influences such as political and economic crisis (e.g., sharp population and industrial output decreases in Eastern Europe).[23] In other words, it is very easy for scenarios to become static and to be presented as "givens," meaning they are more of a prediction of the future than a narrative with options and alternatives that can help lead us to the future we would most want.

In practice, the RAND-style scenarios were copied by many organizations that tended to "black box" them, with a select group of experts describing the future and then presenting it as a given to another group of people.[24] In our experience, many foresight exercises place experts around a table and give them a large piece of paper. These experts are then asked to identify the most important future risks in a given area. The subsequent discussions tend to be dominated by the most forceful personalities at the table, who then emphasize topics that are related to their work. The groups cut out complexity and focus on what is most immediately accessible and believable. Doing so, they anchor the scenarios in such a way that they describe obvious risks and obvious futures. Furthermore, if, during the foresight exercises, acute risk scenarios do not match participants' understanding of the problem, the scenario warnings may be dismissed.[25] At a foresight exercise in Stockholm in 2010, European security experts were presented with scenarios that described events such as food riots in India. One participant, a German federal police officer, noted, "I don't understand why this is important for my job. Can we talk about something else?"

Attempts to reduce complexity of the scenarios eliminate much of the uncertainty that surrounds potential futures. Some scenario discussions, and particularly reports by intelligence agencies, are very careful in their language

"A Comparison of *The Limits to Growth* with 30 Years of Reality," *Global Environmental Change* 18, No. 3 (2008): 397–411.

[22] Herbert A. Simon, "Prediction and Prescription in Systems Modeling," *Operations Research* 38, No. 1 (1990): 7–14.

[23] Assumptions of "set futures" can lead to highly damaging policies when human factors are involved. See Betsy Hartmann, "Converging on Disaster: Climate Security and the Malthusian Anticipatory Regime for Africa," *Geopolitics* 19, No. 4 (2014): 757–83.

[24] There has been some laudable work done on avoiding these "top-down" approaches to scenarios and adaptation planning, with Sweden being a particular example. See Patrik Baard, Henrik Carlsen, Karin Edvardsson Bjornberg, and Maria Vredin Johansson, "Scenarios and Sustainability: A Swedish Case Study of Adaptation," *Tools for Local Decision-Makers*, No. 124 (2011).

[25] Amos Tversky and Daniel Kahneman, "The Framing of Decisions and the Psychology of Choice," *Science* 211, No. 4481 (1981): 453–58.

concerning terms such as *most likely, possibly,* and *rarely.*[26] Yet, even in carefully worded reports, the focus is on the probability of events, rather than on the uncertainty surrounding hazards or risks.[27] The difference here is crucial. When focusing on probabilities, we make calculations according to available information, and we assume that the most believable calculations are those based on the most reliable data. But what if the largest risks lie within the areas of uncertainty? What if we need to be able to plan for the unthinkable? What if we need to push the boundaries of scientific research beyond what is most certain? In such cases, we need a different approach, one that more closely follows the work of Shell Oil.

From Complexity to Disbelief: Enter Shell Oil

The basic philosophy behind the development of a new scenario process was drawn from the work of Pierre Wack and colleagues at Shell Oil in the 1970s. Wack realized the shortcomings of traditional scenarios and was concerned that Shell Oil was basing strategy and investment decisions on potentially faulty assumptions of what the future might bring. After all, for decades, oil companies had enjoyed constant growth. As economies expanded, so too did consumption of fossil fuels, which made it an easy business decision to continue investing in infrastructure and assets like processing facilities, pipelines, and tankers. What Wack wanted the Shell executives to consider was, What if demand doesn't grow? What if an external shock hits the oil markets, leaving the company with expensive and stranded assets? Could the company afford not to consider such potential futures?[28]

Wack was addressing the problem of systemic risk planning, where organizational development had created its own complexity and anchoring. In such cases, future scenarios were simply extrapolations of existing conditions. The senior executives at Shell were unreceptive to questions concerning hypothetical what-if scenarios. These executives had risen to their positions making decisions that matched what the Shell planning system (known as the "unified planning machinery") indicated – ever-increasing investment in infrastructure and ever-increasing growth in demand.

---

[26] UK Ministry of Defence, *Adaptability and Partnership: Issues for the Strategic Defence Review* (London: MOD, 2010).

[27] Thomas G. Belden, "Indications, Warning, and Crisis Operations," *International Studies Quarterly* 21, No. 1 (1977): 181–98.

[28] Pierre Wack, "Scenarios: Uncharted Waters Ahead," *Harvard Business Review* 63, No. 5 (1985); Wack, "Scenarios: Shooting the Rapids," *Harvard Business Review* 63, No. 6 (1985): 139–50.

When the Organization of the Petroleum Exporting Countries (OPEC) oil crisis first hit in 1973, global supply of oil dropped sharply, and the global markets were thrown into turmoil. The Shell executives who had considered Pierre Wack's scenarios were better able to weather the economic storm, compared to other oil companies that had not considered the possibility of a sudden shock to the global market. In retrospect, the OPEC shocks proved Wack to be correct, though even he was ready to admit that the process was not an easy one. For an outsider like Wack, who did not fit the typical mold of an oil executive in Amsterdam or London, getting the executives to engage in the process became crucial. There were cultural expectations that needed to be changed, but such changes could not come from the outside, with experts telling well-paid decision makers that they were wrong. Rather, Wack and his colleagues had to engage with the executives over time, allowing them to become invested in the process of scenario creation so that they "owned" these potential futures.[29]

Wack's work (as well as that of successor organizations like the Global Business Network (GBN)) understood that to overcome the obstacle of disbelief in scenario building, the experts and decision makers had to be involved in the process. In large part, the sense of "ownership" for participants came from the judgments that they were allowed to make and from the ability to shepherd that expertise throughout the process.[30] Scenarios contain any number of embedded assumptions, and as events play out in the narrative, the uncertainty surrounding these assumptions may become more evident. Whichever expert contributes to the process of tackling such uncertainty becomes an important part of the process. For example, a scenario describing the future of the natural gas industry in Europe will have to make assumptions about future prices for gas, oil, renewable energy sources, construction of new pipelines or liquid natural gas terminals. If the scenario is simply presented to an energy expert, he may quickly become frustrated and be tempted to ask questions like, Why does the scenario assume that the new US administration will support construction of the NordSteam 2 pipeline? Likewise, scientists working with a disaster risk scenario that designates a certain area as "safe" from flooding may ask any number of questions about the data or assumptions. An entire scenario could be discounted if the assumptions cannot be explained and the expert is not allowed to provide any input.

In policy and business circles, the GBN approach often became synonymous with one of Wack's colleagues, Peter Schwartz. In 2003, Schwartz and his

---

[29] Ian Wilson, "From Scenario Thinking to Strategic Action," *Technological Forecasting and Social Change* 65, No. 1 (2000): 23–29.
[30] Jay Ogilvy, "Scenario Planning, Art or Science?" *World Futures* 61, No. 5 (2005): 331–46.

coauthor Doug Randall created a short scenario for the US Department of Defense's Office of Net Assessment. The scenario was based on some emerging scientific data concerning the abrupt nature of potential climatic changes and their security implications.[31] In the following years, GBN and its facilitators, such as Susan Stickley, were central to attempts for development of new scenarios to understand energy and environmental security risks of interest to the US Department of Energy. There was just one problem: although the GBN approach and Wack philosophy worked well at creating inclusive networks and overcoming the disbelief obstacle, they were not as well suited for handling the complexity of environmental risks and scientific data.[32] A new scenario approach was needed.

Complex Risk Scenarios

The need for a hybrid approach to scenario creation became evident in the spring of 2009, when the Energy and Environmental Security Directorate (then IN-40) in the US Department of Energy hosted a summit meeting in Washington, DC. Facilitated by GBN, the second day of the event was designed as a scenario creation workshop, with participants carefully selected from a cross section of various fields of expertise. In planning the meeting, a small group of experts wrote several environmental and energy risk scenarios, describing potential futures related to climate change, energy prices, demographics, and other major driving forces. Participants in the summit meeting would then assess security impacts of the risk scenarios that they were given. The scenarios drew on unclassified information often used in futures assessments with the Office of the Director of National Intelligence and IEA and then were sent out to scientists for comment and validation.[33] The scientists, as was their professional nature during peer review, were not kind.[34] The scenarios faced many questions concerning scientific assumptions about the sea level

---

[31] Peter Schwartz and Doug Randall, *An Abrupt Climate Change Scenario and Its Implications for United States National Security* (Pasadena: California Institute of Pasadena Jet Propulsion Lab, 2003).

[32] Carol Dumaine and Irving Mintzer, "Confronting Climate Change and Reframing Security," *SAIS Review of International Affairs* 35, No. 1 (2015): 5–16; Leon S. Fuerth and Evan M. Faber, *Anticipatory Governance Practical Upgrades: Equipping the Executive Branch to Cope with Increasing Speed and Complexity of Major Challenges* (Fort McNair, DC: Institute for National Strategic Studies, 2012).

[33] Office of the Director of National Intelligence, "National Intelligence Council – Global Trends," www.dni.gov/index.php/who-we-are/organizations/nic/nic-related-menus/nic-related-content/global-trends.

[34] Admittedly, I (Briggs) was one of those reviewers, and even with my best attempts to be collegial, I found myself inserting many questions and comments.

rise, air temperatures, ocean temperatures, glacial melt, and dozens of other factors, and it quickly became obvious that the scenarios would not stand up to scrutiny during the meeting itself.

Susan Stickley, a GBN facilitator present, then suggested that we try using some cards that would contain combinations of "drivers." These would constitute a mix of hazards and risks that (unknown to us at the time) had already been developed by Chris Luebkeman as 3×5 notecard sets. I (Briggs) drew up some templates as letter-sized (A4) cards, including potential hazards such as melting of the West Antarctic ice sheet, a short list of potential impacts, and a list of scientific references.[35] By the time of the meeting, the team had developed some two dozen driver cards, covering topics from tropical deforestation to global solar storms. While the initial use of these cards was haphazard (the first such scenario is described in Chapter 4), after experimenting with students at Lehigh University and University College London, the cards were used as the basis for a more formalized approach under the USAF Minerva project.

The idea behind complex scenarios was to create a hybrid approach between extrapolated data of the Kahn/RAND scenarios and the less methodical but more inclusive approach of Wack and GBN. If experts and stakeholders needed uncertainty to feel included in the scenario creation process, then that needed to be provided yet somehow also controlled. At the same time, we wanted to avoid the foresight workshops in which people stated the most obvious and what they considered the most probable future risks. We would still use background scenarios and "linear" forecasts of the future, but in such cases, experts would be presented with four "wild cards" that existed on the far edges of expected probability. In combination, these would provide enough uncertainty that expert groups would have to work together to develop a coherent narrative of how such drivers would fit together. The original template for the DOE cards included a probability function, but the team quickly realized that groups would spend all their time arguing over probability and would likely throw out cards with risks that they considered less probable. While scientists and other experts would sometimes push back on the idea of avoiding probabilistic risk discussions, doing so was necessary to address multiple hazards at once. The hybrid scenario approach contained three primary components:

---

[35] A few years later, I (Briggs) met Luebkeman at the National Defense University and explained that my team had developed cards without realizing that he had already done so – even if in a different format. He was very modest in describing this as "convergent evolution" and was not at all possessive of the idea. His cards, called *Drivers of Change*, can still be bought online.

1 *An "environment" within which the scenario is created.* This is often a predetermined geographical region and time scale, with explicit background assumptions concerning extrapolated conditions (e.g., demographics). Contemporary or short-term scenarios are generally easier to create, because the environment itself does not introduce greater uncertainty.

2 *Four "drivers" of change.* These are often abrupt geophysical changes but can also include political events, resource constraints, technological innovations, or other EES hazards.

3 *Cascading impacts from combinations of the drivers, meaning secondary and tertiary impacts/risks and the ways in which they relate to one another.* These cascade maps help identify points of critical vulnerabilities (critical nodes) and critical uncertainties, identified by participants as the scenario is created. End points are not predetermined – no one should ask "when does conflict erupt?" as that implies a linear chain of causality toward a set end state. When done properly, impacts will often come as a surprise, as risks can spread in different directions and also act as feedback loops onto previous drivers and hazards.

If future climate-related disasters contain multiple variables and drivers, and if each has a probability associated with both impact and occurrence, then mathematically speaking, the related uncertainties will spike beyond the capacity of traditional assessment tools. That is one reason why scientific studies in risk assessments tend to focus on as few factors or variables as possible. The confidence in the studies or assessments decreases as uncertainty increases. Since most of us are taught that probabilities follow a traditional, bell-shaped curve, we might also assume that in cases where we are forced to overlay these probabilities on top of one another, it makes sense to focus on the middle of the curve, where the probabilities are all highest. Yet, many environmental systems do not work this way. As discussed in Chapter 2, complex systems in nature are very often nonlinear, meaning they can jump from one point of stability to another, ignoring what we might consider to be the comfortable middle. If one traces, for example, the probability of lake water being a certain clarity after summer rains, we might be surprised to discover that as nitrogen from runoff feeds into the lake, clarity of the water will steadily increase but then suddenly disappear entirely as the lake is choked with green algae from eutrophication processes. The lake water reaches a tipping point and leaps from one point of stability to another. Likewise, in assessing future security risks from climate change, we are faced with the enormous task of what to do with overwhelming amounts of uncertainty and largely unknown probabilities.[36]

Henrik Carlsen made the same argument with respect to scenarios – that scenario sets needed to look at combinations of extremes rather than most probable combinations of probable states.[37] Even improbable combinations of "normal" hazards could work well, mirroring what is often taught in flight training.[38] By using this approach, the scenarios shifted from a projection of possible futures (Kahn) or narrative of alternatives (Wack) to an exploration of critical vulnerabilities in the system. Laying uncommon combinations of extremes onto a region essentially stress-tested how resilient that community or state was to environmental and other hazards and at what point and how it could become overwhelmed – and thereby become a disaster. Examples of how these scenarios were used will be explored in the next few chapters, but it should be noted that the process of creation of the scenarios often remained as crucial as the final products themselves.

Complex Scenario Creation

The construction of complex scenarios generally involves four main elements: foresight workshops, scenario validation, handling uncertainty, and tracing potential cascading impacts.[39] We describe each in detail below.

Foresight Workshops

The first step in complex scenarios involves scenario creation workshops where experts are brought together and new ideas are formed about potential non-linear changes in relevant systems. Foresight scenario creation workshops were first used by the US Department of Energy and were more fully developed by the chair and associate chair for the USAF Minerva Initiative in the spring and early summer of 2011, in cooperation with University College London, the

---

[36] Timothy M. Lenton, "Early Warning of Climate Tipping Points," *Nature Climate Change* 1, No. 4 (2011): 201.

[37] Henrik E. Carlsen, Anders Eriksson, Karl Henrik Dreborg, Bengt Johansson, and Orjan Bodin, "Systematic Exploration of Scenario Spaces," *Foresight* 18, No. 1 (2016): 59–75.

[38] I (Briggs) met Carlsen in summer 2009 in Sweden, and we presented jointly on this topic later in 2010 at the American Geophysical Union conference in San Francisco. See Chad M. Briggs and Henrik Carlsen, "Environmental and Climate Security: Improving Scenario Methodologies for Science and Risk Assessment," AGU Fall Meeting Abstracts, 2010.

[39] Models for early warning communities of environmental risks have existed since at least 2000. See, e.g., the Pacific Disaster Center at www.pdc.org/ or, more recently, the ASEAN Coordinating Centre for Humanitarian Assistance at www.ahacentre.org/.

International Institute for Strategic Studies in London, and NATO's Emerging Security Challenges Division.

In 2007, DOE and international partners like the Scottish government initiated a project on assessing emerging energy and environmental security risks, meant to provide an unclassified space for scientists, policy makers, security officials, and other experts to prepare for future events.[40] Members of the US security community were concerned with how climate change and associated hazards would impact energy and national security planning. I (Briggs) joined this effort in late 2008 as the leader of the Abrupt Climate Change and Security team. From 2008 to 2010, the team developed tools and methodologies for translating scientific data on climate change to policy-relevant warnings, focusing on scenario planning techniques for complex, high-uncertainty risks. The team developed an international network of experts as part of DOE's GlobalEESE (Global Energy and Environment Strategic Ecosystem) project and, in 2009, began work on developing regional assess-ments, downscaling global challenges of climate change to local impacts.

In 2010, this work and its associated research were transferred to the US Air Force under the Office of the Secretary of Defense's (OSD) Minerva Initiative. OSD tasked the Minerva team with providing usable assessments for US combatant commanders, including Northern Command (NORTHCOM), NATO, European Command (EUCOM), Pacific Command (PACOM), and allies such as Canada, Australia, Iraq, and Singapore. Between 2010 and 2011, the team focused on changes to the Arctic in North America and Europe and, in 2012, also advised the Iraqi National Security Council on planning for food, water, and energy security challenges. Workshops were developed and employed to help assess future, complex risks where combinations of scientific and local expertise could help identify "unknown unknowns" that would not have been considered based on obvious or historical risk patterns.

From 2011 to 2012, the Pentagon redirected the team to the Pacific theater, where they provided the USAF chief of staff (Gen. Welsh) with a comprehensive assessment of how changes to water would affect security within and between China and India. On its own initiative, the team also carried out an assessment of emerging environmental changes to islands in the Pacific, in cooperation with the University of Hawaii. One assessment workshop identified specific vulnerabilities to the island of Oahu, which was then devel-oped into a full scenario warning of potential hurricane risks that had pre-viously not existed (see Chapter 5). At the time, Hawaii had not been hit by

---

[40] David A. Bray, Sean Costigan, Keith A. Daum, Helene Lavoix, Elizabeth L. Malone, and Chris Pallaris, "Perspective: Cultivating Strategic Foresight for Energy and Environmental Security," *Environmental Practice* 11, No. 3 (2009): 209–11.

a hurricane since 1992. The assessment was made just prior to Hurricane Sandy. In 2013–15, the Hawaiian Islands were hit by multiple hurricanes, as outlined in the scenario. The Hawaii scenario was later briefed to the White House National Security Council and to the Office of the Director of National Intelligence (ODNI).[41]

Other scenarios were developed for the 2012 International Polar Year Conference held in Montreal. The conference focused on scientific research on Antarctica and the Arctic region, with groups converging on concerns of overseas investment in mining and resource extraction in locations such as Greenland. I (Matejova) was a principal collaborator in this project, serving as a workshop facilitator at the conference. I have since remained involved in the EES network, for example, leading a scenario workshop on Europe's energy security in May 2012 in Kyiv, Ukraine.

The scenarios developed during the foresight workshops provide a snapshot of possible futures in a given region in five to ten years, with a focus on energy and environmental security challenges. The scenarios are designed to force participants to imagine a world that has not yet happened and may not be obvious. Since decision-making in the face of uncertainty is difficult, the main purpose of the workshops is to expose participants to different perspectives, encourage collaborative exploration of complex ideas, and find new areas of uncertainty that may otherwise be neglected in the contingency planning process.

Each workshop generally is a full-day intensive exercise, with experts spread into several groups, each with a trained facilitator. The group distribution is chosen in advance to force participants to create scenarios using improbable combinations of plausible events. This process allows participants to be invested in the process rather than simply comment on it. The workshop format employs use of background research cards (i.e., "drivers") to provide information and structure to the discussion, with card material tailored to energy and environmental variables in and related to the area of interest. The structure ensures that participants must rely on the group to develop emergent knowledge (i.e., experts cannot simply fall back upon their own expertise), yet is not so broad as to be overwhelming or inconclusive. Specifically, the participants are asked to identify emerging, complex hazards; critical uncertainties; potential tipping points; and crucial risk priorities for the area of interest.[42]

---

[41] This process is described in more detail in Chapter 5.

[42] The workshops drew upon the 2009 DOE meeting and the work of Stickley and Robson, both of whom supported efforts to refine the approach and use it elsewhere. The original cards written for DOE were rewritten and expanded into a "deck" of some fifty potential drivers, which were customized and chosen for the target group. The experiments with the workshops in 2010–11

In practice, the workshop format allows identification of plausible scenarios that do not yet receive wide attention. This approach recognizes that energy and environmental systems are closely interconnected and that security concerns are not defined only in terms of violent conflict. The results of the workshops are refined by team members with input from both workshop participants and related experts. This ensures that critical details are not missed and are referenced properly.

Scenario Validation

The second step of complex scenario creation involves scenario validation, or a process of verifying that the science, politics, and various other considerations used in the scenarios are all plausible and match the existing knowledge as closely as possible. Although this process of "wind tunneling" is common in business scenarios as well, with energy and environmental risks, the scientific input from experts becomes critically important. Part of the validation process therefore takes place during the creation workshop itself, and then later, during more in-depth research, once an initial scenario narrative has been established.

Validating scientific data can be difficult for two reasons. First, many future physical conditions, from crude oil production to air temperatures over the Himalayas, depend on human actions and responses – whether directly (such as how much crude oil Saudi Arabia produces in a given month) or indirectly from second- or third-order impacts. For example, increased heat waves in China will likely spark human responses, with some of these (such as the use of air conditioners) producing positive feedback effects that worsen climate change via fossil fuel–generated energy use. Other reactions may produce negative feedback loops, such as increasing greenspace in cities and turning to renewable energy sources. Trying to predict human reactions to events requires the use of simulations and wargames, discussed in detail in Chapter 6.

The second difficulty is that scientific studies rarely produce exact numbers to describe physical conditions. Variance and uncertainty are generally present, and with future projections of potential conditions, the uncertainty becomes considerably more pronounced. This problem can be alleviated by consulting scientific, engineering, and other experts who can provide seasoned judgments on a plausible future condition. Such judgment is usually made in cooperation with the scenario coordinator, who may choose to highlight certain hazards over others.[43]

were never intended as a major focus for the Minerva work, but they became useful tools for the assigned scenario work.

[43] The judgments of scenario coordinators are at times more art than science. Complex scenario development can be done quantitatively, as with Carlsen's methodologies, but the DOE/USAF

Scenario validation, however, means more than simply fact checking; it is also a way of ensuring that the scenario process allows experts to "shepherd" their information rather than hand over a fact sheet and allow others to interpret it. Creating scenarios in advance by small group of people and then introducing them to experts may lead to these experts collectively shrugging and wondering why the scenarios are important to them when they were not involved in their development. This is a common problem observed during other scenario workshops and one we wished to avoid.

Furthermore, when experts are faced with the hypothetical scenario in which they do not understand the assumptions and motivations behind its creation, a real risk is that the boundary conditions of that scenario will be rejected out of hand. For example, at a meeting that I (Briggs) attended in Baghdad in 2012, a group of European planners had been contracted to develop scenarios for future river flows for the Tigris and Euphrates. Iraq had few data points concerning environmental conditions, and water monitoring stations were often targets for insurgent or terrorist attacks. Therefore, the scenarios became important for allowing Iraqi security officials to understand how much water might be available for energy production and processing, agriculture, and urban populations in the future. Drawing on information available from upstream users, such as Syria and Turkey, an expert displayed hard numbers for how many meters per second flow could be expected from these rivers in the future. After the presentation, and exasperated Iraqi official stood up and asked, "Why don't we just assume that these numbers are zero?" To him, the numbers were not plausible, because he did not trust the sources of information and thought it was better to stress the extreme boundaries rather than a median outcome. Considering the instability in the region and the subsequent outbreak of the Syrian civil war, he may have had a point.

The scenario creation and validation process requires experts to continue with the development of the narrative, allowing discussions of plausible and possible events. In many areas, reliable scientific studies simply do not exist. During the scenario process, the role of experts is to help interpret what that uncertainty means and how it can be handled. The process requires contributions from people "on the ground" who can say "I know the official government report says there is no selenium contamination of drinking water, but here are all the reasons that report was wrong . . ." In many ways, uncertainty helps fuel the scenario process.

scenarios often relied more on intuition of what would fit best with the given security framework. This is one reason, among many, why the scenarios avoided violent conflict framing (except for operational scenarios) and instead used broader human security definitions. So-called hard security frames tended to predetermine the outcome, which could create a form of 'tunnel vision' and box in experts.

Uncertainty Boundaries

Uncertainty, especially in academia and politics, is often viewed with suspicion and disdain; it is something to be avoided and minimized at all costs. Scientific journals require a 95 percent confidence interval for studies to pass peer review, and many politicians point to uncertainty surrounding climate change studies as a reason to "wait and see" before passing legislation or taking risk mitigation actions. In PhD programs, we are taught that knowledge expands incrementally from established sources and that jumping too far into uncharted waters is unprofessional. There are good reasons for scientists to be conservative and cautious in making conclusions. We are taught in scientific risk assessments to favor Type 2 errors (false negatives) and to avoid making pronouncements that might turn out to be false later. No one wants to be the proverbial boy who cried wolf. Yet, we are increasingly faced with risk complexities that confound traditional methodologies, and we cannot afford to ignore these new risk constellations.[44]

Uncertainty takes various forms. For example, information may be unavailable due to secrecy or lack of monitoring or due to methodological uncertainty intrinsic to models, measuring errors, extrapolation factors, and others.[45] In risk assessments and scenarios, analysts must be able to identify and describe uncertainty, using it as a positive aspect of the assessment. Rather than pretending that nothing exists in the dark, scenarios can help explore hazards and associated risks that have not yet been studied or confirmed. Uncertainty, after all, generally does not mean that no information is available, only that for various reasons and to varying degrees, the information is questionable. Therefore, experts must be encouraged to explain what is *not* known as much as what is known, and why.

Militaries and intelligence services have long understood this reasoning. In the 2007 CNA report, retired general Gordon Sullivan explained, "People are saying they want to be perfectly convinced about climate science projections, but speaking as a soldier, we never have 100 percent certainty. If you wait until you have 100 percent certainty, something bad is going to happen on the

---

[44] Postwar environmental health assessments have been highly instructive in this regard. Public health experts must often assess complex systems under conditions of intense uncertainty and short time horizons. In areas where even the most basic data are not available, policy and investment decisions must still be made. Understanding the ways in which unmet critical needs can lead to further deterioration of the system or stability becomes crucial. See David J. Briggs, Clive E. Sabel, and Kayoung Lee, "Uncertainty in Epidemiology and Health Risk and Impact Assessment," *Environmental Geochemistry and Health* 31, No. 2 (2009): 189–203.

[45] Kristin Shrader-Frechette, "Methodological Rules for Four Classes of Scientific Uncertainty," in *Scientific Uncertainty and Environmental Problem Solving*, ed. Johns Lemmons (Cambridge, MA: Blackwell Scientific, 1996), 12–39.

battlefield."[46] Historical examples from Pearl Harbor to the German Navy "Channel Dash" in 1942 showed that lack of information concerning a threat should not be interpreted as evidence of lack of threat.[47] In more recent years, this weight-of-evidence argument shifted to the United States's so-called 1 percent doctrine, where even a 1 percent chance of a terror attack was justification for concerted action, almost regardless of the uncertainty involved.[48] While EES disaster planners and assessors need not go to post-9/11 extremes of labeling everything as risk, a more balanced approach is certainly warranted. The obstacles associated with shifting prevailing rules on such contributions are discussed in Chapter 8.

For the scenarios, uncertainties provide points of reference and questions. Why have more scientific studies not been done in this area? Why have local concerns been ignored? What are the monitoring limitations of ecosystem health in interior Brazil? Is it possible for the monsoon rains simply to stop? Often, experts provide valuable insights, but the assessment process must be tailored to allow their voices to be heard and integrated into a measure of risk. As Kristin Shrader-Frechette wrote, one should not confuse risk assessments with scientific publishing, even though rules of evidence often call for solid scientific information. The lack of scientific data or continued existence of uncertainty is not an excuse for inaction.[49] Solid identification of "known unknowns" can be highly instructive in describing potential disaster risks, especially those with cascading impacts.

Scales and Cascades

The original DOE scenarios had to deal with scaling challenges and tracing cascading impacts. Why should European Union or NATO planners be interested in water pollution issues from a new coal plant in rural Kosovo? Why should changes in sea surface temperature in the Indian Ocean affect logistics planning for the US military in Hawaii? How do we take an enormously uncertain and global process such as climate change,

---

[46] *Science Daily*, "Climate Change Poses Serious Threat to US National Security," press release, April 17, 2007, www.sciencedaily.com/releases/2007/04/070417092232.htm.

[47] See Chad M. Briggs, "Developing Strategic and Operational Environmental Intelligence Capabilities," *Intelligence and National Security* 27, No. 5 (2012): 653–68.

[48] Ron Suskind, *One Percent Doctrine: Deep Inside America's Pursuit of Its Enemies since 9/11* (New York: Simon and Schuster, 2006).

[49] Kristin Shrader-Frechette, *Risk Analysis and Scientific Method: Methodological and Ethical Problems with Evaluating Societal Hazards* (Dordrecht, Netherlands: Springer Science and Business Media, 2012).

scale down the impacts to local levels, and then trace those impacts back to the global level?[50] Tackling this challenge required a combination of vulnerability analyses and scenario planning, including the methods for integrating local knowledge and identifying environmental tipping points.

The problems of scales and cascades are interrelated and particularly wicked issues, and they are at times ignored in risk assessments. In complex systems, small changes at one level can propagate and affect much larger systems. Conversely, larger systems and changes may eventually reach down and affect individuals and communities at a local level. For example, the disaster at the Fukushima Daiichi nuclear power plant in 2011 illustrated how a large natural force can overwhelm a critical node in a system (i.e., the backup diesel generator) and how the impacts can cascade back outward, quickly affecting systems across the globe.[51] The challenge for assessing EES risks is therefore not merely that systems are complex or full of inherent uncertainty but that they defy our psychological tendency to focus on just one level of analysis or one geographical region.[52] In many of the earlier environment security studies, changes to natural resource stocks in a given region were often attributed to the local population, without considering broader factors such as the global trade or international security policies.

During the complex scenario process, a follow-up workshop sometimes helps streamline the selected scenarios and trace cascading effects in a network analysis. The purpose of network analysis is to draw out as much detail as possible about the potential cascading impacts of a single environmental event. The selected scenarios may also be joined with other planning scenarios in comprehensive regional assessments. This process engages field experts, partner governments, and nongovernmental organizations across different countries and regions. The process allows planners to see where the critical vulnerabilities and cascading impacts intersect with other missions and strategies. The comprehensive assessment takes the validated scenario and asks, How does a larger environmental tipping point (e.g., a change in ocean currents) affect specific infrastructure and operations? How would failures in

[50] Credit should go to the earlier security theorists who advocated for this global-local interaction framing. See Barry Buzan, "New Patterns of Global Security in the Twenty-First Century," *International Affairs* 67, No. 3 (1991): 431–51.

[51] See Dung T. Nguyen, Yilin Shen, and My T. Thai, "Detecting Critical Nodes in Interdependent Power Networks for Vulnerability Assessment," *IEEE Transactions on Smart Grid* 4, No. 1 (2013): 151–59.

[52] N. W. Arnell, Matthew J. L. Livermore, Sari Kovats, Peter E. Levy, Rob Nicholls, Martin L. Parry, and Stuart R. Gaffin, "Climate and Socio-economic Scenarios for Global-Scale Climate Change Impacts Assessments: Characterising the SRES Storylines," *Global Environmental Change* 14, No. 1 (2004): 3–20.

existing infrastructure (e.g., ports) impact other parts of the country and/or region? What would the loss of specific built environment mean for national and regional strategic operations? Answering such questions allows planners to see where potential risks exist and where investment is needed to strengthen the existing systems. Merely knowing that a risk is possible minimizes indecision and allows quick adaptation once the risk emerges.

Conclusion

The aim of this chapter was to discuss the basics of scenario planning in EES risk assessment. Putting together convincing and scientifically sound narratives is extremely difficult and requires input from a diverse array of experts with varying perspectives. Scenario creation has several benefits, including regional cooperation, cost reduction, and partnership building. For example, in the Asia-Pacific region, the complexity of the strategic environment and potential impacts of extreme environmental events may spur advance cooperation between Indonesia, the Association of Southeast Asian Nations (ASEAN), the United States, and China as well as others in the Pacific Rim who would be willing to share resources. Aside from reduction in costs, such cooperation may motivate a political dialogue on United States–China cooperation with a third party (Indonesia) that had been advocating such cooperation, and where the new ASEAN disaster center is located (in Jakarta). Scenario workshops provide opportunities for socialization of scientists, researchers, activists, and policy makers. Thus, while the scenario approach focuses on disaster planning, important lessons also derive from partnership building and diplomatic benefits. Yet, persisting obstacles, some of which are described in more detail in Chapter 8, prevent effective sharing of information and acceptance of new realities.

The following two chapters describe several attempts to develop energy and environmental security/disaster risk scenarios, primarily under the DOE and USAF programs between 2008 and 2012. Rather than presenting the process of scenario creation as fixed and proven, we admit that we made significant mistakes along the way, though ones from which we learned how to improve future efforts. Many scenarios were largely forgotten and made no significant impact on the understanding of disaster risks, while others became influential and memorable to their creators. It is therefore worthwhile to ask why some of these scenarios were more successful than others in describing shifting disaster risks and vulnerabilities. We then go on to discuss the use of scenarios in further applications, such as wargames and simulations (Chapter 6). We emphasize that scenarios, once developed, are not easily digestible and rarely come replete with a list of clear policy recommendations. As Wack noted, the process of shifting preconceived assumptions about the future is often messy and painful and must work against the inertia of past predictive success and fears of anticipating the unknown.[53]

---

[53] Stephen M. Millett, "The Future of Scenarios: Challenges and Opportunities," *Strategy and Leadership* 31, No. 2 (2003): 16–24.

4

From Lima to New York

The theory of scenarios is far easier than their actual construction. In practice, some scenarios never seem to coalesce into a narrative that makes much sense, others have solid logic behind them but with hard-to-believe conclusions, and yet others have dramatic endings that catch people's attention and spur action. The following chapters attempt to explain why some scenarios work and others fall flat. We draw upon those that were created for and used by the US military and intelligence services, seeing with some hindsight what worked well and what did not. The examples are meant to be illustrative, as the theory and application for risk and disaster scenarios can be far removed from one another, and there are no easy guidebooks on how to proceed with addressing newly emerging risks like climate change.

In the spring and summer of 2009, the climate security team at the US Department of Energy discussed which scenarios to use in illustrating potential abrupt shifts in climate risks. The team had been charged with not only creating risk assessments but also determining which methodologies worked best for such assessments and how to communicate them to policy makers. As discussed in previous chapters, due to complexity of environmental systems, downscaling climate change from a global to local risks was challenging. Which climate changes (i.e., "forcings") should be chosen first? Where would the impacts be most obvious? Would those chosen locations be of interest to policy makers in Washington, DC, London, or other major cities? With these questions in mind, two scenarios were chosen in 2009 as the primary focus for assessment: Peru and New York City.

The former focused on the impacts of abrupt climate change on scarce water resources and energy security in Peru. This was a trial scenario, developed to test new scenario creation methods and design. Since its broader security implications were somewhat unclear, the scenario was of little more than instructive interest to US officials. The second scenario addressed the possibility of a hurricane impact on New York City, a situation that became all too true in October 2012 with Hurricane Sandy. The initial warnings were published with the US Army in late 2010. These warnings, however, were not well received, nor were they communicated outside of a small community of disaster planners.

This chapter explores how the two scenarios were constructed, critically examining the ingredients that allowed them to produce accurate warnings of potential future disasters and associated vulnerabilities. The two scenarios (as well as those in the subsequent chapter) are presented systematically and follow the same structure. We first explain the main assumptions and drivers and then discuss the predicted impacts, postassessment, and lessons learned. Each scenario is also introduced through a summary table that presents the timeline, geographical scope, drivers, security frame, assumed vulnerabilities, intervention points, and critical uncertainties. Since concerns over abrupt climate change prompted the development of the initial EES scenarios, we first discuss this issue below.

The Nature of Abrupt Climate Change

Participants in the GlobalEESE program within DOE met in December 2008 to identify key areas of risk for energy and environmental security. These included issues such as water scarcity in Afghanistan and sea level rise impacts on oil infrastructure. One of the main areas of concern was abrupt climate change, and it was here that the security scenarios (both at DOE and later USAF) discussed in this book originate. Abrupt climate change was considered distinct from the more common perception (at least at the time) that climatic changes would be linear and gradual, meaning that both temperature changes and their associated impacts would be felt in short steps over a long period of time. A significant group of climate scientists had long argued that this perception was misleading and that environmental systems exhibit *phase shifts* in system behavior, otherwise known as tipping points where minor changes to external inputs result in major changes to a system.[1] These abrupt or nonlinear changes could be witnessed in terms of impacts, as well – a system may become overwhelmed, and due to critical vulnerabilities and/or feedback effects, a relatively minor impact may be amplified into a disaster. Such impacts had long been observed in power grids, for example, where minor failures cascade into large-scale blackouts.

Scientific research had identified increasingly sensitive components of the global climate system and related ecosystems. For example, due to polar

---

[1] Marten Scheffer, Stephen R. Carpenter, Timothy M. Lenton, Jordi Bascompte, William Brock, Vasilis Dakos, Johan Van de Koppel, Ingrid A. van de Leemput, Simon A. Levin, Egbert H. van Nes, Mercedes Pascual, and John Vandermeer, "Anticipating Critical Transitions," *Science* 338, No. 6105 (2012): 344–48.

amplification, the Arctic system is very sensitive to changes in greenhouse gases. Some of the greatest temperature shifts have been recorded in the Arctic regions, with major changes to sea ice, loss of permafrost, and shifts in average air temperature being at least twice that of the global average.[2] In other areas of the world, smaller shifts in temperature show sensitivity in other ways. Increased air and water temperatures can trigger acute shifts in precipitation, ecosystem health, and disease vectors. The term *abrupt climate change* therefore encapsulates a wide range of sudden shifts in environmental stability, any of which could potentially impact energy and environmental security.[3]

The idea behind assessing abrupt climate change was therefore twofold: first, to find emerging scientific data on climate change and identify potential tipping points in environmental systems, and second, to identify and assess those areas related to energy security where the abrupt environmental changes could result in unexpected disasters. In some ways, the model for the team was based on ideas originally set out by Schwartz and Randall in their 2003 Department of Defense paper but aimed to include scientists and other experts in the assessments. Rather than employing a "thought experiment" (how Schwartz personally described his paper), DOE hoped to identify real and specific risks to EES in terms of climate-related disasters. The two scenarios discussed below did just that.

Assessing Energy and Environmental Security Risks in Peru

Timeline: five to ten years in the future
Geographical scope: the country of Peru and immediate neighbors
Drivers: melting of highland glaciers; urban growth and water scarcity; sensitivity of Amazonian rainforest; abrupt climate change in Latin America
Security frame: human security with focus on basic needs of water and food; energy security as a secondary concern
Assumed vulnerabilities: food and water scarcity; ecosystem sensitivity
Intervention points: unknown
Critical uncertainties: rate of climate change; rural-urban migration factors; urban response to water scarcity; ecosystem response

[2] Edward A. Schuur, A. D. McGuire, Christina Schadel, Guido Grosse, J. W. Harden, D. J. Hayes, Gustaf Hugelius, Charles D. Koven, P. Kuhry, David Lawrence, Sue Natali, David Olefeldt, Vladimir E. Romanovsky, Kevin Schaefer, M. R. Turetsky, Claire C. Treat, and Jorien E. Vonk, "Climate Change and the Permafrost Carbon Feedback," *Nature* 520, No. 7546 (2015): 171.

[3] Alistair W. R. Seddon, Marc Macias-Fauria, Peter R. Long, David Benz, and Kathy J. Willis, "Sensitivity of Global Terrestrial Ecosystems to Climate Variability," *Nature* 531, No. 7593 (2016): 229.

The Peruvian scenario grew out of discussions at a conference on abrupt climate change in Columbus, Ohio, in June 2009. The American Geophysical Union (AGU) holds periodic Chapman conferences, focused on specific aspects of geosciences and with a smaller set of scientists than the much larger annual meeting held in December. The 2009 Chapman conference included most of the world's leading scientists on abrupt climate change, many of whom were associated with the Ohio State University. In 2009, a large amount of media attention was directed to new evidence of rapid melting of the Greenland ice sheet, seemingly in contradiction to the warnings from the IPCC Fourth Assessment that had just been published two years earlier. The Chapman conference in many ways illustrated how climate science was misunderstood in the broader media and political spheres and was somewhat divided even within universities and geoscience departments. Peru was one of the areas suggested by conference participants that was likely to be affected first and most visibly by climate change.

Constructing the Scenario: Assumptions and Drivers

With senior professors, such as Lonnie Thompson, tracking the retreat of Andean glaciers for many years, Peru appeared to be a good test case for designing a security assessment scenario under DOE. Background information on the scientific basis of the glaciers in Peru was well documented. Working from the initial "drivers" of climate change impacts on glaciers and urban pressures in cities, the team had to assess potential cascading impacts from retreating glaciers. The initial research assumed that loss of glaciers, which effectively act as freshwater reservoirs in mountainous regions, would affect agriculture, hydropower generation, civilian populations in cities like Lima, and nearby ecosystems. A background assessment of various conditions was prepared by Jennifer Gonzales in late 2009, and preliminary findings were published a year later in the US Army War College's journal *Parameters*.[4]

Peru's experience with abrupt climate change came from its glacial formations in the Cordillera Blanca mountain range of the South American Andes, a 180-kilometer stretch of high-altitude mountains containing nearly one-

---

[4] Jennifer Gonzalez, "Abrupt Climate Change Scenarios and Security Foresight: Climate Change and Water in Peru," US Department of Energy Background Study (2010); Briggs, "Environmental Change, Strategic Foresight, and Impacts on Military Power."

quarter of the world's tropical glacier deposits (see Figure 4.1). The glaciers in the Cordillera provide a slow release of water to river basins such as the Upper Rio Santa, carrying water from the highlands to the Pacific coast. With most of the Peruvian population near coastal regions, the glaciers provide an important and necessary reservoir of freshwater in areas that are otherwise arid. Lima itself, located in Peru's central coastal region, has a population of some 8.5 million. Since annual precipitation in the region is nearly nonexistent, Lima relies on upstream supplies of water that can easily be disrupted by changes to weather and climate patterns.

Glaciers in the Andes are particularly sensitive to changes in climate conditions. The snow tends to be replenished in the wetter summer season, but as temperatures rise, the accumulation zone for snow rises in elevation, leaving the lower areas of the glacier to melt. Even if the precipitation patterns themselves do not change, loss of snowpack means that glaciers shrink over time, with downstream flows being less consistent and dependent on rain events. Other changes, such as an increase in ground-level humidity or an increase in cloud cover, can further accelerate melting and overall shrinkage of the glacial cover.

The Peruvian scenario focus benefited from consistent monitoring of the Cordillera glaciers since the 1920s, including previous retreats during the 1930s, and an accelerating retreat since the 1970s. In 1930, the Cordillera spanned between 800 and 850 square kilometers, and by 1970, it was reduced to 660 square kilometers.[5] Since then, the glaciers in the Peruvian highlands have lost half their total volume and over 30 percent of their area, with 81 percent of glaciers below five thousand meters in elevation disappearing entirely.[6] Some estimates suggest the Cordillera glaciers could disappear within four decades, with the remaining low-lying glaciers gone long before then.[7]

---

[5] Christian Georges, "20th-Century Glacier Fluctuations in the Tropical Cordillera Blanca, Peru," *Arctic Antarctic and Alpine Research* 36, No. 1 (2004): 100–107; Adina E. Racoviteanu, Yves Arnaud, Mark W. Williams, and Julio Ordonez, "Decadal Changes in Glacier Parameters in the Cordillera Blanca, Peru, Derived from Remote Sensing," *Journal of Glaciology* 54, No. 186 (2008): 499–510.

[6] Chelsea Whyte, "Ancient Andes Glaciers Have Lost Half Their Ice in Just 40 Years," *New Scientist*, October 10, 2016, www.newscientist.com/article/2108455-ancient-andes-glaciers-have-lost-half-their-ice-in-just-40-years/.

[7] Krista Eleftheriou, "World's Highest Glaciers, in Peruvian Andes, May Disappear within 40 Years," *ABC News*, November 5, 2015, www.abc.net.au/news/2015-11-05/perus-highest-disap pearing-glaciers-climate-change/6915668; Mathias Vuille, Bernard Francou, Patrick Wagnon, Irmgard Juen, Georg Kaser, Bryan G. Mark, and Raymond S. Bradley, "Climate Change and Tropical Andean Glaciers: Past, Present and Future," *Earth-Science Reviews* 89, No. 3–4 (2008): 79–96.

Figure 4.1 Map of Peru.
Source: Dafina Berisha

Predicted Impacts

The immediate impacts of the glacial melt were already seen in lakes and reservoirs of the Rio Santa basin. Increased inundation or flood events had spurred concerns over the ability of dams to withstand the more sudden inflows of water. A few landslide tsunamis have occurred in these lakes, with glacier breakup in 2010 creating a twenty-three-meter-high wave that claimed three lives.[8] Concerns

---

[8] Marco Aquino, "Glacier Breaks in Peru, Causing Tsunami in Andes," *Reuters*, April 12, 2010, www.reuters.com/article/us-peru-glaciers/glacier-breaks-in-peru-causing-tsunami-in-andes-idUSTRE63B69Y20100412.

have been raised over similar events in places like Lake Palcacocha, a 1.5-kilometer-long lake with a dam that could be breached by a thirty-meter wave, flooding the downstream city of Huaraz and its two hundred thousand inhabitants.[9] Numerous lakes and reservoirs rely upon glacial melt, and are stressed with increased meltwater flows (a phenomenon that is also counterintuitive for water resource planning). As glaciers melt, downstream flows may increase for a while, giving a false sense of security before the sources dry up and water availability drops below historical averages.

The downstream flows are particularly important for the Santa Rio basin in Peru, which includes the capital city of Lima. With water scarcity already an issue, roughly one-quarter of Lima's 8 million inhabitants have no secure access to water. Freshwater is sometimes provided by delivery trucks and sold to local residents. While this is not uncommon in large cities in South America, the lack of local rainfall makes Lima especially vulnerable to changes in upstream freshwater supplies.[10] Should water levels drop enough, basic services and sanitation would be difficult or even impossible to maintain. The exact consequences of severe drought and water unavailability are very specific to geographies and cultures but in general result in increased risks of water-washed and waterborne-related diseases such as scabies and cholera, higher health mortality among children, less resilience to extreme heat events, and economic damages from loss of productivity and production. Very few large cities have experienced absolute loss of water resources, which makes prediction of future such events difficult. However, a common assumption we held was that one major adaptation would be migration from the city to other areas with more available water. Whether that destination would be in or near Peru was unknown.

More worrying were the impacts on agriculture and energy production. The agricultural sector is the largest consumer of water in Peru, using some 85 percent of total freshwater resources in 2009.[11] This use of water for irrigation has been acute, since half of the country's agricultural production is located in the arid coastal region where little to no rainfall occurs. Peru's food production is highly reliant on both exports and imports, a common legacy of

---

[9] See, e.g., Dan Collyns, "Climate Change Has Turned Peru's Glacial Lake into a Deadly Flood Timebomb," *Guardian*, June 29, 2018, www.theguardian.com/environment/2018/jun/29/climate-change-has-turned-perus-glacial-lake-into-a-deadly-flood-timebomb.

[10] Joan Calzada, Susana Iranzo, and Alex Saenz, "Community Managed Water Systems: The Case of Peru," *Journal of Environment and Development* 26, No. 4 (2017): 400–428.

[11] Jeffrey Bury, Bryan G. Mark, Mark Carey, Kenneth R. Young, Jeffrey M. McKenzie, Michel Baraer, Adam French, and Molly H. Polk, "New Geographies of Water and Climate Change in Peru: Coupled Natural and Social Transformations in the Santa River Watershed," *Annals of the Association of American Geographers* 103, No. 2 (2013): 363–74.

former colonial states where much agricultural output is designed as cash crops for North America and Europe. Peru, for example, has become the world's leading exporter of asparagus, a crop known for its high water consumption. The more traditional water-intensive crops of sugar and cotton also remain prime exports.

At the same time, Peru remains heavily reliant on imports of basic foodstuffs, which account for nearly 40 percent of production. Local production of wheat, soybean, and corn has decreased in recent years, with imports from the United States nearly doubling between 2014 and 2017.[12] These trends suggest an increasing vulnerability of the Peruvian agricultural sector to external influences, one that was not recognized in the original scenario work. With water-intensive export crops growing rapidly, Peru's reliance on basic foodstuff imports from the United States and Canada leaves less of an internal market for food security in case Chinese demand drops or American exports become more difficult to secure. The high-value exports are also highly reliant on water availability and low prices, two factors that cannot be guaranteed in the future as climate change increases pressure on water supply.

The energy sector in Peru has also faced increasing demands, with local demand for electricity growing 90 percent between 2005 and 2015. The country benefits from a large hydropower capacity (measured in 2013 as 165,377 megawatt potential) and the ability to expand into wind power in the future.[13] However, total energy consumption is still tilted heavily toward fossil fuels, with 80 percent of total energy consumption in the country provided by oil, coal, and gas in 2013.[14] With rapidly increasing demand, Peru's Ministry of Energy and Mines and financier Inter-American Development Bank rely heavily on hydropower for future electricity production. The National Energy Plan (2014–25) identifies fifteen hydropower dam projects with another sixty identified sites, mostly in the Amazon region of the eastern Andes.[15] The hydro plans have come under criticism that they do not take account of potentially severe climate impacts or consider social and environmental impacts from large dam and reservoir construction risks. Nonhydro renewables, such as wind and solar power, are downplayed in the national strategy.

---

[12] US International Trade Administration, "Peru Country Commercial Guide: Agricultural Sectors," September 22, 2017, www.export.gov/article?id=Peru-Agricultural-Sectors.

[13] Peruvian Private Investment Promotion Agency, "Electricity Sector Data," www .investinperu.pe/modulos/JER/PlantillaStandard.aspx?are=1&prf=0&jer=5940&sec=50.

[14] These are updated figures and differ slightly from the 2009 data used in the Gonzalez/Briggs report.

[15] The National Energy Plan is available at www.minem.gob.pe/minem/archivos/2ResEje-2014–2025%20Vf.pdf. See also Monti Aguirre, "Peru's Energy Future," *International Rivers*, June 9, 2016, www.internationalrivers.org/blogs/233/peru-s-energy-future.

Like the urban water consumption risks, Peru's geography allows some leeway in how it allocates energy production and adapts to climate change realities. The problem is that energy infrastructure planning takes decades to realize and, once installed, represents large sunk costs that are difficult to remove or refurbish. Smaller-scale grid and renewables allow for more flexibility, but these tend to be ignored in large national energy strategies, partly owing to historical traditions of centralized grids and utility control and partly from pressures of the companies who stand to benefit from large construction projects like dams. As seen in the subsequent scenarios, however, climate and disaster risks are forcing some reconsideration of small- and micro-grid investment benefits.

Post-assessment

Although the original mechanism for environmental change was well understood and well documented, there was no clear format or template available for how a scenario should be constructed. The GlobalInt scenario creation workshops often emphasize the need to create narratives around future scenarios or stories that could easily be communicated. However, at first, it was not clear what should be emphasized or how to integrate science into the security assessment. The theoretical basis was simple: take initial conditions and then trace cascades throughout the system. The loss of water could affect the production of hydropower electricity, and this would in turn have impacts on other sectors related to energy production. Likewise, food production would be affected both by loss of freshwater resources and by changes to the electrical system, but how these would be mapped out or interact was predictably complicated. While putting the scenario pieces together could be worked out through trial and error, the bigger challenge for the Peruvian scenario was determining where a threshold existed for security concern and intervention.

As explained in Chapter 3, scenarios can be designed to describe any number of potential future events, but what makes them interesting or compelling depends on the subject as well as the audience. For the military and intelligence communities, some geographical regions were automatically of high interest because of current or historical activity. Environmental security scenarios dealing with Iraq, for example, would have no trouble in justifying the regional focus but would have to make a case for why lack of freshwater was more important than a car bomb campaign near the Green Zone in Baghdad. The Peruvian scenario was not of automatic interest to the US military or intelligence communities, save for some Latin American experts at US Southern Command (SOUTHCOM) or think tanks like the CNA

Corporation. In a way, Peru was chosen as an initial test case because it was not obvious and because there was no competition for "hard" security activity beyond continued concern over the Shining Path insurgency. In the end, while freshwater resources remain a serious concern in the country and region, the Peruvian scenario effort was ended and did not attract much attention outside of a few smaller circles. In retrospect, the following valuable lessons were learned on how to approach abrupt climate change scenarios, which helped in later efforts.

Lesson: Work with Local Experts on Potential Impacts and Resilience

Some of the scenario assumptions about first-order impacts from glacial melt turned out not to be true, such as the reliance of upland farmers on glacial melt water for agriculture. Farmers in the Peruvian mountains often relied on rain that was not seriously affected (at least yet) by climate change, an error that was pointed out by sociopolitical researchers with field experience in the country. We had relied on scientific findings only for the initial driver, instead of working with local experts on determining where impacts might occur and how resilient communities were in weathering those changes. It turned out that Peruvian farmers were hardly as fragile as we assumed, which affected the trajectory of the cascading impacts and risks.

Another aspect of water use in Peru that was not recognized in 2009–10 was the high per capita use of water in cities like Lima.[16] At 250 liters per capita per day in 2010, Lima was extremely inefficient in its use of water. In comparison, cities in the European Union average only 120–40 liters, while the per capita water use in Cairo (considered somewhat comparable as a large desert city) was 100 liters.[17] While this fact was hardly a secret at the time of the DOE assessment, we erred in focusing on the absolute scarcity of water to the city and did not recognize that inefficiency was itself a form of resilience.

The issue of efficiency, or in other terms a "just-in-time" economic model, became more of a focal point for the alter USAF team when examining Asia-Pacific countries such as Japan, where it was recognized that efficiency is a form of vulnerability. If a system is highly efficient, there is little room for

---

[16] Antonio A. R. Ioris, "Water Scarcity and the Exclusionary City: The Struggle for Water Justice in Lima, Peru," *Water International* 41, No. 1 (2016): 125–39.

[17] *Peruvian Times*, "Aird Lima among Most Wasteful Cities for Water Consumption," September 21, 2010, www.peruviantimes.com/21/arid-lima-among-most-wasteful-cities-for-water-consumption/9195/.

improvement or change when external pressures exert themselves. With a highly inefficient system, such as that in Lima, outside pressure from water scarcity can force a change in water usage and infrastructure, and this is precisely what Lima has done in subsequent years. The climatic changes in Peru have been gradual and predictable enough that scarcity has not come as a sudden shock, but instead has created incentives for changes in resource use.

Peruvian president Alan Garcia began instituting changes in 2006, with an Agua para Todos program to provide water for all residents, with a particular emphasis on Lima. While in 2009, large parts of Lima had no access to water, only a few years later, this had changed, and much of the remaining population was provided with fifty to sixty liters per day (it remains unclear whether this includes the informal settlements (*asientamientos humanos*)). The state water agency also began metering water, attributing much of the wastefulness of water use in Lima to lack of measuring. These changes have allowed the city to adapt to the risks from glacial melt, at least in the short term, though ground-water withdrawals and continued growth of the city have maintained pressure on overall water resource availability.[18]

Lesson: External Influences Are Crucial for Scenarios over Time

The abrupt climate change team at DOE had an understandable focus on how geophysical changes could affect the larger security picture. This remains the focus of much of academic research. Studies have examined, for example, the correlation between changes in rainfall with conflict risks in Africa and Asia, and the 1990s Homer-Dixon research was centered on scarcity of natural resources.[19] Reflecting on the Peruvian scenario development, however, it was obvious that outside political factors also changed the environment within which disaster risks were measured. Just like changes to climate boundary systems shifted the types and severity of risks, so too would changes to political conditions alter the risk landscape. In the case of Peru, we missed both the outside influence of countries like the United States and China and the temporal nature of change. Since 2009, China has become a prime export market for Peruvian goods, accounting for much of the growth in the local agricultural

---

[18] For a background on water scarcity issues in Lima, see Antonio A. R. Ioris, "The Geography of Multiple Scarcities: Urban Development and Water Problems in Lima, Peru," *Geoforum* 43, No. 3 (2012): 612–22.

[19] Homer-Dixon, "Environmental Scarcities and Violent Conflict"; Cullen S. Hendrix and Idean Salehyan, "Climate Change, Rainfall, and Social Conflict in Africa," *Journal of Peace Research* 49, No. 1 (2012): 35–50.

industry, exporting crops (in addition to asparagus) such as grapes, cranberries, avocado, citrus fruits, mango, pomegranate – all water intensive.[20]

The temporal dimension has always been a thorny issue. The initial assessment took a snapshot of environmental conditions and projected changes like glacial melt into the near future. The cascading impacts, however, lacked any sense of change over time – we asked how changes to glacial melt would affect the agricultural sector in Peru in the future, but the agricultural sector itself was rooted in present conditions. That meant that we missed the Chinese dimension completely, not recognizing that increasing wealth and consumption in China would alter the nature of food production and vulnerabilities in Peru within only a few years. Taking a lesson from the more traditional scenario methods of Kahn et al., we had to make more of an effort to track multiple trends at once and see how they interacted into the future.[21] Although it would greatly complicate scenario development, it made sense to assess, for example, how housing and transportation development in a region intersected with future sea level rise risks. We just had to admit that the people buying those houses might be from abroad and not fit historical patterns or assumptions.

Lesson: Begin with Science

One very positive lesson from the Peru work was the recognition that scientific communities can be an excellent source of information, far beyond the usual peer-reviewed literature and scientific articles. The experience with AGU suggested three things that we had suspected earlier and that turned out to be substantially true. The first takeaway was that scientists know far more than they will readily admit publicly, about both the nature of their studies and the future risks associated with what they see from research. The nature of scientific publishing means that articles must contain only data with high confidence and low uncertainty, pushing the edges of established knowledge only slightly with every new study. Scientists monitoring abrupt climatic changes are often reluctant to make solid public conclusions about what the changes mean or

---

[20] Public Radio International, "Peru's Cash Crop Asparagus Is Bleeding the Region Dry," January 24, 2012, www.pri.org/stories/2012-01-24/perus-cash-crop-asparagus-bleeding-key-region-dry; Rebecca Ray, K. P. Gallagher, Andres Lopez, and Cynthia Sanborn, "China in Latin America: Lessons for South-South Cooperation and Sustainable Development," in *China and Sustainable Development in Latin America*, ed. Rebecca Ray, K. P. Gallagher, Andres Lopez, and Cynthia Sanborn (New York: Anthem Press, 2015), chapter 1.

[21] Dana Mietzner and Guido Reger, "Advantages and Disadvantages of Scenario Approaches for Strategic Foresight," *International Journal of Technology Intelligence and Planning* 1, No. 2 (2005): 220–39.

what associated risks might exist. This reluctance has created a substantial barrier between the scientific and military/intelligence communities.

Even scientists within the intelligence and military establishments are highly reliant on the academic communities for new information and research. The methods for obtaining this information, however, do not fit well with environmental and disaster risks. As discussed later in Chapter 8, the traditions of secrecy in national security discussions meant that scientists were understandably wary and distrustful of simply handing over their data, and this was certainly true with the scientists in the abrupt climate change community. They first had to trust that the person they were talking to had at least a basic understanding of the scientific concepts, so that the security assessment would not grossly misrepresent or misunderstand the complex scientific issues involved. The Peruvian scenario was the first real example we had of the importance of establishing trust within the scientific community. Admittedly, this was made easier by the association with DOE, which itself employs tens of thousands of scientists and engineers and was headed at the time by a Nobel laureate.

Once trust was established, it was surprising how much the scientists were willing to talk and how much information they made available. If anything, we were flooded with information and data, including long, invaluable explanations on what was not known and why. Understandably, many, if not most, of the scientists had developed personal attachments and feelings to their area of study, meaning they were worried about environmental conditions from climate change and what those changes meant to their families, communities, and country. Many were frustrated with lack of recognition of the magnitude of the problem but felt constrained by professional ethics on what they could say and how outspoken they could be when communicating warnings. Scholarly community measures success according to published peer reviewed articles and research grants, while engagement with the wider community (i.e., the public, policy makers, and security communities) not only does not contribute to one's career but can sometimes hinder it.

The need to establish trust was also an important lesson on the use of unclassified information. As Carol Dumaine had said on numerous occasions, the most crucial information for assessments comes from open secrets, meaning information that is both unknown and unclassified. Often, experts have already collected data and perhaps even created risk assessments on emerging environmental and disaster hazards. This information can only be obtained by working with expert communities (meaning both scientific and local experts). In some areas, such as geospatial intelligence and satellite reconnaissance, substantial information must remain classified. For the most part, however, disaster risk data exist in the open realm, but they take work to uncover. In the

Peruvian assessment, the issue of glacial retreat was not at all a secret, but it turned out to be critical to the expert judgments on how serious the emerging risks might be and the explanations on the nature of uncertainty surrounding those risks.

Lesson: What Is Not Known Can Be More Important than What Is Known

The work on climate change in Peru highlighted as well the importance of mapping uncertainty in disaster risk assessment. If the scenario had been based solely on well-established data from peer-reviewed publications, the overall risk assessment would have been very conservative and would not have accounted for what was not known and why. Following the AGU Chapman conference in June 2009, several of the senior scientists provided detailed assessments concerning the state of the field and knowledge regarding abrupt climate change. According to Ohio State professor Richard Alley, cryology as a science had lagged behind the atmospheric and oceanic sciences in the United States, in large part because meteorology and oceanography, being critical to military operations, received substantial funding from the Department of Defense over the decades. Without advanced modeling of how ice sheets moved, the default in preparing the *IPCC Fourth Assessment Report* (4AR) was to treat land glaciers as "essentially unmoving blocks of ice." All the potential knowledge of how quickly the glacier might melt or move was not communicated to policy makers, nor were associated uncertainties.

The work of modeling ice sheet flows and integrating them into long-term climate change assessments was difficult and complex and by the mid-2000s had not matured enough to make it into the IPCC 4AR. In 2009, some of the critical work on ice sheet modeling was being done by an Ohio State University graduate student named Patrick Applegate. Applegate and others were not only advancing the field but concerned about preliminary findings and what those might mean for the stability of ice sheets in Greenland and West Antarctica. As scientists like Applegate and Alley explained, a good deal was already understood and observed about how glaciers shrink and destabilize, but it was not as simple as an ice cube melting in the summer sun.[22]

In Greenland, for example, pools of melted water collect on the surface of a glacier, bright aquamarine blue in color, and visible if one flies over Greenland

---

[22] Personal communication, June 2009. Also see Patrick J. Applegate, Nina Kirchner, Emma J. Stone, Klaus Keller, and Ralf Greve, "An Assessment of Key Model Parametric Uncertainties in Projections of Greenland Ice Sheet Behavior," *Cryosphere* 6, No. 3 (2012): 589–606.

in an airliner. Researchers working in Greenland noted that these pools often suddenly disappear and attributed the disappearance to the creation of moulins, vertical hollow shafts up to ten meters wide that carried meltwater from the surface to the base of the glacier. This meltwater could then act as a lubricant between the glacier and the bedrock, allowing a smoother flow of the ice sheet toward the ocean and accelerating destabilization of the entire structure. In 2009, this information was known but needed to be communicated as a critical uncertainty within the climate change community – people tended to underestimate the stability of glaciers. Subsequent research has validated these ideas not only in Greenland but also in West Antarctica, an area that in 2009 was considered stable and not of potential risk to global sea level rise until at least late in the twenty-first century.[23]

What the AGU scientists had laid out was a collective explanation of emerging risks that had not yet been communicated and areas that were not yet monitored or researched well enough to draw conclusions. While one section of the scenario assessment, led by Jennifer Gonzales, focused on what was known on the Peruvian situation and trends, a parallel section of the scenario was needed to outline the nature of scientific and other uncertainties surrounding these disaster and climate risks. I (Briggs) wrote the first of the so-called dark reports in a hotel in Stockholm in early July. I had just met the Swedish defense scientist Henrik Carlsen in Karlstad the week before, and his work on modeling disaster risk extremes in scenarios overlapped well with what we were trying to accomplish at DOE.[24]

Lesson: Local Impacts Don't Always Translate into Global Concerns

It was evident that Peru, while an interesting start and test case for scenario design, was not dynamic enough in terms of scenario creation, or relevant enough for policy makers in the United States. Admittedly, we had been warned about this pitfall from the beginning: local impacts may not always translate into global concerns. Perhaps in some ways, Peru was not meant to be a resonating scenario, since the methodologies were still in the nascent phase. The assessments were careful not to jump to easy conclusions about violent conflict between states, and the link to insurgents such as the Shining Path was unclear. With impacts largely falling on poorer populations in the slums of

---

[23] Christina Hulbe, "Is Ice Sheet Collapse in West Antarctica Unstoppable?," *Science* 356, No. 6341 (2017): 910–11.

[24] Henrik Carlsen, Richard J. T. Klein, and Per Wikman-Svahn, "Transparent Scenario Development," *Nature Climate Change* 7, No. 9 (2017): 613.

Lima or affecting ecosystems high in the Peruvian mountains, the security implications for the United States were hardly overwhelming. The findings from the assessment were deemed interesting for DOE and USAF as an initial test case, but officials strongly hinted that more "substantial" impacts were needed to illustrate the real nature of abrupt climate change and its links to disasters. Another example was needed, one that more vividly illustrated impacts in a way that would resonate with both American and European audiences. While Hurricane Katrina was still vividly and horrifically remembered, the response failure following the storm was not clearly climate related and did not force people to rethink assumptions concerning *where* unexpected climate change impacts could occur. Recognizing from the start that this might be a problem, a parallel scenario was under development that would prove more attention-grabbing: New York.

Anticipating Sandy

Timeline: present day to ten years into the future
Geographical scope: New York City and metropolitan region
Drivers: risk of hurricane from rising sea surface temperatures; sea level rise; vulnerability of transport and energy infrastructure
Security frame: human security; focus on energy and transport vulnerabilities and associated military disaster response
Assumed vulnerabilities: location of energy and transport infrastructure
Intervention points: disaster mitigation plans; energy and transport system redundancies
Critical uncertainties: exact mechanism for increased storm risk was unknown; cascading impacts beyond New York City and tristate region were unknown

For the next scenario, the choice of New York City was not difficult. During the spring and summer of 2009, I (Briggs) was shuttling back and forth between the United States and Europe, primarily on Continental Airlines flights between Newark and Brussels.[25] I had written many of the longer strategy documents while sitting at Newark airport, where one could look out the window and see

---

[25] For any who care to point out the contradiction of working on climate risks while emitting carbon dioxide from flying, the point is well taken. I had a responsibility for reaching out to scientists in Europe, and much of the connection had to be face-to-face, yet my jobs were based

water just beyond the main runway. While waiting for a flight to Athens in May, I was reminded of the history of the 1938 hurricane that hit Long Island as a Category 3 storm, killing some six hundred people.[26] Given the large amount of construction that had been done on the ports and shores since the Second World War, it was an interesting question whether such a storm was plausible again, and what impacts there might be, should it happen. At the time, it was simply a question. There was no clear climate change mechanism that could make the storm more likely, save for additional sea surface warming increasing the intensity or duration of Atlantic tropical storms.

The question became more practical two days later in Athens. I had been invited to speak about environmental migration at an Organization for Security and Cooperation in Europe (OSCE) ministerial meeting in Greece on behalf of the Institute for Environmental Security. The room was laid out with a long rectangle of tables, with the speaker mirrored on television screens placed in front of the ministers and ambassadors. The arrangement allowed them to tune out when they were disinterested – which they largely seemed to be. I concluded my speech by illustrating future risks and asked the delegates to imagine a storm like Hurricane Katrina hitting New York City instead, with the airports and Lower Manhattan flooded and evacuations from New York to the outer boroughs or upstate. That caught people's attention. In contrast to other examples, which often focused on regions like Africa or Asia and the possibility of migration into Europe, New York City was a place that everyone in the room knew. I could see concerned faces as I stood to leave. While some delegates came afterward to voice appreciation for the warning, the most memorable comment came from the US delegate: "You shouldn't try scaring everyone using examples of improbable events that will never happen!"

Was it truly improbable? As noted in Chapter 3, the DOE team had agreed to avoid too many discussions of probability, but a New York hurricane had historical record, with numerous tropical storms occurring in the 1800s. The latter half of the twentieth century was, if anything, an unusually quiet period for tropical storm impacts on the region. A scenario of a direct hit by a hurricane was entirely plausible and fit within the idea of posing a tipping point for emerging risks. Tropical storms form because of warming sea surface temperatures. They gain energy from the water when the sea surface temperature rises above 26.5°C. When the water is particularly warm, a tropical storm will continue to gain strength from ocean convection, which explains why such

in Pennsylvania and Washington, DC. The frequent travel was the reason for "forward-basing" in Europe (Berlin and London) during 2010–11, and more recently in Kosovo.

[26] See National Weather Service, "The Great New England hurricane of 1938," https://www.weather.gov/okx/1938HurricaneHome.

storms weaken over land or cooler waters. While the number of storms can be highly variable, overall, the concern is that tropical storms can become more powerful with climate change.[27] The 2017 Atlantic hurricane season was a case in point, with seventeen named storms and several especially powerful hurricanes hitting Mexico, Texas, Florida, the islands of the Caribbean, and even Ireland.[28] In 2009, the question was whether Katrina was a historically powerful and damaging storm or whether it was a sign of things to come.

In the past, hurricanes and tropical storms moving over land lost energy and were considerably weakened by the time they reached the New York City region. The worry in 2009 was the possibility that a storm would travel up the East Coast over unusually warm water and then suddenly shift westward up Long Island Sound. The westward movement would create a storm surge in advance of the eye wall. The narrowing of the sound toward New York and New Jersey would effectively "funnel" and amplify the surge by the time it reached shore. Assuming a slight northward movement overall, the water would not only hit the Jersey shore but wrap around into Queens and Lower Manhattan. Discussions of such an event were already under way in 2009, though perhaps limited to certain audiences and policy circles. DOE was certainly not the first to consider the possibility.[29]

In the summer of 2009, the DOE team contacted the New York City Office of Emergency Management to ask what work might have already been done on the possibility of a Katrina-like storm hitting the region. According to one official from the office, the possibility was well known and recognized among New York City disaster planners, but he admitted that they faced a dilemma. Although detailed scenarios and evacuation plans could be worked out in advance, he felt that the work could not be shared with the public. The worry was that any real public admission of the risk could set off a series of reactions from residents, with wealthier residents in vulnerable areas selling and moving elsewhere, leaving more vulnerable and less wealthy residents shouldering the risks. What he was describing was a classic pattern with disaster refugees seen elsewhere. While the media and policy focus is often on those fleeing, the most

---

[27] Kevin E. Trenberth, Lijing Cheng, Peter Jacobs, Yongxin Zhang, and John Fasullo, "Hurricane Harvey Links to Ocean Heat Content and Climate Change Adaptation," *Earth's Future* (2018), https://agupubs.onlinelibrary.wiley.com/doi/10.1029/2018EF000825.

[28] US NOAA, "Extremely active 2017 Atlantic hurricane season finally ends," 30 November 2017, www.noaa.gov/media-release/extremely-active-2017-atlantic-hurricane-season-finally-ends.

[29] Ning Lin, Kerry A. Emanuel, J. A. Smith, and E. Vanmarcke, "Risk Assessment of Hurricane Storm Surge for New York City," *Journal of Geophysical Research: Atmospheres* 115, No. D18 (2010).

vulnerable populations are those left behind.[30] In the case of New York City and New Jersey, property flight could undercut the tax base for areas that needed revenue for adaptation measures. The other issue, the official hinted, was that politicians were uncomfortable voicing warning about something in which they did not have confidence. It was well and good to make plans in advance, but admitting that to the public was another matter.

New York City and DOE had slightly different priorities in terms of scenario focus. While the city of New York was understandably worried about its citizens, for the DOE team the risks over infrastructure took precedence. The ports of New York and New Jersey were the twenty-third busiest in the world for container volume. They involved extensive auto carrier deliveries, oil and liquid fuel import/export, and ferry passenger traffic. Oil and gas refineries were located in potential flood areas, such as the Port Reading and Perth Amboy areas between Newark and New Brunswick in New Jersey. The three major airports of the region were also located directly in flood areas, including Newark, JFK (in Queens), and LaGuardia, central hubs for both domestic and international flights, and in total responsible for around 100 million passengers a year. The infrastructure of New York itself was also a concern, since much of it was located underground.

Constructing the Scenario: Assumptions and Drivers

The scenario was based on the assumption that impacts could clearly be traced from potential flooding, but the exact mechanism by which the storm would occur could not be known in advance. Sea surface warming was not enough to uncover newly plausible mechanism for storms – those would not be known or understood until after the storm actually hit in 2012. In written communications among the team that summer, members agreed that the emphasis should be on plausible scenarios to avoid getting bogged down in underestimating potential risks due to uncertainty. Rather than the "high-impact, low-probability" risks described by Nicholas Taleb in writings on "black swans,"[31] the preference among many in the intelligence community was for "high-impact, unknown-probability" events. The writings on black swans did not seem to apply well to climate issues. They assumed that probability was already well known, and the concern was over probabilistic "long tails" (i.e., the far ends of logarithmic

---

[30] Candice A. Myers, Tim Slack, and Joachim Singelmann, "Social Vulnerability and Migration in the Wake of Disaster: The Case of Hurricanes Katrina and Rita," *Population and Environment* 29, No. 6 (2008): 271–91.

[31] Nassim Nicholas Taleb, *The Black Swan* (New York: Random House, 2007).

probability functions where extreme effects would occur but only rarely). Changes to the climate system had possibly shifted systems into more extreme conditions, or into a state where extremes (such as the 2003 heat wave in Europe) became more common than the historical record suggests.

In climate terms, this meant that the boundary conditions had shifted. Boundary conditions refer to the range of normal variance in a climate system, which are constrained by interactions of the systems as they relate to solar radiation, albedo (i.e., reflection of energy back into space), and the amount of energy in the system. Due to the large amounts of greenhouse gases that have been emitted into the atmosphere, more energy is trapped, more energy collects in the earth's environmental systems, and not as much is reflected back into space (creating a feedback loop). The boundaries of "normal" climate variation have therefore changed, whether it means warmer winters than had been the average, more extreme heat waves in the summers, shifts in ocean and air currents, or shifts in ecological systems. Since the environment is a complex system, the impacts and risks associated with shifts to boundary conditions cannot easily be predicted in advance.

We assumed it was plausible that tropical storm risks to the region would be real, that we could no longer consider the probability to be low (assuming it ever was), and that the potential impacts were so high as to justify advance planning and assessment. It was also obvious that a scenario focusing on New York City would grab the attention of policy makers more easily than one based on Peru. The salience of the scenario was not merely in the importance of policy makers' familiarity with the region but in using a hurricane as the trigger event built upon two additional factors. First, people's familiarity with the events and visual images from Hurricane Katrina provided both anchoring and priming effects on their ability to visualize a similar event occurring in New York City and believe in such possibility. Second, the scenario described a discrete geophysical event rather than a more diffuse shift in background environmental conditions. The usefulness of having triggering events became more obvious to us over time, and the New York case provided a way for people to focus and trace cascading events rather than keep track of, for example, eighteen different variables shifting at once. In disaster psychology, abrupt shocks and events gain more political and media attention than slow-moving disasters. Shocks can also be a greater test for systemic resilience – to see, for example, how much the energy infrastructure in the New York region could withstand or recover from.

Predicted Impacts

The DOE program ended before the scenario could be fully fleshed out, but enough details were available by 2010 that they were presented in the US Army War College's journal *Parameters* later that year.[32] The event assumed that a Category 3 hurricane would travel up the East Coast of the United States, then turn sharply west up Long Island Sound. The storm surge would funnel its intensity while traveling up the sound, hitting hardest on the Jersey Shore and industrial areas of New Jersey, wrapping around to hit Lower Manhattan and Queens. A storm surge of up to ten meters was considered possible; it would inundate and close the Newark, LaGuardia and JFK airports, and create severe disruption of energy and transportation grids in the region. The security impacts for the military would largely relate to disaster response, with the National Guard and elements of the federal military needed for recovery efforts. Further cascading impacts would include financial damages from disruption of the Wall Street sector, large insurance claims from storm-related damages, and potential costs from infrastructure adaptation investments against future storms.

The Reality Was Stranger than Fiction: Post-assessment

Unfortunately, we did not have to wait long to see how accurate the scenario was to a real-life event. Only two years after publishing some of the scenario warnings, a hurricane did hit the New York City and New Jersey Shore region. In fact, Hurricane Sandy was one of two tropical storms that hit the New York region in two consecutive years. In August 2011, Hurricane Irene, weakened to a tropical storm, made landfall on the East Coast of the United States, claiming lives, damaging infrastructure, flooding roads, and knocking out power. More than nine hundred thousand homes were left without power in New York alone, where the storm caused destruction of infrastructure and the closure of roads, airports, and the public transit system.[33] In October 2012, the city was at risk once again.

On October 23, 2012, Tracy Briggs and I (Briggs) were in London to work with colleagues from the Department of War Studies at King's College, when I received an email from our GlobalInt associate Laura Deutsch. Laura was passing along a warning about a new tropical storm, named Sandy, that had

---

[32] Briggs, "Environmental Change, Strategic Foresight and Impacts on Military Powers."

[33] CBS, "Impacts from Irene, State by State," *CBS News*, August 29, 2011, www.cbsnews.com/news/impacts-from-irene-state-by-state/; David K. Mears and Sarah McKearnan, "Rivers and Resilience: Lessons Learned from Tropical Storm Irene," *Vermont Journal of Environmental Law* 14 (2012): 177.

formed in the Caribbean. At the time it was near Jamaica, but was projected to travel up the East Coast of the United States. Our immediate concern related to our own logistics – we had to travel from London to Ottawa on October 30, and then I had to turn around and head to Baghdad via Newark on November 2. By late 2012, our assessment focus had been on the Asia-Pacific region, and the Hawaii scenario (see Chapter 5) was already well under development. But having looked in some detail at hurricane impacts on New York, it was horrifying to see the scenario unfold on the global news.

After wreaking devastation in the Caribbean, Sandy moved past the Bahamas and, as a Category 1 hurricane, continued parallel to the coasts of Georgia, South Carolina, and North Carolina. By October 28, meteorologists had warned that due to an unusual alignment of weather factors, the storm was likely to become a powerful superstorm and turn northwest toward Baltimore, Washington, DC, Philadelphia, and New York.[34] It did exactly that, drenching the coast and coming ashore near Atlantic City in New Jersey. The surge then flooded parts of Lower Manhattan and hit Staten Island as well as the surrounding communities. On October 30, Sandy moved over Pennsylvania and dissipated a day later, leaving behind a path of destruction – lost lives and billions of dollars in damages (Figure 4.2).[35]

The events around Hurricane Sandy were instructive, but the lessons were somewhat bittersweet. Although we happened to be correct, prediction was never what we had intended with the scenarios. The massive storm hitting New York and New Jersey was always a possibility. What remained was to assess whether warnings had been heeded, and what adequate measures could have been taken in advance.

Lesson: "Cassandra Scenarios" Aren't Very Helpful

Warnings about a storm hitting New York City had been discounted ever since the scenarios first surfaced following Katrina in 2005. The reaction of the US diplomat in Athens was little different from others, who, when faced with the possibility of a horrific event hitting a place they knew well, retreated into a mix of horror and disbelief. To disaster psychologists, this would not have come as any surprise. Risk psychologists such as Paul Slovic had demonstrated that warnings, if meaningful, threaten the "cognitive normality" humans use to

---

[34] Tony McNally, Massimo Bonavita, and Jean-Noel Thepaut, "The Role of Satellite Data in the Forecasting of Hurricane Sandy," *Monthly Weather Review* 142, No. 2 (2014): 634–46.

[35] Willie Drye, "A Timeline of Hurricane Sandy's Path of Destruction," *National Geographic*, November 2, 2012, https://blog.nationalgeographic.org/2012/11/02/a-timeline-of-hurricane-sandys-path-of-destruction/.

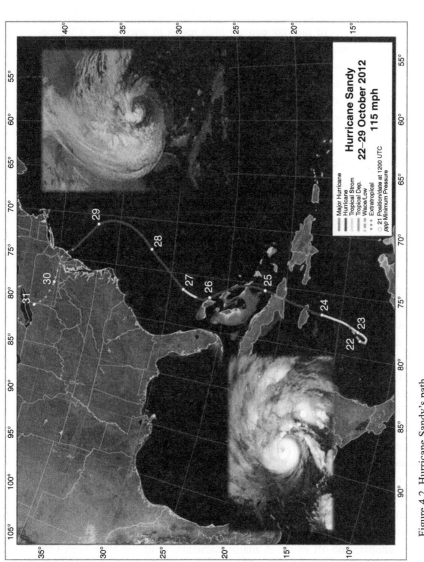

Figure 4.2 Hurricane Sandy's path.
Source: NOAA

deal with risks from day to day.[36] Unless warnings are packaged with clear and achievable steps to reduce the risk, the perception of the risk tends to be minimized. This discounting of risk is especially true if the issue is complex, seems vague, is not rooted in someone's personal experience or knowledge, and when the predictions of the risk contain high levels of uncertainty. Climate-related disasters such as superstorms fit all those criteria, and therefore make transmission and acceptance of warnings difficult. While we will return to these and other challenges in Chapter 8, in the aftermath of Sandy, we felt we could have done more to communicate these risks. After all, what good is a disaster scenario if it is ignored?

Lesson: Scenarios Must Accept Substantial Uncertainty

The uncertainty surrounding Sandy meant that scientific discussions over the role of climate change in accelerating such storms and disasters remained unsettled. While the hypothesis over the connection between Rossby waves[37] and shifting weather patterns was based on sound science, the systems were so complex that accurate prediction remained elusive, at least when it came to long-term climate risks. Sandy was also a clear example of what our USAF team had warned about vis-à-vis disasters in environmental intelligence assess-ments earlier that year – that most disasters are improbable combinations of probable risks, and it was the combination itself that made the storm so power-ful and damaging. Had it not been for the high-pressure system over Greenland that forced the storm westward, Sandy would have made a glancing blow on Newfoundland, passed into the North Atlantic, and dissipated. Had a cold front not met the storm as it hit the Jersey Shore, Sandy might not have been nearly as powerful, and so on. It was a combination of factors that made the storm as destructive as it was, and the combination of so many risks and drivers at once made the uncertainty surrounding it quickly mushroom.

The key question on those drivers remained: will they increase in the future, and therefore in different combinations overwhelm the vulnerabilities of the New York City/New Jersey region? Some of the drivers may become more common or powerful in the future, leading to an overall increase in risks. A disaster may appear as a result of different combinations of factors, and not as a unique, one-off event. A major vulnerability of the New York City

---

[36] Paul Slovic and Ellen Peters, "Risk Perception and Affect," *Current Directions in Psychological Science* 15, No. 6 (2006): 322–25.

[37] Jennifer Francis and Stephen J. Vavrus, "Evidence Linking Arctic Amplification to Extreme Weather in Mid-Latitudes," *Geophysical Research Letters* 39, No. 6 (2012), https://agupubs .onlinelibrary.wiley.com/doi/10.1029/2012GL051000.

infrastructure was having much of the city (including electrical transformers, subways, and computer systems) placed below ground. When compared to regions where such infrastructure is placed above ground, critical infrastructure is more vulnerable to storm and wind risks, as was seen in Puerto Rico in 2017. Sandy flooded the lower half of Manhattan, leaving it without electricity or transport, as these nodes became overwhelmed. While there is now retrofitting to protect electrical grids, the question remains under what other disaster scenarios would flooding or other hazards overwhelm this underground infrastructure. The DOE scenario focusing on hurricanes was based on historical events, but with rising sea level, every inch of incremental storm surge rise displaces another six thousand people, and becomes an exponential growth after some time.[38] Are there other disasters we had missed? Will there be new combinations of hazards and events that will overwhelm other underground infrastructure? We had focused on the obvious, but future scenarios may not be based on historical analogues, and may both surprise and overwhelm us. The trick is to get ahead of that surprise.

Conclusion

The two scenarios presented in this chapter were the first attempts at assessing future EES risks in complex systems. Aside from exploring new potential security problems, both produced valuable lessons for future scenario and policy work. Although it was a test case, the Peru scenario revealed that working with local experts is necessary to produce more accurate impact assessments, and that gaining trust from scientists opens the gates to a rich world of data. We have also learned that much like environmental stressors, external political influences can shift the underlying conditions, that engaging with uncertainty is crucial, and that local impacts are not always easily translated into global concerns (and perhaps neither they should be). The New York scenario offered further lessons. Hurricane Sandy was a "Cassandra situation" where the warnings had been fairly accurate but largely ignored outside of small circles of experts.[39] Sandy also showed the limitations of translating science into plausible scenarios, since the mechanisms of the actual storm could not have been known or predicted in advance.

---

[38] The one inch–six thousand people assumption was based on earlier US government climate studies and now appears to be an example of evidence that has since disappeared from US government websites.

[39] Chiara De Franco and Christoph Meyer, eds., *Forecasting, Warning and Responding to Transnational Risks* (New York: Palgrave Macmillan, 2011).

In practical terms, scenarios must be packaged for each audience. However accurately one anticipates potential future disasters, merely giving the warning in a generic sense is not enough. In the intelligence community, this was both a benefit and a challenge. The intelligence community has a strict separation between their responsibility to give warnings, and their involvement in policy making. This separation is intended to keep politics out of intelligence assessments, and help prevent assessments from merely telling policy makers what they want to hear. During the DOE work, the separation allowed us to take scenarios to more extreme conclusions. At the same time, this meant that the final "product" was often met with disbelief by those outside of the intelligence and military realms. When the New York City scenario was first developed in 2009, there was no obvious solution, and we were not expected to find one at that time. By 2012, we had a greater responsibility to communicate our findings and realized that a two-step process was necessary. The scenarios had to be developed under the rules of an intelligence assessment, looking to potential extremes without regard for what was more publicly believable. Once the assessments were complete, we had to find critical nodes where the final audiences could understand why the disaster risks directly affected them. These lessons and their attendant solutions later found their application in the Pacific scenarios, which are discussed in the next chapter.

5

From Pearl Harbor to Pearl Harbor

In December 2011, seventy years after the Japanese attack on US naval forces at Pearl Harbor, I (Briggs) arrived as head of a USAF research team at Pacific Command headquarters at Camp H. M. Smith, Hawaii. After spending much of the previous year in London and Ottawa, focused on Arctic issues, the Pentagon had reassigned the team to examine how changes to energy and environmental conditions would affect strategic security in the Asia-Pacific region. While a theater-wide assessment was submitted to the USAF chief of staff the following year, one of the more interesting scenarios involved, not China or India, but the Hawaiian island of Oahu. Based on emerging scientific research that suggested potential changes to sea surface temperatures and tropical storm tracks, our team identified critical vulnerabilities to energy and transport infrastructure affecting nearly 1 million people. With distant echoes to intelligence failures of 1941, when US intelligence expected an attack much farther west in the Pacific, so too did the energy and environmental assessments suggest that our security concerns might be focused in the wrong places.

This shift in focus to the Pacific region was in many ways return to the basics. Many of the lessons concerning failures of intelligence in the United States have been based on the experiences of the Pearl Harbor attack of 1941, specifically the failures of translating available intelligence into effective warnings and action. One set of lessons that comes from the intelligence warning literature and profession concerns translating the so-called weak signals. The idea behind the weak signals is that information may be available on impending disasters or risks but we lack the capacity to collate and analyze it in a way that can be used for effective warnings.[1] This chapter largely focuses

---

[1] Paul J. H. Schoemaker, George S. Day, and Scott A. Snyder, "Integrating Organizational Networks, Weak Signals, Strategic Radars and Scenario Planning," *Technological Forecasting and Social Change* 80, No. 4 (2013): 815–24; Sandro Mendonça, Miguel Pina e Cunha, Jari Kaivo-Oja, and Frank Ruff, "Wild Cards, Weak Signals and Organisational Improvisation,"

on the experiences of translating weak signals into workable scenarios for energy and environment security.

In translating weak signals into actionable intelligence, scenarios can help categorize information that otherwise would be left out of context. One of the first scenarios developed by the DOE team in 2009 was related to energy security and environmental factors in Japan, a narrative that would counter-intuitively tie together events as seemingly disparate as climate change–related disasters and Fukushima. The scenario described the energy security implications of undersea methane deposits near Japan and helped increase our understanding of the fragility of Japanese security leading up to the events of March 2011.[2] Appropriately, the final set of scenarios developed for the USAF Minerva project several years later returned to the Pacific and described vulnerabilities in the Hawaiian Islands, putting the concepts of weak signals to their most effective use. In this chapter, we introduce both scenarios along with their lessons. First, however, we discuss the main underlying concepts – surprise attacks and weak signals.

Surprise Attacks and Weak Signals

Many analyses of the Pearl Harbor attack focus on the concept of a surprise attack, which is an event linked to different planning preconditions – information is available but ignored, precautions can be taken but are not, and the sense of risk is lessened because of a belief that the worst impacts will be felt elsewhere. In December 1941, while the US military was genuinely worried that war with Japan was imminent, the strong belief persisted that any attack by the Japanese would take place much farther west in the Pacific, most notably in the US territories in the Philippines.[3] In analyzing Pearl Harbor and similar strategic surprises, Ephraim Kam has explained surprise attacks through three primary elements.[4] First, such events are disproportionately damaging, meaning having impacts far greater than expected and outside of historical norms. Second, surprise attacks are not anticipated. While this might seem tautological, the

---

Futures 36, No. 2 (2004): 201–18; Pierre Rossel, "Early Detection, Warnings, Weak Signals and Seeds of Change: A Turbulent Domain of Futures Studies," *Futures* 44, No. 3 (2012): 229–39.

[2] See Nobuhito Mori, Tomoyuki Takahashi, and 2011 Tohoku Earthquake Tsunami Joint Survey Group, "Nationwide Post Event Survey and Analysis of the 2011 Tohoku Earthquake Tsunami," *Coastal Engineering Journal* 54, No. 1 (2012): 1250001.

[3] David Kahn, "The Intelligence Failure of Pearl Harbor," *Foreign Affairs* 70, No. 5 (1991): 138–52; Richard K. Betts, "Analysis, War, and Decision: Why Intelligence Failures Are Inevitable," *World Politics* 31, no. 1 (1978): 61–89.

[4] Ephraim Kam, *Surprise Attack: The Victim's Perspective* (Cambridge, MA: Harvard University Press, 1988).

statement emphasizes the psychological and organizational barriers that can dampen expectations and minimize expected risk. Finally, surprise attacks indicate underlying unpreparedness – combinations of physical vulnerability (e.g., the geography of Pearl Harbor), cultural and social vulnerabilities (e.g., an attack on Sunday morning), and lack of willingness to prepare for potential risks (e.g., aircraft parked in rows, battleships anchored in line). Although Kam focused on military actions and deliberate threats, the same three elements could be said to describe disaster risks associated with abrupt climate change.

Since 2005, a series of hurricanes and other storms – Katrina, Sandy, Harvey, Maria, and others – have caused disproportionate damage in the United States. Simultaneous unnamed disasters have ravaged California with drought, followed by extensive wildfires and subsequent floods. The sheer scale of disasters fueled by climate change around the globe in recent years has been inconsistent with historical records, leaving organizations from insurance companies to emergency responders scrambling to cope with new realities.[5] Prior to Hurricane Katrina, officers in the Army Corps of Engineers warned Washington, DC, about potential floods in the ninth district of New Orleans.[6] Environmental planners warned about increasing flood risks from sub urban sprawl in the Houston, Texas, region prior to Hurricane Harvey.[7] These expert warnings, however, went unheeded. "Unimaginable" disasters are reflections of our ability to prepare for disasters, not of the information available to warn about them. We have ample evidence that disasters – whether climate related, such as Hurricane Maria in Puerto Rico, or nonclimate events, such as the 2011 Tohoku tsunami and Fukushima disaster – indicate underlying unpreparedness in our societies. Data may be available on risks, and experts may give warnings about potential disasters, but for various reasons (some discussed in Chapter 2), we tend to minimize such warnings and underinvest in infrastructure, which leaves us vulnerable to disasters on a grand scale.

Broadly speaking, the concept of weak signals may mean different things, depending on the background and goals of experts. In some cases, for example, weak signals could refer to attempts to interpret what little information is available in a closed system. For example, during the Cold War, the concept

---

[5] Carolyn Kousky, "Informing Climate Adaptation: A Review of the Economic Costs of Natural Disasters," *Energy Economics* 46 (2014): 576–92.

[6] Personal communication with B.Gen. Wendell "Chris" King, November 2009. See also Charles F. Parker, Eric K. Stern, Eric Paglia, and Christer Brown, "Preventable Catastrophe? The Hurricane Katrina Disaster Revisited," *Journal of Contingencies and Crisis Management* 17, No. 4 (2009): 206–20.

[7] Lise Olsen, "Record Reservoir Flood Predictions Kept Secret before Hurricane Harvey Hit Houston," *Houston Chronicle*, February 22, 2018, www.chron.com/news/houston-weather/hur ricaneharvey/article/Record-reservoir-flood-predictions-kept-secret-12633506.php.

of *Kremlinology* was the attempt to understand the workings of Soviet leadership based upon otherwise minor signals such as who was standing closest to the Soviet premier during the annual May Day parades or the removal or size of various paintings in offices. The term *Kremlinology* has since adapted to refer to any study of a powerful and closed organization on which very little information is available.[8]

In contrast, weak signals for disaster risks refer to a far different problem – there is so much information available that it is difficult to know what is most crucial for understanding potential future events. Often, the most obvious markers for risk trends may be misleading, but because they fit a pattern and meet our expectations, we tend to accept them and then end up focusing on the wrong things. Such a problem is compounded if we devote resources to monitoring potential risks in the wrong areas or underinvest in research and therefore underestimate the associated risk simply because the data are not readily available. The political and diplomatic focus on average air temperatures, at the expense of understanding and appreciating the risks associated with the hydrosphere and cryosphere in climate systems, is only one example. In the face of newly emerging disasters, determining which signals are important and how to interpret them is a paramount challenge.

In 2012, Nate Silver published a book entitled *The Signal and Noise*,[9] which in part attempted to address this problem. Silver, who was unusually successful at predicting the outcomes of the US elections in 2008 and 2012, wrote about how many seemingly unpredictable concepts could be understood if one looked beyond typical measurements and applied statistical analyses from related realms. While Silver's analyses are interesting, his approach and goals were still significantly different from the needs of the disaster risk community. He has focused on predictions of identifiable events, such as elections or the stock market. Scenarios and related foresight methods, however, are not meant to predict specific events. Instead, they are meant to help our understanding of what events might happen and what they mean for risk mitigation and adaptation.

In a critique of Silver's methodology, climate scientist Michael Mann objected to the attempted application of methodologies from social sciences, such as economics, to scientific concepts such as climate change. Mann had several problems with Silver's portrayal of climate science and the nature of uncertainty within the scientific community. One essential critique boiled down

---

[8] Patrick Cockburn, *Getting Russia Wrong: The End of Kremlinology* (New York: Verso Books, 1989).

[9] Nate Silver, *The Signal and the Noise: Why So Many Predictions Fail – but Some Don't* (New York: Penguin Press, 2012).

to the issue that Silver was attempting to interpret data from a field in which he had little knowledge or expertise.[10] The idea for weak signals described in the following two scenarios in this chapter came from very different experiences. We realized early on that experts in various fields had to be involved in the scenario creation process and maintain their involvement throughout. It was only in this way that various signals could be interpreted in context.

Similar problems often arise with risk approaches such as environmental impact assessments and scenario planning. As we described earlier, risk methodologies often attempt to predict future events or at least provide a quantification of probability. Data that do not fall under easily identifiable categories are often considered "outliers" and may be ignored or removed from data sets. Particularly when faced with information that contradicts the "accepted wisdom," humans and organizations have a tendency to downplay or ignore potential future risks, especially if the information falls outside of the respective fields of the experts involved. An American political scientist trained in quantitative approaches to national security studies, for example, may favor methodologies that focus on statistical relationships between changes in air temperature and the probability of interstate violent conflict. If presented with data on how climatic changes can lead to shifts in soil alkalinity in tropical rain forests, the political scientist may find it largely meaningless. Weak signals can provide information and warnings of potential cascading impacts and future disasters, but the signals need to be interpreted and communicated within a proper framework.

From our perspective, then, weak signals referred to emerging data that could only be fully understood through the collective effort of a network of experts. These experts could not only contribute their knowledge of respective fields but also help others understand the importance, significance, uncertainties, and limits of information that might otherwise pass notice. The idea of expanding concepts of environmental politics to address complexity is hardly new, and this was largely the reasoning behind creation of expert EES networks like GlobalEESE.[11] However, it was not enough to bring experts into a network

[10] Michael E. Mann, "FiveThirtyEight: The Number of Things Nate Silver Gets Wrong about Climate Change," *Huffington Post*, September 24, 2012, www.huffingtonpost.com/michael-e-mann/nate-silver-climate-change_b_1909482.html.

[11] Chad Briggs, "The Emperor's Clothes: International Relations Theory beyond the Cold War," *Political and Economic Review* 1, No. 1 (1996): 1–13. This article had been my first attempt at explaining how the overly narrow focus of mainstream political science helped explain why the fall of the Berlin Wall had been a surprise and how ignoring complexity would be disastrous for environmental politics. It would take years of further study, collaboration, and research to flesh out those ideas. See also David A. Bray, Sean Costigan, Keith A. Daum, Helene Lavoix, Elizabeth L. Malone, and Chris Pallaris, "Perspective: Cultivating Strategic Foresight for Energy and Environmental Security," *Environmental Practice* 11, No. 3 (2009): 209–11.

to discuss potential EES risks. A framework had to be developed for each set of hazards and risks – we needed a structure by which outsiders could understand trigger events and potential pathways of future disasters. Without clear methodological and policy frameworks, discussions of future risks can be interesting without taking clear directions toward resolution.

Starting in spring 2009 at DOE, scenarios helped provide those interpretive structures, with one of the first being an expert narrative concerning methane hydrates (clathrates) near Japan. As a first attempt at scenario creation under the GlobalEESE program, there were no instructions on where to focus or how to proceed. With the help of colleagues and invited experts, the resulting narrative became something of a prescient warning about how to interpret weak signals in the years leading to the Fukushima disaster of 2011.

Methane Hydrates Scenarios

Timeline: ten to twenty years in the future
Geographical scope: Japan and maritime areas to the east
Drivers: melting permafrost; nuclear power safety; declining fisheries; Arctic sea warming
Security frame: national energy security; environmental disaster risks
Assumed vulnerabilities: warming oceans; uncertainty in energy markets
Intervention points: technological innovation
Critical uncertainties: technology transfers; warming of intermediate waters

During the April 2009 summit meeting in Washington, DC, participants were asked to use random mixes of environmental risks and hazards and apply them to a security risk template developed by Susan Stickley and David Robson. One group, which included experts such as Cleo Paskal and Ko Barrett, found it difficult to fit the four chosen drivers into a likely scenario. We struggled with finding ways to fit declining fisheries with nuclear power safety and climate change and decided to forgo a structured template to describe a scenario with "trigger points" for others to warn them of a progression toward a potential disaster. While it was possible to put two or three of the drivers together in a given narrative, fitting all of them into a coherent scenario proved to be an enormous challenge. One of the drivers always seemed to be a wildcard and an outlier that had no meaningful relationship to the other factors. What we learned, however, was that tackling these outliers was the key to approaching novel disaster scenarios. Understanding the scenario requires some background explanation to the hazards and drivers we were juggling.

The first issue was that of methane releases in the Arctic. In 2009, this was already recognized as a potentially large problem, although not flagged in the IPCC Fourth Assessment.[12] Discussions about the melting permafrost suggested that the subsequent global disruption of carbon budget was not going to be great, since sudden massive releases of terrestrial methane were not considered likely in the near future. Yet, we had been hearing more strident warnings from scientists working in the field, particularly those focusing on hydrologic methane deposits.[13] Despite the risk that melting permafrost poses to the global carbon budget, a much larger risk seemed to be hidden out of sight and often out of mind: methane hydrates (or clathrates).

Methane hydrates are fragile crystalline ice formations of methane, kept in place underwater under conditions of generally stable temperature and pressure. The expanse of these hydrate formations is extraordinarily vast, with estimates of twenty thousand trillion cubic meters of carbon being stored in continental shelf regions of the ocean around the world.[14] These are not only found in the Arctic regions – vast reserves are known to exist in areas like those off the coasts of Japan and South Carolina. For many years, the hydrate formations were not well studied and were not considered important components in climate change or risk discussions, save for the abrupt climate change community and discussions of the "clathrate gun hypothesis."[15] Largely, this lack of attention stemmed from a belief that ocean temperatures would not change at such depth, nor would they see pressure change significantly enough to disrupt the fragile methane lattices. Hydrates are generally found around five hundred meters deep in the oceans, with some shallower deposits in the Arctic. Some thought only these shallow deposits would be affected by climate-related

---

[12] Bruce Buffett and David Archer, "Global Inventory of Methane Clathrate: Sensitivity to Changes in the Deep Ocean," *Earth and Planetary Science Letters* 227, No. 3–4 (2004): 185–99.

[13] Katey Walter-Anthony's videos of burning methane plumes from lakes in Alaska were a good example of an eye-catching visual. See Katey M. Walter, S. A. Zimov, J. P. Chanton, D. Verbyla, and F. S. Chapin III, "Methane Bubbling from Siberian Thaw Lakes as a Positive Feedback to Climate Warming," *Nature* 443, No. 7107 (2006): 71.

[14] Timothy S. Collet, "Natural Gas Hydrate as a Potential Energy Resource," in *Natural Gas Hydrate in Oceanic and Permafrost Environments*, ed. Michael D. Max (Dordrecht, Netherlands: Kluwer Academic, 2003), 132.

[15] James P. Kennett, Kevin G. Cannariato, Ingrid L. Hendy, and Richard J. Behl, "Methane Hydrates in Quaternary Climate Change: The Clathrate Gun Hypothesis," American Geophysical Union, 2003.

warming before 2100.[16] Unfortunately, both assumptions about temperature and pressure may have been wrong.

In 2008, there was a small abstract notice in the scientific research journal *Geophysical Research Letters* indicating that a joint Swedish/ Russian research team in the Barents Sea witnessed a significant increase in subsea methane gas emissions.[17] While the full article detailing the research team's findings was not to be published until the spring of 2010, information was significant enough that the research was brought up as potential hazard at the 2009 summit in Washington, DC.[18] The working group experts agreed that in many ways, the implications were profound. If water at intermediate depths (approximately four hundred meters) was, in fact, warming significantly enough to destabilize subsea methane hydrate formations, many other assumptions about the rate of climate change and the risks of abrupt changes themselves may have been ill-founded. At the same time, information emerged that technologies were being developed to enable commercial extraction of natural gas from marine methane hydrate formations.[19] Ironically enough, this technology partly came from DOE.

Constructing the Scenario: Assumptions and Drivers

The scenario was built around methane hydrates after our inability to link hazards related to nuclear power, fisheries, and Arctic warming. A potentially alternative energy source in the ocean that was both in the Arctic and temperate zones, hydrates seemed to fit as a factor that was not otherwise considered in the initial mix of drivers. For the scenario to make sense as a narrative, the group identified potential impacts from rapid destabilization of methane hydrates and then described the "trigger points" that would alert others to these potentials being realized.

---

[16] David Archer, "Methane Hydrate Stability and Anthropogenic Climate Change," *Biogeosciences Discussions* 4, No. 2 (2007): 993–1057.

[17] Natalia Shakhova, Igor Semiletov, Anatoly Salyuk, and Denis Kosmach, "Anomalies of Methane in the Atmosphere over the East Siberian Shelf: Is There Any Sign of Methane Leakage from Shallow Shelf Hydrates?" *Geophysical Research Abstracts* 10, EGU2008-A-01526 (2008).

[18] Natalia Shakhova, Igor Semiletov, Anatoly Salyuk, Vladimir Yusupov, Denis Kosmach, and Orjan Gustafsson, "Extensive Methane Venting to the Atmosphere from Sediments of the East Siberian Arctic Shelf," *Science* 327, No. 5970 (2010): 1246–50.

[19] Ray Boswell, "Resource Potential of Methane Hydrate Coming into Focus," *Journal of Petroleum Science and Engineering* 56, No. 1–3 (2007): 9–13.

Potential Impacts

Several potential scenario outcomes involved extensive environmental risks from hydrate mining, including excess release of methane into the ocean and atmosphere, unspecified ecosystem impacts, and even potential collapse of sections of the continental shelf. This last risk was known as the *Storegga effect*, named after a geological event some eight thousand years ago in which a 180-mile section of subsea continental shelf collapsed and triggered a massive North Atlantic tsunami that hit Scotland and affected areas as far as fifty miles inland from the coast.[20] Some researchers believed that the mechanism for the collapse was an explosive detonation of methane hydrates, resulting in a massive underwater rockslide. In a number of the scenario run-throughs, climate change destabilization of hydrates served as an impetus for even more mining of the methane before it was released into the atmosphere, since the CO_2 released from burning the gas would be a less potent greenhouse gas than methane itself. The more hydrates became destabilized, the more mining of such deposits for fuel would serve as a form of greenhouse gas mitigation. The group concluded that, given the technological requirements, ready locations of subsea hydrate formations, domestic natural gas supplies, and history of cooperation with the United States, there would be a relatively small number of countries to be watched. Japan was chosen as the focus for the scenario, since the Nankai Trough off the coast of Japan was a major deposit of marine methane hydrates (see Figure 5.1).[21] The following weak signals served as potential warnings for triggers of the scenario risks:

1 *Evidence of warming of intermediate waters, allowing destabilization of hydrate formations.* The Swedish/Russian research already suggested that this process was under way by 2009.

2 *Development of technology allowing commercial mining of marine hydrate deposits.* This technology was already under development, though experimentally.

3 *National commercialization of such technology for use in Japan.*

4 *A shock to the Japanese energy landscape, requiring sudden demand of gas reserves.*

---

[20] Jurgen Mienert, Maarten Vanneste, Stefan Bunz, Karin Andreassen, Haflidi Haflidason, and Hans Petter Sejrup, "Ocean Warming and Gas Hydrate Stability on the Mid-Norwegian Margin at the Storegga Slide," *Marine and Petroleum Geology* 22, No. 1–2 (2005): 233–44.

[21] Yoshihiro Konno, Tetsuya Fujii, Akihiko Sato, Koya Akamine, Motoyoshi Naiki, Yoshihiro Masuda, Koji Yamamoto, and Jiro Nagao, "Key Findings of the World's First Offshore Methane Hydrate Production Test off the Coast of Japan: Toward Future Commercial Production," *Energy and Fuels* 31, No. 3 (2017): 2607–16.

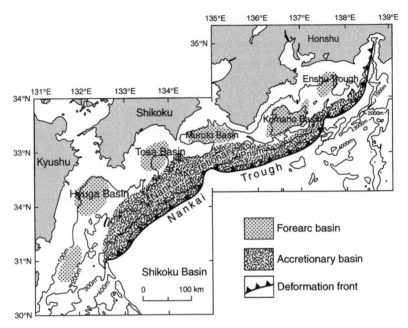

Figure 5.1 Methane clathrate deposits in Nankai Trough off the coast of Japan.
Source: Baba and Yamada (2004)

From the Scenario to Real-World Events: Postassessment

In August 2010, with the USAF Minerva projects starting, I (Briggs) traveled to the Pentagon to brief US Navy Capt. Timothy Gallaudet on the methane scenario. The Norwegian government had expressed interest in the issue to the US Navy, but there was no disaster risk framework to understand how the issue might have played out, other than serving as a greenhouse gas amplification effect. Although Gallaudet (who would later become a rear admiral and Oceanographer of the Navy) said the scenario was interesting and provided a broader understanding of the risks associated with methane hydrates, the scenario's timeline appeared to be futuristic.

Only one month later, Japan announced commercial investment in methane hydrate extraction technologies, to be carried out in cooperation with the US Department of Energy.[22] By itself this would be an unremarkable piece of news to most security analysts, but in the context of the scenario developed the year before, this otherwise weak signal had potential energy and

---

[22] E.g., Michael Fitzpatrick, "Japan to Drill for Controversial 'Fire Ice,'" *Guardian*, September 27, 2010, www.theguardian.com/business/2010/sep/27/energy-industry-energy.

environmental security implications. The first three steps of the scenario had woven together otherwise disparate and unconnected pieces of scientific and technological information. The scenario narrative suggested that a disaster in Japan could be a trigger for further developments, meaning that the energy and environmental landscape could shift quickly. Unfortunately, we did not have to wait long for that trigger to occur.

The March 11, 2011, Tohoku earthquake and resulting tsunami triggered a chain of events in Japan that would cripple its nuclear power industry, and create a sudden, intense need for natural gas supplies.[23] While in the short term, supplies came from Russia, the long-term prospects for marine methane hydrate mining took on a very real appearance.[24] The USAF Minerva project had just officially started a few months earlier, and a number of Pentagon officials and intelligence analysts wanted immediate answers concerning the wider energy and environmental security situation in Japan. The devastating impact from the tsunami on cities like Sendai, and the unfolding nuclear disaster at the Fukushima Daiichi plant both received most of the attention, and deservedly so. For strategic planners, however, there was an intense need to know what would happen next, and how the cascading impacts from the disasters would set up new risks and new vulnerabilities. Until that point, EES briefings had typically spent a fair amount of time introducing the subject of energy and environmental security, but after the Tohoku earthquake and tsunami, the ability of environmental forces to impact energy systems was no longer disputable. What remained were questions on how the impacts would play out, and what decisions needed to be made to avoid a development path that would create new disaster risks.

Lesson: Future Comes Quickly

The original methane hydrate scenario had been developed as a thought exercise, not a directed planning project. Yet, the narrative turned out to be highly useful for understanding the complex nature of environmental systems and energy security once the 2011 disasters occurred in Japan. What was most surprising was the speed at which everything occurred, from the initial reports of methane hydrate destabilization in the Arctic to the predicted scenario points and finally the Fukushima disaster. Most scenarios, and particularly those with

---

[23] Masatsugu Hayashi and Larry Hughes, "The Policy Responses to the Fukushima Nuclear Accident and Their Effect on Japanese Energy Security," *Energy Policy* 59 (2013): 86–101.

[24] Yoshihiro Masuda, Koji Yamamoto, Shimada Tadaaki, Takao Ebinuma, and Sadao Nagakubo, "Japan's Methane Hydrate R&D Program Progresses to Phase 2," *Fire in the Ice* 9, No. 4 (2009), www.netl.doe.gov/File%20Library/Research/Oil-Gas/methane%20hydrates/MHNewsFall09.pdf.

climate change as a driving factor, established time horizons of twenty years to the end of the century – due to the general belief that environmental systems were stable and would not change too abruptly. That assumption turned out to be wrong, especially when environmental changes were accelerated by other natural forces as well as the vulnerability of human and energy infrastructure systems. Subsequent scenarios, such as those described in this book, then tended to focus the time horizon on the present day out to perhaps five years, understanding that time had become a precious resource.

Lesson: Unpublished Data Are Crucial

This scenario highlighted the usefulness and necessity of using scientific data in prepublication form. We diverged from the usual practice of waiting for publication of peer-reviewed studies to draw on their conclusions. By the time Dr. Shakhova and her colleagues published their findings in the journal *Science* in 2010, the scenario – based on their initial data – had already been fully developed and communicated both to the US Department of Energy and US Department of Defense. When the article was published, several news articles warned of potential environmental consequences of methane hydrates.[25] Upon reading one of the articles, one DOE official contacted us asking if we had seen it and could make sense of it. We replied with, "yes, we gave that to you last year." Although we cannot always be relying on emerging scientific data, it was worth making the effort to do so.

The DOE could appreciate early warnings. DOE officials have been working under the rules of warning intelligence – accuracy in prediction is valued but not if a delay makes preventive action impossible. The workings of the scientific and intelligence/military communities tend to differ both in terms of secrecy (an issue we discuss in Chapter 8) and the use of evidence. Understandably, the use of data and scientific conclusions for which there is no full confidence may make scientists uncomfortable. This is another reason why it is crucial to keep scientists involved in the assessment process – to allow their expert judgments on uncertainty and to prevent erroneous interpretations of complex information.

Lesson: Scenarios as Collective Knowledge

The early scenario work on methane clathrates in Japan provided some grounding for future scenarios and discussions on related topics. In general, previous

---

[25] Environmental News Service, "Unstable Siberian Arctic Shelf Leaking Greenhouse Gas Methane," March 8, 2010, www.ens-newswire.com/ens/mar2010/2010-03-08-03.html.

scenarios helped with approaching what would otherwise be highly unique and complex topics. In practical terms, scenarios could therefore be useful beyond standalone products. While most of the scenarios created between 2009 and 2012 were not developed into anything beyond the documents used in the original workshops, the cumulative "library" of scenarios represented a form of collective knowledge and experience that could be passed along if needed.

For example, in September 2011, another USAF Minerva scenario group was examining potential impacts of climate change, attempting to link changes in Arctic ice sheets to increasing coastal hazard exposure in South and Southeast Asia. After many and varied attempts to link these issues through plausible mechanisms, Dave Pieri, a volcanologist with NASA's Jet Propulsion Laboratories (JPL), suggested a novel but very real mechanism. Many ice sheets in coastal areas, Pieri explained, not only rested on mountainsides but also held them together. With such ice sheets melting, the risk of parts of the mountainside sloughing off into the ocean (a process known as sector collapse) increased.[26] The impacts would be serious. Although subsequent scientific validation indicated that tsunamis from such events would be unlikely (at least not directly), methane hydrate formations in the affected area could not only be disrupted but also detonated. Preliminary calculations suggested that the explosive potential from such an event could be on the order of one or more megatons and potentially orders of magnitude higher, depending on geological factors (equivalent to a hydrogen bomb explosion). The scenario was not meant to be predictive; it was a cautionary reading of how different geological forces could combine to create, quite literally, explosive results.

One other risk aspect of methane hydrates has not been developed into a scenario – ironically, because both the confidence of the event and its impacts are high. In some preliminary work, researchers at Virginia Tech University indicated that methane hydrates are highly sensitive to changes in water pressure. Even modest increases in sea level – as little as thirty centimeters – may trigger clathrate destabilization and massive subsea methane releases. At this point, even more conservative predictions of sea level rise indicate that such levels will be reached well within the century. If and when this occurs, the world may find itself in what scientists refer to as the "clathrate gun" scenario.[27] The clathrate gun hypothesis was an attempt to explain abrupt climatic changes in the past, suggesting that sudden changes in temperature were the result of massive methane releases from clathrate deposits. Although

---

[26] Lucia Capra, "Abrupt Climatic Changes as Triggering Mechanisms of Massive Volcanic Collapses," *Journal of Volcanology and Geothermal Research* 155, No. 3–4 (2006): 329–33.

[27] Gerald R. Dickens, "A Methane Trigger for Rapid Warming?" *Science* 299, No. 5609 (2003): 1017.

the influence of methane hydrates in past geological events is disputed, given the environmental conditions of the twenty-first century, the world may find itself in a scenario that does become true. Massive releases of methane from subsea clathrate formations, coupled with terrestrial methane from melting permafrost, could trigger an extraordinary cycle of ever-increasing warming.

In the case of Japan, discussion of methane hydrates may still be important for understanding the ripple effects from the 2011 Fukushima disaster as well as the ways in which the disruption of the nuclear energy industry in Japan may create new disaster risks. In a similar fashion, in 2012 a new set of scenarios was developed to assess potential risks and cascading disaster impacts to the energy system of Hawaii.

The Need for the Hawaiian Scenarios

The USAF Minerva team was originally tasked with examining areas of the northern hemisphere, particularly the Arctic and contiguous areas involving the United States and NATO. This changed by late 2011, in line with general Pentagon priorities toward the Asia-Pacific region, and in cooperation with the Air Force Research Institute (AFRI). AFRI was preparing a report for the USAF chief of staff, the top general in USAF, on future trends in Asia-Pacific region, a massive expanse of water and land that stretches from the west coast of the Americas to the east coast of Africa. In setting out directions for how the Minerva Program could contribute to the report, one request was to consider "any energy-environmental risk that could affect Pacific Command in the next thirty years." The parameters were overwhelming, and it was difficult to fashion scenarios that could encompass such a broad spectrum of geography and potential risks.

The USAF/AU team focused on the impacts of critical water and energy resources on regional security, with a special focus on Japan, China, and India. A report from AFRI would include challenges to the Pacific for the USAF Chief of Staff, and the Minerva team was retasked from an Arctic/European focus to working with Pacific Command (PACOM) in Hawaii. The Asia-Pacific assessment consumed most of the team's efforts throughout the spring and summer of 2012, but during that time a side project grew, one that would ultimately gain more attention from policy makers and intelligence community in DC: the vulnerabilities of the Hawaiian Islands themselves.

A great deal of assistance came from the Center for Island, Maritime, and Extreme Environment Security (CIMES), a research group at the University of Hawaii, largely funded by the Department of Homeland Security, whose projects included undersea mapping and disaster data planning. Its associate director, Kevin Kelly, took me (Briggs) and my wife Tracy to meet the biologists and oceanographers at the university's Institute for Marine Biology on Coconut Island. The island (originally named Moku-o-loe) is located off the eastern shore of Oahu near the Kaneohe Bay Marine Corps Air Station (MCAS). There, we were introduced to three of the institute's scientists, Greta Aeby, Rob Toonen, and Ruth Gates, proceeding to explain our efforts at trying to translate scientific data into security assessments. As we have done many times before, after the scientists explained their work and the general conclusions of their research, we asked a single question: What about your work keeps you up at night?

The question was inspired by an advice given to me (Briggs) by Simon Dalby early in my doctoral dissertation process: "Write about what keeps you up at night." Environmental scientists are often motivated not just by analytical puzzles, but also by a sense of urgency about what their research might find. When it comes to environmental systems, the concern is not only over visible physical risks, but also over the methodological challenge that we may not be able to explain or predict abrupt change until after it occurs. The three scientists at the Coconut Island described a process, which they understood would be nearly impossible to prove until after it happened. The Hawaiian Islands sit within a nearly permanent atmospheric high-pressure system, the unique result of ocean currents as they flow around the volcanic islands. The ocean currents could shift as a result of as little as half a degree Celsius rise in sea surface temperatures. Half a degree was already well within the warming trend for the tropical Pacific, and a shift in the ocean currents could significantly change the weather patterns on the islands.[28] Most notably, the state of Hawaii enjoyed not only sunny skies from the high-pressure system, but was also able to deflect tropical storms away from the islands. While tropical storms are hardly rare in tropical seas, Hawaii has suffered remarkably few impacts from hurricanes, the notable exception being Hurricane Iniki in 1992.[29]

During the discussion, Tracy and I realized that we had found the perfect starting point for a cluster approach to complex scenarios. This was an example of weak signals within an environmental system potentially leading to an

[28] Stephanie C. Herring, Martin P. Hoerling, James P. Kossin, Thomas C. Peterson, and Peter A. Stott, "Explaining Extreme Events of 2014 from a Climate Perspective," *Bulletin of the American Meteorological Society* 96, No. 12 (2015): S1–S172.

[29] Andrew B. Kennedy, Joannes J. Westerink, Jane M. Smith, Mark E. Hope, Michael Hartman, Alexandros A. Taflanidis, Seizo Tanaka, Hans Westerink, Kwok Fai Cheung, Tom Smith, Madeleine M. Hamann, Masashi Minamide, Aina Ota, and Clint Dawson, "Tropical Cyclone Inundation Potential on the Hawaiian Islands of Oahu and Kauai," *Ocean Modelling* 52 (2012): 54–68.

ahistorical disaster, with cascading impacts across security systems. Since we did not understand just how vulnerable the islands were and where the critical nodes might be, we decided to set up a scenario process that ran in parallel to the Air Force Pacific Command assessment. A year after the Fukushima disaster in Japan, it was a safe bet that energy systems and infrastructure would be vulnerable if they had never really been tested before.[30] The Hawaiian tropical storm scenario would take a year to complete, and by the end would resonate to a surprising degree with both the observed environmental changes in the Pacific, and national security concerns back in Washington, DC.

The Pacific Tropical Storm Scenarios

Timeline: present day
Geographical scope: three concurrent scenarios – pan-Pacific, all Hawaiian Islands, and the island of Oahu
Drivers: Pacific tropical storms; tsunami inundation; deforestation; vulnerability of energy infrastructure; ocean acidification; cyberattack on infrastructure
Security frame: human security with focus on disaster response and attention to food and energy security
Assumed vulnerabilities: shift in atmospheric conditions; increasing acidification of ocean waters
Intervention points: existing military facilities in Hawaii
Critical uncertainties: response of insurance companies; humanitarian needs for tourists; increased risks of storms

While the assessments of Japan and China continued throughout the spring and early summer, background research for the Hawaiian workshop process was put into place, with the scenario creation workshop scheduled at the University of Hawaii for August 2012. The workshop was set up with three groups using similar starting points but looking at different geographic scales that ranged from transpacific perspective (i.e., the Hawaiian Islands west toward Singapore) down to a very specific focus on the island of Oahu itself. Before the August workshop took place, we had already planned for

---

[30] Cleo Paskal, *The Vulnerability of Energy Infrastructure to Environmental Change* (London: Chatham House, 2009).

a follow-up event to take place in Washington, DC, in January 2013 at the National Council on Science and Environment conference. The Washington workshop was intended as a "wind tunneling" effort, with the intervening months spent choosing the most interesting observations from August scenarios, and validating the scientific and infrastructural assumptions behind how the scenarios played out.

Constructing the Scenario: Assumptions and Drivers

Given a common starting point of an increase in tropical storm risk, we could use the Hawaii scenarios to help map whether hazards introduced into the system would cascade outward in multiple directions in a chaotic system, or whether different combinations of drivers would converge back toward common disaster risks and vulnerabilities. The latter involved an identification of environmental tipping points for future, complex disasters. Tropical storms and potential shifts in ocean currents due to marginal changes in sea surface temperature were treated as significant drivers of complex disasters in Hawaii.

The three groups at the UH-Manoa campus were led by Tracy Briggs, Kevin Kelly, and myself (Briggs). The groups worked for about five hours, and by the afternoon created an intriguing framework and identified critical vulnerabilities that came as a surprise to everyone. The larger geographic scope developed by Tracy's group provided a strategic context within which to understand environmental changes and disaster risks, including everything from undersea fiber-optic cables to vulnerability of small island states. Kevin's group, looking at the entire state of Hawaii, provided more detailed context for the political and economic background of the islands, including fisheries, tourism, and broader environmental changes affecting coastal regions. Focusing on the island of Oahu, the third group considered some potential impacts of a combination of four events: flooding due to deforestation, landslides after heavy rains, continued ocean acidification (with impacts on coral reefs that provide protection for Oahu's freshwater and coastal areas), and a cyberattack wildcard. Some of the main questions asked were: How does a larger environmental tipping point (i.e., a change in ocean currents) affect specific infrastructure and operations? What would the loss of built environments mean for national and regional strategic operations? And how would failures in existing infrastructure (mainly ports) impact the whole region?

Predicted Impacts

The most eye-opening assessment came with the examination of the island of Oahu, with its 1 million inhabitants, its tourist destination of Waikiki, and its military installations from Pearl Harbor to Kaneohe Bay. As with most scenarios, we did not focus on a single event such as a hurricane but tried to examine combinations of disaster hazards with underlying and emerging vulnerabilities. The group was asked to consider a one-two punch, or two tropical storms with hits in rapid succession. Given the lack of historical experience on the island with such a potential disaster, the group expressed concerns over erosion and flooding, but it was the idea of potential storm surge that was most worrying.

Deforestation was an obvious link to tropical storms and their impacts, as increased urbanization of the islands had changed local topography, increasing erosion, decreasing groundwater infiltration, and channeling water runoff. Although deforestation was merely one factor, it highlighted the risks of erosion, flash flooding, and landslides, especially given the unique geography of the Hawaiian Islands. Many houses on Oahu were built on ridges that were highly vulnerable to extreme rain events, and the group discussed how a lingering tropical storm (akin to Tropical Storm Irene over Vermont in 2011) may have been more damaging than the high winds but relatively lower rainfall of a full hurricane.[31] Hawaii had recently experienced high-rainfall events in 2012, and the island of Oahu was unable to cope with storm flooding.[32]

The issue of sewers and wastewater treatment led to the cyberattack driver. It was pointed out that the wastewater treatment facilities on Oahu were uniquely vulnerable to cyberattack or manipulation, and that disabling the treatment facilities in Honolulu would result in a choice of allowing toilets to back up in the Waikiki hotels, or flushing of untreated wastewater into the waters off Waikiki beaches. Such a choice had already been faced due to accidental breakdowns in the system (or more often, from flooding), with resulting impacts on local tourism.[33] Repeated events would likely create permanent damage to tourist travel. The cyberattack driver also included potential disruption of military facilities, though it was felt that local installations (e.g., Camp Smith or Pearl Harbor) were suitably resilient now due to

---

[31] A good source of data on flooding and other risks came from the Pacific Disaster Center in Hawaii. See Pacific Disaster Center, "Modeling Dam Failure Scenarios for the Hawaiian Islands," www.pdc.org/about/projects/hawaii-dam-failure-modeling/.

[32] *Hawaii News Now*, "Flash Floods Inundate East Honolulu," March 7, 2012, www.hawaiinewsnow.com/story/17097126/flash-floods-inundate-east-honolulu.

[33] *Honolulu Star Advertiser*, "Nearly 9 Million Gallons of Sewage Spilled in Windward Waters after Weekend Storms," May 23, 2018, www.staradvertiser.com/2018/02/22/breaking-news/sewage-brown-water-advisories-posted-for-windward-oahu-beaches/.

investment in alternative energy sources, backup power systems, and grid protection from programs like SPIDERS.[34]

Much of the scenario discussion focused on the connection between tropical storms and ocean acidification. It was understood that ocean acidification would reduce the health and growth of coral reefs, with factors such as coral bleaching, ocean temperatures, urban runoff, human disease, and others also contributing to reduced health. A tropical storm damages coral reefs when storm surges race inland, particularly in shallow waters such as those around Waikiki and the eastern shore of Oahu (near Kaneohe Bay MCAS) (see Figure 5.2). Given the historically rare incidence of tropical storms in the Hawaiian Islands (roughly once every twenty years), coral reefs have had plenty of time to regrow after each storm event. Reefs in Hawaii therefore provide ample protection from storm surges, as they provide friction against wave action and lower surge height. Research to date had consistently assumed that "worst case" storm surge inundation would involve existing bathymetry, meaning that friction from coral reefs would remain constant.[35] However, should coral reefs be damaged by a storm, the islands' vulnerability to storm surges would increase significantly, and existing hazards maps may severely underestimate potential damage.

There were emergency risk management plans and significant federal, state, and DOD resources in place to mitigate the damage caused by a single storm event in the short term. This was to ensure that basic functioning capabilities are resumed as quickly as possible. The focus therefore shifted from military security to civilian disaster response, as DOD would be able to adapt to severe events and maintain basic operations. It was agreed, however, that the vulnerabilities exposed by shifting storm patterns within the Hawaiian Islands would be amplified and more difficult to recover from with each passing tropical storm, especially with civilian infrastructure. All three groups of experts highlighted a number of critical nodes in the Oahu energy and environmental security systems. These are summarized in Table 5.1.

Postassessment

The August scenarios from the University of Hawaii were taken and validated, meaning that research was undertaken to back up claims made in the scenarios, and to collate the three scenarios into one workable narrative. The August workshop

---

[34] Tina Casey, "In First Test, US Military's SPIDERS Microgrid Uses 90% Renewable Energy," *Clean Technica*, February 12, 2013, https://cleantechnica.com/2013/02/12/u-s-militarys-new-spiders-renewable-energy-microgrid/.

[35] Kennedy et al.

Table 5.1: *Critical Nodes in the Energy and Environmental Security Systems of Oahu, Hawaii*

Barbers Point: This harbor was the only import and refining facility for the island of Oahu and had an open channel to the south, leaving it highly vulnerable to tropical storm tracks and storm surges. Significant damage to this facility would leave the island without any appreciable source of energy. In large part, electricity on the island was provided by diesel generation. Most civilian supplies on Oahu had few significant reserves, meaning that electricity and transport fuels would run out before repairs could be made to the port and refineries. The expert group suggested that increased investments in renewable fuel sources may provide alternatives in the case of such disasters.

Sand Island and Parkway: The port facilities of Oahu (including the US Coast Guard base) also exist on a sandy, low-level island south of Honolulu, with only one bridge from the island to the city. This container port would be highly vulnerable to flooding. In particular, food imports could be disrupted if the island and/or parkway were damaged. Oahu only kept a three-day reserve of food on the island, and disruption to the port facilities would create an immediate food insecurity situation.

Hickam and Kaneohe Bay: The airbases at Hickam and Kaneohe Bay are at sea level, and loss of protective coral reefs would mean higher vulnerability to wave surges. The PACOM experts were particularly concerned about the risks of a tsunami following a hurricane, owing to the debris scattered on the airfields and the weeks it would take to clear the fields for operation (hurricane-related storm surges would presumably be easier to clear and repair). Damage to these airfields would pose two primary difficulties to the security community: first, disruption of operations might impede military ops elsewhere in the Pacific, and second, such fields would not be available for disaster relief operations for the island itself.

Waikiki: The tourist area of Waikiki (including Fort DeRussy) lies on reclaimed land and is highly vulnerable to flooding. Given the shallow waters off the beach and existence of extensive coral reefs, a scenario of flooding coupled with reef damage would result in complete flooding of the area and a shutdown of Oahu's tourist industry. The expert group could not determine how long the area would economically survive without hotels being open and raised questions about the role of insurance companies in allowing repair and reopening. Workgroup members mentioned that several hotels in Kauai remained closed twenty years after Hurricane Iniki because of insurance companies refusing to reinsure vulnerable locations. Should the tourist industry on Oahu collapse, the group predicted significant out-migration of islanders to the US mainland.

Although the group could not explore all aspects of the scenario, the outline of events was as follows:
- Rising ocean temperatures shift Hawaiian trade wind patterns, and a hurricane hits the island of Oahu. Significant damage occurs in some coastal and inland areas, but overall the island can withstand the storm and recover economic activity. DOD air and naval operations are only disrupted for a matter of days, as ships are put to sea and aircraft are diverted to other bases.
- Due to the storm and a combination of ocean acidification, coral bleaching, and urban runoff, Hawaiian coral reefs are significantly damaged following the initial hurricane. Ecological damage is present and may affect some tourism, but the primary concern remains increased vulnerability to wave inundation to Oahu.

Table 5.1: (*cont.*)

- Another event within one to five months then occurs. This trigger can be either another tropical storm/hurricane or a tsunami (less than three meters), whose impact is then disproportionate to previous events or previous "worst case" projections.[a] The Barbers Point harbor is flooded and damaged beyond use, Sand Island is flooded and container facilities are rendered inoperable, and airfields at Hickam/HNL and Kaneohe Bay are out of operation for at least one week.
- Island transport networks are damaged by erosion and flooding, hampering relief efforts.
- Food and energy security becomes a primary concern, as civilian reserves on the island are insufficient and port facilities cannot be used. Relief operations by air are initially limited to C-130 flights into Wheeler Field. Adequate energy supplies for civilian use cannot be restored for at least several weeks.
- Fresh water supplies for the island may also be damaged. The expert group pointed out that Oahu's groundwater supplies are protected by undersea coral formations and that damage to coral by storm/acid and other pressures may result in saltwater intrusion into the freshwater supplies of the island.
- Hotels around Waikiki are evacuated and may fail to reopen due to lack of insurance coverage for areas now deemed flood zones. The economic impacts on the island are severe. We later learned that some five hundred thousand tourists reside in Waikiki hotels at any given time and that the Hawaii Emergency Management Agency had planned, as a first measure, to remove and fly out all tourists in the event of disaster. With no working airports, it was not clear how that would occur.

Recommendations from the expert group included:
- Further study potential impacts from shifting environmental conditions, with an emphasis on tropical storms, coral reefs, and freshwater supplies.
- Increase energy port facilities for Oahu, coupled with alternative energy sources.
- Discuss with DHS/FEMA potential catastrophic risks to Hawaii and related military cooperation in response.

---

[a] See Karl Kim, Pradip Pant, and Eric Yamashita, "Evacuation Planning for Plausible Worst Case Inundation Scenarios in Honolulu, Hawaii," *Journal of Emergency Management* 13, No. 2 (2015): 93–108.

also highlighted that a key disaster hazard was tsunamis, a nonclimate variable that provided additional data on how vulnerable infrastructure such as Barbers Point and Sand Island were to a constellation of risks. This risk was highlighted a few days before landfall of Hurricane Sandy in October, when a tsunami warning was issued for the island of Oahu. Brian Macadoo from Yale University had been asked to help advise on such risks even prior to the Hawaii workshop in August, but his responsibilities in Singapore led us to cooperate with new partners from Virginia Tech, tsunami expert Robert Weiss and coastal engineer Jennifer Irish.[36] Dr. Weiss

---

[36] Weiss and Irish were crucial in post-USAF continuation of the scenarios.

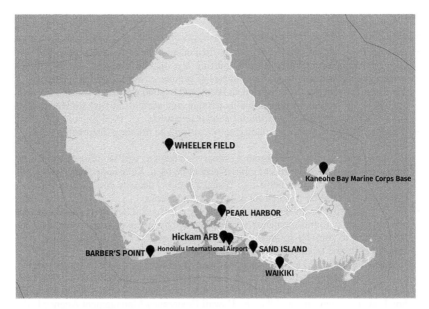

Figure 5.2 The Hawaiian island of Oahu.
Source: Dafina Berisha

was instrumental in assisting with the January 2012 workshop, along with national security experts from the United States and abroad, climate scientists, and foreign military experts such as Birgitta Liljedahl and Annica Waleji.

By the fall of 2013, nearly a year after the USAF Minerva project had ended, the Hawaii scenarios effectively resonated within Washington, DC, much more so than previous efforts or most of the official reports produced. The Oahu scenario effectively encapsulated and translated emerging scientific data in ways that by 2013 appeared prescient once a series of tropical storms began to threaten the islands. Importantly, the audience was extended beyond military commands – the issue was taken up both by environmental journalists and experts from the Centers for Disease Control working on Pacific island resilience. The disaster scenario was briefed to the US Global Change Research Program, and from there to members of the US National Security Council, Department of Homeland Security, and the office of the Director of National Intelligence. One senior intelligence officer remarked that this was the first clear example he had seen of the link between climate change and security risks.

Indeed, that is precisely what we had set out to do from December 2008. There is plenty of academic research on potential links between climate change and security, and many think tank reports emphasize the environmental aspects of conflicts such as the Syrian civil war. The trouble with such reports for policy makers in country capitals such as Washington and Ottawa, however, has been that since the 1990s, most of these reports have emphasized risks to places far away from the capitals. Following Hurricane Katrina, people increasingly sensed this may not be the case. After the Japanese tsunami in 2011 and Hurricane Sandy in 2012, security and intelligence officials began looking for more concrete examples of these emerging disaster risks potentially hitting home. At the same time, however, some politicians have resisted bad news even when coupled with irrefutable proof, which is a political obstacle to which we will return in a later chapter.

Like the New York scenario, the Hawaiian assessment foreshadowed actual events in 2013 and 2018. Emerging scientific research explained the factors and climate "signals" in the shifting risk landscape.[37] Yet, unlike New York, the Hawaiian scenario was not meant merely as a learning tool, but served as a legitimate warning of future disaster risks. While the tropical storms of 2013 were notable primarily for their number and potential track, Hurricane Lane in August 2018 was a far more powerful storm, and one which unfortunately followed the same storm track and inflicted some of the same damage described in the scenario. The state of Hawaii had taken concrete steps to mitigate these risks, but, at times, the environment can change more quickly than our abilities to formulate and implement disaster risk mitigation and management policies.

Lesson: The Most Obvious Risks Are Not Always the Most Important

Perhaps the most important lesson from the Hawaii scenarios was that the assessment process, if done properly, could lead us in directions that we could not hope to predict from the beginning. The initial scenarios for the AFRI study drew from the project concept informally known as Scattered Lantern (see Chapter 6 for more detail). This proposed set of case studies within USAF Minerva was intended to examine the archipelago of islands extending from

---

[37] Hiroyuki Murakami, Gabriel A. Vecchi, Thomas L. Delworth, Karen Paffendorf, Liwei Jia, Richard Gudgel, and Fanrong Zeng, "Investigating the Influence of Anthropogenic Forcing and Natural Variability on the 2014 Hawaiian Hurricane Season," *Bulletin of the American Meteorological Society* 96, No. 12 (2015): S115–19; Hiroyuki Murakami, Gabriel A. Vecchi, Thomas L. Delworth, Andrew T. Wittenberg, Seth Underwood, Richard Gudgel, Xiaosong Yang, Liwei Jia, Fanrong Zeng, Karen Paffendorf, and Wei Zhang, "Dominant Role of Subtropical Pacific Warming in Extreme Eastern Pacific Hurricane Seasons: 2015 and the Future," *Journal of Climate* 30, No. 1 (2017): 243–64.

Hawaii west through Oceania and Indonesia to the Malayan Peninsula and Singapore. AFRI felt that this approach was not "substantive" enough, and led the team to focus on China and India instead. This, it was argued, would be of more interest to the Pentagon staff.

The Hawaiian Islands were not the obvious place to look for energy and environmental security risks, but in the end, they formed the most compelling narrative created during either the DOE or USAF Minerva projects. The project assessment on China and India was solid but predictable, not uncovering information or conclusions that had not been reached elsewhere. It was the Hawaii assessment that everyone remembered – despite it starting as a tangential effort, which had to be juggled in Minerva's final months along with the China/India report, the NATO project in Brussels, and reports for the Iraqi National Security Council in Baghdad.[38] It was very much a case of following the data by listening to the experts who knew the information best.

Lesson: There Is No Substitute for Local Experts

While we emphasized the role of local experts in the Peruvian scenario, by the time we were working in Hawaii, this lesson became critical. We spent months speaking to local scientists, lawyers, environmentalists, engineers, and military officials to identify emerging risks and learn what those risks meant and how they connected to others. During the initial workshop, Tracy and I (Briggs) were careful to invite an unusual but relevant cross-section of experts in each group (itself a lesson passed on from the original 2009 DOE summit meeting). My scenario group, as an example, was composed of experts including one USAF flag officer and one environmental expert from PACOM (Chris Sholes), one cyber expert, a Chinese political scientist, a cetacean/fisheries expert, and a sociologist. Other groups' participants included Maxine Burkett (a migration lawyer), a Coast Guard commander, and a Polynesian diplomat.[39]

Given such wide range of viewpoints, when one member of the group discussed potential risks from ocean acidification to coral formations on the

---

[38] Chad M. Briggs, "Water Scarcity, Regional Security and Comprehensive Planning," remarks as prepared for the Al Nahrain Center workshop Water, Food, Energy and the Security of Iraq (Maxwell AFB: USAF, 2012).

[39] If there were ever a scratch-built exercise, the Hawaii scenario workshop would be a sterling example. Following closely on the heels of the GAO travel scandal, USAF put into place severe restrictions on necessary travel and, more importantly, a prohibition on hosting any conference or workshop without high-level Pentagon approval. We therefore had to put together the workshop without any money and set the date for a weekend when Tracy and I (Briggs) would already be in Honolulu to attend an Asia Pacific Security Center (APCSS) event. Curiously, perhaps our most valuable USAF findings were done off the clock and with zero budget. We also have to thank Kevin Kelly and CIMES for their hospitality.

island of Oahu, an interesting discussion on the islands freshwater "lens" emerged between Major General Pawling and Katie Adamson, two individuals so different in age and background that they would never otherwise meet. Likewise, during discussions of tidal surges onto Sand Island, an expert from the city of Honolulu pointed out specific roadways that would also be affected, helping sketch out cascading impacts on car traffic and cargo distribution throughout the city. In other words, the experts could provide detailed resolution on risks, impacts, and cascades that would merely be hypothetical in a closed scenario creation process.

Lesson: Effective Disaster Planning Hinges on Reducing Political Barriers

One lesson learned from the Hawaii scenarios was similar to a conclusion from the China/India assessment: the US Department of Defense was limited in its own capabilities. Although the US military has enormous capabilities for humanitarian assistance and disaster response, most attempts at risk mitigation or civilian adaptation are beyond DOD's jurisdiction and responsibilities. When successive tropical storms hit the Hawaiian Islands, the US Navy and Air Force already had contingency plans for putting ships up to sea and relocating aircraft, including plans for protection of critical infrastructure at bases like Pearl Harbor. Such plans had been in place well before any recent scenario efforts.

The military interest in the scenarios therefore came not from the primary concern over military forces and assets, but from an understanding that massive civilian damage to the islands would seriously hamper military readiness. Mitigating these disaster risks, such as by allowing widespread installation of solar panels on civilian houses, was merely something we could recommend to the state of Hawaii. When conducting aerial reconnaissance of Oahu, it was notable that in 2012 solar panels were installed on military housing and Walmart, but were being blocked by the state utility for civilian houses. Identification of hazards and risks was one thing, but there still remained political barriers to translating such assessments into effective action.

Conclusion

The scenarios in this chapter highlighted the importance of weak signals in EES risk assessments. The methane hydrate scenario demonstrated how scenarios could provide context for new information on complex and rapidly changing systems. Attempting to assess the importance of every piece of information is an impossible task, but with the right framework, certain news items or reports of scientific data can emerge as crucial pieces to a larger puzzle. The steps leading to potential disasters may be recognized if there are historical pathways, but with emerging disaster risks, weak signals may be the only available warning, and they require analytical narratives for their importance to be recognized in advance. The methane scenario also drew attention to the importance of unpublished data and shorter time horizons when assessing EES risks.

The warnings around Hawaii tropical storms and climate security resonated more than the earlier warnings about New York, even before Hurricane Sandy hit in late 2012. The Oahu scenario contained clear causal mechanisms for a disaster that could be triggered by any number of environmental hazard combinations. Whether we examined two tropical storms in succession, a tropical storm mixed with tsunami, or several other starting points, the critical nodes of the island remained at high risk, suggesting a strong attractor in a complex system. Even though the scientific data concerning shifts in the Hawaiian high-pressure system remained unpublished, this was a plausible mechanism that we lacked prior to Hurricane Sandy (which required a subsequent explanation on the role of the polar vortex and Rossby waves).[40] When tropical storms did start hitting the Hawaiian Islands in 2013, the context for climate-related disaster risks was better understood and more widely accepted.[41]

The scenarios, after all, were never intended to be accurate predictions of a certain future, but instead were meant to help guide understanding of how environmental changes could affect disaster risks and vulnerabilities, and point out the context within which weak signals could be interpreted and recognized. The process of creating and validating the scenarios emphasized that they could not be written by a closed team working with limited streams of information. The process required active participation from a wide variety of experts, particularly those willing to share information that included either unpublished scientific data or local/indigenous knowledge that would otherwise be unavailable for desk studies. The Hawaii scenario also began the process of including decision-making in response to the identified hazards, risks, and vulnerabilities. Decision analysis and training, however, often requires a distinct approach where the emphasis is on using scenarios as part of a structured wargame or simulation.

---

[40] Jennifer Francis and Natasa Skific, "Evidence Linking Rapid Arctic Warming to Mid-latitude Weather Patterns," *Philosophical Transactions of the Royal Society of London, Series A* 373, No. 2045 (2015): 20140170.

[41] Andrew Freedman, "Hawaii at Growing Risk of Hurricanes, Studies Show," *Climate Central*, May 8, 2013, www.climatecentral.org/news/hawaii-at-risk-for-more-hurricanes-studies-show-15966.

6

Beyond Scenarios: Wargames, Simulations, and Net Assessment

In late April 2011, a conflict simulation was held at the US Air Force Wargame Institute at Maxwell Air Force Base in Montgomery, Alabama. A modern facility that looks like it was created for a movie set, the institute was designed both for testing military strategies and helping train officers enrolled at the USAF's Air University. The wargame participants were typically field grade officers, meaning air force majors or their equivalents, at a point in their careers where many of them would be promoted to lieutenant colonel and given responsibility for providing strategic advice to their military and civilian superiors. In the military, this may not be an easy transition, as officers go from making tactical decisions about their squadron or battalion to making strategic decisions about much larger and complex military threats.

The simulation group, led by retired Col. Stephen "Wilbur" Wright, designed a simulation that forced officers to make difficult decisions about different priorities. Over two days, participants were presented with four concurrent scenarios where they would have to give advice to senior leadership on what the US military should do. Scenarios included a collapse of the government in Mexico, Iran carrying out a nuclear test, China taking control of the Spratly islands in the South China Sea, and the eruption of the Mount Spurr volcano in the Aleutian Islands of Alaska. Many of the officers laughed off the fourth scenario as being relatively unimportant, focusing instead on the South China Sea situation and the need to move massive air resources from North America to Japan and the Philippines.

Over the two days, however, the participants slowly realized the importance of the volcanic eruption, as the event disrupted many of their assumptions about aerial navigation to Asia, and threw many of the logistics plans out the window. The simulation had been intended that way. Using data from NASA's Jet Propulsion Laboratory (specifically, volcanologist Dave Pieri), the scenarios were designed to interact so that participants had to make difficult choices under high stress and high uncertainty, with the environmental "layer" of a polar volcanic ash cloud creating a blind spot for assumptions about how to proceed. The real world also interceded on April 27, 2011. During the morning briefing, while officers in flight suits were shown radar images of an approaching line of thunderstorms in Alabama, they were warned about tornado risks and necessary emergency procedures. Knowing that two of the professors (Chad and Tracy Briggs) sitting behind them were environmental experts, one pilot leaned over and asked: "Is this tornado risk real, or is this part of the simulation?"[1]

As noted in Chapter 3, there is a close link between scenarios and wargames. The development of scenarios after the Second World War was intended to expand understanding of potential future conditions, but in many cases, these scenarios were disconnected from consideration of decisions and responses that could be made in these potential futures. Scientists preparing climate change scenarios for the IPCC, for example, would be careful not to inject too much politics into the climate models, even though future climate change conditions depend on political and economic decisions for greenhouse gas mitigation. Likewise, in the intelligence community, scenarios would be developed with the intention of warning policy makers of potential future risks, but they would lack recommendations on which future was most desirable or how to achieve it. The initial scenarios that the DOE team developed in 2009–10 encountered both obstacles, as scientists and intelligence analysts participating in the scenario process wanted to insulate the warnings from charges of being too political in their assumptions.

Yet, it is not enough to warn of impending and emerging hazards – governments and communities must also be aware of their response capabilities and decision pathways. The USAF Minerva scenarios included aspects of decision-making, particularly in the Hawaii scenario (see Chapter 5), but typically these are later steps that involve distinct groups of experts. While scenarios tend to emphasize the goal of identifying hazards, risks, and vulnerabilities, the use of simulations and wargames focuses more on training decision makers to respond to newly emerging environments and conditions of uncertainty. At the US Department of Energy, Carol Dumaine often noted that the risks that may be most damaging in the end exist at the "critical peripheries," where hazards, risks, and vulnerabilities intersect in a way that no one had anticipated. Although wargames and simulations are hardly foolproof when it comes to their predictive capacities, they can be useful in identifying such critical peripheries and in training for interpreting weak signals.

---

[1] Sadly, the tornado risk was real, and that evening across Alabama, sixty-four people were killed and more than fifteen hundred were injured.

This chapter provides a discussion of wargame origins and development, along with examples from disaster-related exercises used with both civilians and military over the past ten years. Our intention is to show how wargames have helped train military officers and civilian security experts on the complex nature of emerging disaster risks. Advocating for a role of wargames in disaster planning, we discuss the US military disaster response in the Pacific, and specifically the Multinational Planning Augmentation Team (MPAT) as an example of a program that uses wargames as a central training tool for risk assessment. We also introduce two of Minerva's unfinished projects – Bishop North and Scattered Lantern – as examples of application of the concept of net assessment on complex energy and environmental security risks.

Why Wargames?

Wargames and simulations (terms sometimes used interchangeably) are a distinct and applied step in using disaster risk scenarios for risk assessments. They are meant to provide an immersive atmosphere to practice decision-making, and test strategies in an environment that can often replicate real-world conditions. Telling decision makers ahead of time that "energy risks are quite complicated" or "natural disasters will affect your military strategy" may elicit a nod but little real understanding. The ability to make decisions in changing environments, to deal with uncertainty and not be paralyzed with doubt are vitally important skills.

The disaster community has used simulations and exercises for decades, and it is not our place to suggest they have not done so well. Instead, our objective here is to discuss how scenarios can be applied once they are developed. The point of scenarios is to uncover blind spots and emerging risks that have not yet been identified. In doing so, it would be irresponsible to give warnings of new risks without any idea of how they interact with existing risks, the standard operating procedures and assumptions as well as given resources and response capabilities. The use of wargames and simulations can be a tool both for training decision makers and for identifying how emerging risks and vulnerabilities interact.[2]

The use of simulations to test future conditions and strategies can also help calibrate disaster response strategies in sensitive political environments.

---

[2] Timothy W. Gillaspie, "Focused Logistics Wargame," *Air Force Journal of Logistics* 25, No. 2 (2001): 35; Xiao Lei Li, Huan Li, Min Gang Cheng, and Zhong Qi Fan, "Framework for Emergency Decision Exercise System of Urban Crisis based on Wargaming," *Applied Mechanics and Materials* 373 (2013): 1139–43.

In 2008, for example, in response to a devastating ice storm in eastern Canada, the Canadian Army sent soldiers into Eastern Ontario and Quebec to assist civilians, including going house to house to check on residents. However, deploying Canadian soldiers inside Quebec was a politically sensitive issue to many residents who resented the federal government sending military forces into a province that had only recently voted on separation from Canada.[3] In contrast, when the US military responded to the 2011 tsunami in Japan, US forces were quickly deployed to affected areas, including the US Air Force 353rd Special Operations Group to the Sendai airport. As part of Operation Tomodachi, the air force group restored airport operations very quickly, but when the official reopening ceremony took place, the US forces were hardly to be seen. This reflected knowledge of the sensitivity of the situation. Although the Japanese acknowledged the US help, it was important in official ceremonies to give responsibility to the Japanese forces.[4] Again, simulations help planners recognize such potential situations in advance.

In the following two sections, we discuss the origins and ingredients of wargame development, including the underlying objectives, scenarios, rules and roles, and wargaming environment. We then follow up with a discussion of three previously ran wargames along with their lessons and application in disaster risk assessment.

Wargaming: Main Ingredients

Chapter 3 discussed the development of dietary scenarios by the Prussian military. By later in the nineteenth century, German officers were employing *Kriegsppiel*, tabletop wargames in which officers would play out military operations under a variety of potential real-world scenarios.[5] The basic ingredients of present-day wargames generally remain the same. A wargame contains set objectives that the simulation is meant to achieve. The purpose can be to test strategic or tactical doctrines, train decision makers in responding to new environments, or test how shifting environments affect existing responses and resources. Each simulation has set rules, which are established in advance and adjudicated by a referee or group of referees. Time is generally measured in

---

[3] Cleo Paskal, *Global Warring: How Environmental, Economic, and Political Crises Will Redraw the World Map* (New York: St. Martin's Press, 2010).

[4] Martin Fackler, "US Airmen Quietly Reopen Wrecked Airport in Japan," *New York Times*, April 13, 2011, www.nytimes.com/2011/04/14/world/asia/14sendai.html.

[5] The terms *wargame* and *simulation* will be used interchangeably here, although some experts shy away from *game* terms for fear that they diminish the seriousness of the exercise.

turns with the rules specifying who acts first or has a chance to respond. The games have elements of chance – not all intended actions can be successful, and surprises occur.[6]

Objectives

Wargames and simulations can be designed and conducted to achieve one or more objectives: identify new risks, train decision makers, and test new tactics and strategies. When designing a scenario for use in a simulation, it is important to clearly identify specific objectives, and determine the rules and environment within which the simulation will take place. Commonly, a wargame used for one purpose (such as instruction) may be able to provide additional insights once the events and outcomes are analyzed. This process of evaluation, termed a "hotwash" in the military (or more formally, an after-action review (AAR)), is a critical step both for the wargame designers and the participants. As participants are generally operating independently of one another in different groups, they are unable to see the bigger picture until an after-event evaluation has been performed.

One of the most famous examples of using wargames to test strategies was the decades-long process of the US military developing War Plan Orange in the early twentieth century. War Plan Orange was the US strategy to defeat Japan in the event of war, with informal studies beginning in 1906 and a formal plan adopted in 1924. Wargames were used at the US War College and Naval War College to test various strategies, given specific resources and geography. These wargames ultimately led to confidence in the island-hopping strategy, which was eventually used in World War II. Many of the senior US commanders in the Pacific during the war had been participants in the earlier wargames, which had given them additional insight into the advantages and potential pitfalls of the strategy they were ordered to undertake.

In the end, the nature of the simulation objective determines how the underlying scenario and rules of the simulation are constructed. A simulation that focuses more on multilateral cooperation will construct multiple teams working toward a common goal. If the objective is to identify problems with implementing new strategies, tactics, and logistical systems, the wargame scenario can be constructed to provide difficulties and challenges where failure to reach objectives can be assessed in the hotwash. Learning how to defend against actions of an adversary will place emphasis on the role of a "red team,"

---

[6] Peter P. Perla, *The Art of Wargaming: A Guide for Professionals and Hobbyists* (Annapolis, MD: Naval Institute Press, 1990).

who is tasked with undermining the mission of the other teams. Most wargames and simulations will contain a mixture of these elements.

Underlying Scenarios

All wargames and simulations are based on a specific scenario that sets the background and boundaries within which the simulation takes place. These scenarios are designed with close attention to the simulation's core objectives. Boundaries can be given by geographical factors, time periods, main actors, and adversaries. For example, a wargame meant to test potential alternative strategies for a real historical event could develop a scenario set in North Africa in 1941, where participants take the role of directing strategic decisions for the German and British armies. For many of these historical wargames, the intention may be to consider how different decisions affect known outcomes. Other scenarios focus more on the uncertainty surrounding potential futures.[7]

In wargames, scenarios can be designed in four different ways, according to two criteria. First, scenarios can be either fictional or representing real-world conditions. Fictional scenarios do not necessarily mean a complete Dungeons & Dragons style fantasy world; they balance historical and/or political accuracy with conditions that help achieve the simulation's objective. For example, defense or disaster scenarios often use fictional countries to help focus participants on the simulation, and prevent pushback from participants who may say: "that's not really how it is in country X." If the goal of the simulation is to test how country X would respond in a specific situation, then a real-world scenario may be called for. Second, the scenarios can be closed or open, meaning if set in the current day, the scenario may be affected by real-world events taking place over the course of the simulation. Most simulation scenarios are closed, meaning the participants will only respond to the information given to them by referees.

Scenario authors often conduct extensive research into the worlds they are describing, so they can answer participants' questions. These questions may be quite specific: What type of trees were used to create ship masts in the Royal Navy in 1812? How wide are the streets in a fictional capital that is being hit by flash flooding? The more specific a referee can be in describing the scenario world, the more believable the simulation becomes for participants, and the better they can act in a realistic fashion. Scenarios dealing with environmental

---

[7] Peter P. Perla and E. D. McGrady, "Why Wargaming Works," *Naval War College Review* 64, No. 3 (2011): 1–20.

hazards and risks therefore require significant input both from scientists and those with local knowledge of environmental conditions and ecosystems. In such cases, wargame designers generally recommend that scenarios are tested several times, allowing for identification of knowledge gaps on topics ranging from the design of hillside erosion control measures to the resilience of local nomadic herders and farmers.

Wargame scenarios often contain a basic narrative, although the type of "story arc" used depends on the intentions of the scenario designer. A common scenario arc for introductory training includes a setup and several predefined, acceptable outcomes. In this formulation, simulation participants are expected to make decisions that will lead them to the best possible outcomes. More challenging scenarios have no predetermined resolution, and in these wargames, participants' actions are judged relative to their assigned roles and missions. Such wargames contain higher levels of decision uncertainty, which itself can be an intentional component of training. With the emerging environmental risks, simulations may be so novel that the potential outcomes are simply unknown, and the simulations themselves are intended to produce some insight into possible futures. Finally, some wargame scenarios are known to have only negative possible outcomes. These "Kobayashi Maru" wargames (one related to Ukraine will be described below) can be either training exercises, or used as validation that certain possible futures must be avoided.

Wargame scenarios may be created around particular objectives, but can also contain "layers" that add realism and secondary objectives intended to complicate achievement of the overall goals. In the 2011 USAF wargame, for example, the Minerva team worked closely with NASA/JPL and the Air Force Weather Office to create the volcanic eruption in Alaska mentioned previously. The intention of this layer was to highlight the influence of natural hazards in strategic planning, one that would at first appear as a small wrinkle, and then propagate throughout the simulation actions. If the primary focus of a simulation is response to a natural disaster, a useful layer, for example, could be a cyberattack that complicates response or worsens the impacts.[8] Participants are not always aware of the existence of complicating factors at first, and in some wargames, these serve to test whether participants can focus on the most important risks without being caught up in constant crisis response.

---

[8] Col. Mark Read's "California Screaming" scenario in September 2011 used this approach, describing a cyberattack that closely followed an earthquake and considerably amplified impacts.

Rules and Roles

Wargame designs also vary according to their type of interactivity, ranging on a spectrum from rules-based "mechanical" approaches to more open role-playing approaches. The original *Kriegsspiel* approach as well as the one that first appeared in civilian commercial games in the 1950s follow a more mechanical approach, focusing on decision-making according to strict rules and turn-based timetables. These "tabletop" wargames tend to be based on scenarios where details on resources and capabilities are important and are generally well known. Maps are often detailed and laid out with hexagonal grids, with counters or miniatures representing groups of (usually) military forces. These wargames can be designed to represent anything from battles between ancient Greece and Persia to futuristic science fiction battles between fleets in Star Trek. The outcomes of the games are very much dependent on how the rules are designed. Representations of real-world conditions are more accurate when they portray groups with clear hierarchies and easily identifiable units – such as in naval battles. The US Naval War College has run wargames as part of its curriculum since 1894, and later famously conducted naval war-games on the checkerboard floor of Pringle Hall.[9]

While the wargame tradition started in the military and eventually became popular among civilians, the role-playing tradition was first developed within fantasy gaming groups in the 1970s, and subsequently influenced the military. An emphasis on role-playing and simulations shifts the focus away from rules and turn-by-turn movement of units, and instead focuses on interaction between the participants themselves.[10] In a simulation, role-playing can better teach participants the elements of decision-making within a group, especially under the conditions of large uncertainty. The USAF wargames, for example, routinely involve a role-playing component in which officers were challenged by various assistant secretaries of defense (played by the referee group) to defend their decisions at the Pentagon. Individual roles, as described in some of the examples below, may have objectives that intentionally create conflicts within teams, and therefore more accurately represent real-world political conditions. While some wargame participants may be unhappy with being assigned the role of a corrupt politician, creating these backgrounds in advance

---

[9] Roger Smith, "The Long History of Gaming in Military Training," *Simulation and Gaming* 41, No. 1 (2010): 6–19; David A. Kohnen, "The US Navy Won the Battle of Jutland," *Naval War College Review* 69, No. 4 (2016): 123–42.

[10] Jon Peterson, *Playing at the World: A History of Simulating Wars, People and Fantastic Adventures, from Chess to Role-Playing Games* (San Diego, CA: Unreason Press, 2012); Richard Rouse and Steve Illustrator-Ogden, *Game Design Theory and Practice* (Sudbury, MA: Wordware, 2000).

(i.e., during scenario preparation) saves time during simulations. This also lets the scenario designer inject more real-world elements into the simulation. US military officers, for example, would rarely create conditions of corruption on their own initiative. Rules and relationships between players also differ, depending on whether the wargame is held over a few days (this is more common), or whether it can be conducted over several weeks or months. In general, our experience has been that the longer the wargame/simulation, the more fully participants take on roles and duties assigned to them.

Wargaming Environment

Historically, wargames have been carried out either in a live environment or in a common, physical space ("tabletop"). However, increasingly, it is possible to conduct wargames and simulations remotely. This is not an entirely new phenomenon. Wargamers and role players in the civilian world developed rules for play-by-mail beginning in the 1970s. In the 1980s and 1990s, they developed standards for how to play using early Internet technologies of email and discussion boards. Modern IT allows for remote conduct wargames and simulations, with realism fidelity (e.g., availability of maps and databases) that far exceeds any previous capabilities. There are complex software packages to conduct wargames and simulations, though many of these were developed for the US Department of Defense and are not publicly available. The use of online wargames and simulations can be promising in its ability to connect participants around the globe, but there are some limitations that should be considered.

Most wargames and simulations are still organized around a common physical space, and this is done primarily for two reasons. First, the game referees need some access to participants and their discussions, and even more importantly, they must be available for answering participants' questions. Although online technologies allow for questions, practically speaking, it is much easier to ask for clarification in person. Second, physical proximity to others in a group, including body language cues, are important components of decision-making, at least in those scenarios where decision makers would be in physical proximity to another. There can also be software and communication limitations. US students with security clearances, for example, might not be allowed to use certain phone apps, and as one former student (who worked for the FBI) remarked, he did not want certain "trigger words" (e.g., "our team should attack the refugees once the flood subsides") to appear even in his personal email account. Gritty realism in the simulation may be useful, but it is important to keep such scenarios compartmentalized. The wargames discussed below are meant to provide examples of where different mixes of objectives and rules have shed light on the nature of disaster security, much more so than a desk assessment or training course could do on their own.

Wargaming for Disaster Security: Three Examples

Wargames have been able to test the sensitivities to disaster response, gauging not only how effective actual risk reduction and response capabilities may be, but also how those actions affect the larger political and security environments. The following three scenarios – Bechuana, Aybilistan, and Danchuana – were written for different wargames carried out at various institutions between 2008 and 2018. The simulations were to test energy, environmental, and disaster risks and response in West Africa, the Mediterranean, and the Middle East. Together, they draw attention to the salience of changing environments, long-term planning, and hybrid warfare strategies in risk assessment.

Changing Environments: Bechuana Scenario (2008–2010)

> **Setting:** present-day West Africa
> **Type:** fictional country; open scenario
> **Focus:** refugees; natural disasters; potential NATO intervention in Africa

In 2008, the Swedish Defense Research Agency (FOI) held a NATO Advanced Research Workshop in Umeå, Sweden. Canadian Army Maj. Jeff Lewis designed a wargame scenario called Bechuana to test environmental and disaster risks and response in West Africa. The scenario was expanded and used during four-week wargames at Lehigh University in the United States in 2009 and 2010. The civilian students at Lehigh were given roles as leaders of a fictional West African country, the United Nations and humanitarian organizations, NATO military forces from the United Kingdom and Germany, and rebel insurgents/pirates.

The role-playing aspect of the simulation illustrated the difficulties the participants playing European and NATO groups had in knowing how to approach regions of instability where insurgencies, corruption, and violence made it difficult to know whom to trust when considering a response to refugee crisis or natural disaster. Although the students had read about natural disasters and environmental security, many said afterward that they had not appreciated the complexities involved in trying to respond.

From the participant perspective, the wargame highlighted the complexity of disaster management and response, particularly in conflict environments where natural resources were both currency and collateral damage, and where multinational organizations had little information concerning environmental conditions and a limited ability to operate. Opposing teams (in military terms, cells) found it useful to exploit and trigger disasters, including forcing refugee flows and attacking refugees when they were vulnerable. For those participants playing NATO, it was extremely difficult to identify intervention points in the wargame, where they could take actions that could assist the local population and not escalate existing conflicts. The natural hazards introduced in the scenario were relatively mundane, involving monsoon-type floods and sporadic disease outbreaks at refugee camps. In the given political and security context, however, these natural conditions created acute disaster risks for refugees.

This wargame was the first of the three to experiment with divisions within the home government of Bechuana (green cell), creating ethnic divisions between the fictional Mbiki and Setswana tribes. The wargame also experimented with running the simulation over the course of an entire month rather than several days. The combined result was that students reported taking on their assigned roles and divisions even outside of class, the experience becoming a memorable one that they referred back to some years later.[11] One of the students, Victoria Herrmann, who herself ran the Bechuana wargame in 2018 at the American University in Washington, DC, reflected on her experience: "Ultimately, the course and war-game experience taught me more than any lecture could about resource rights, environmental degradation, and fossil fuel extraction."[12] As a training tool, the simulation could give practical lessons of the challenges faced with responding to a disaster or complex emergency, the frustrations involved in working with a multinational organization like the UN, the necessity of cautious action by NATO, and the role of uncertainty in decision-making.

---

[11] One student participant in 2009, now an intelligence analyst, reportedly cornered and interrogated members of the red cell, obtaining information on illicit weapons shipments. This necessitated future restrictions on "extraordinary measures" outside of class, though Kosovo students would later push those boundaries by planting listening devices in classrooms and hacking into opposing teams' email accounts and phones. While wargames are useful instructional tools, there are ethical considerations that instructors should not ignore.

[12] Victoria Herrmann, "Why Sustainability Is Important to Me: Victoria Herrmann '12," *Goblet*, July 14, 2017, www.lehighgoblet.com/why-sustainability-is-important-to-me-victoria-herrmann/.

Lessons learned. Bechuana used a limited application of an open scenario, but since the neighboring countries were also fictional, the real-world news cycle did not appear to have much impact on the course of wargame actions or information. When the Eyjafjallajökull volcanic ash cloud closed European airspace in April 2010, however, real-world events intervened. The NATO/EU players found themselves unable to receive airlifted supplies from Europe, and so turned to the United States to ask for assistance. At that point in the wargame, participants were so taken with their roles that even humanitarian military assistance from the United States ignited a political firestorm. Although all the Lehigh students were American and the African country was fictional, a potential US military intervention sparked violence and instability as rival factions feared a complete change in the security environment. The simulation outcome suggested that European forces would be distrusted for their colonial pasts, but more important, any US military involvement (even humanitarian response) was potentially destabilizing. The results were so curious that they were passed along to US Africa Command (AFRICOM) in Germany as a condition to be tested in future planning.

Pretending We're Not Talking about Ukraine: Aybilistan Scenario (2014)

Setting: present-day Mediterranean **Type:** fictional country; closed scenario **Focus:** energy disaster; refugees; potential EU/NATO intervention

The Aybilistan scenario was written in late 2013 as part of a joint NATO/EU training program to be held in Yalta, Ukraine in May 2014. The wargame was intended to help provide training for security experts from Ukraine and neighboring countries in responding to a combination of insurgency, energy security, and natural disasters. Tested at Johns Hopkins University in spring 2014, events on the ground in Ukraine ran ahead of the simulation itself, and Russian military forces found their way to Yalta before the NATO program did.[13] As the original simulation was intended to include Russian participants, Aybilistan was an example of where the use of the fictional country could help illustrate analogous security and disaster risks without tripping over political sensitivities and nationalism of participants.

---

[13] The wargame was ultimately held in Kyiv, Ukraine, in May 2014.

The scenario was therefore set on a fictional island in the Mediterranean, an independent state with a history of European colonization, troubled relations with its neighbor Libya, an important pipeline from Africa to Europe, and a growing refugee problem as a result of the Arab Spring and subsequent conflict. Teams were divided into local government, NATO, EU, and a terrorist group, with the Europeans (NATO and EU) tasked with finding an effective way to intervene in the country. In both simulation runs in the United States and Ukraine, the NATO groups found themselves unable to find a way to help the island. They were caught between politics in Brussels, strict rules of engagement, and suspicion over potential corruption in the local government. This became a recurring lesson in disaster-related simulations – intentions and even plans for humanitarian intervention become extraordinarily difficult to implement in presence of "harder" security risks.

Although the wargame was meant to simulate some conditions present in Ukraine in early 2014, some participants noted that the history and religious make-up of the country was in many ways analogous to the country of Lebanon. As with the Bechuana simulation, the presence of refugees on the island became a bargaining chip, with opponents of the government attempting to incite extremism within the population, and the Europeans promoting policies that would keep the refugees from continuing their travel toward Europe. Immediate crises sparked by the conflict, incoming refugees, and potential disruption of energy flows to Europe overshadowed long-term consequences to the environment and disaster risks to the small island country. Even when participants were instructed to keep long-term human security needs and risks in mind, intervening events, internal strife of the government, and delays with getting permission to act from Brussels all conspired to prevent effective action and planning for long-term strategies.

Lessons learned. During the simulation in Ukraine, the senior professor leading the EU group managed to broker a deal with the local government, European leaders, and Russian leadership, confidently finding a way to send several thousand Italian soldiers onto the island to assist with disaster response and stabilization. Here, the after-action analysis was immensely important. The scenario briefing indicated that Aybilistan had once been colonized by Italy, and the red team (terrorists/insurgents) was able to capitalize on the perception that the country was being recolonized by Europe. The common wargame setup is to hold periodic press conferences with public statements by each team/cell, which in time-constrained simulations takes the place of propaganda in official statements. In this case, the final statements by the red team persuasively undercut European political arguments, and suggested long-term instability for the country. The EU group also had not established a clear strategy for what the Italian soldiers would do once they found themselves on the beach. It was an important lesson that although a solution had seemingly been found, the long-term consequences to certain interventions were acutely destabilizing.[14]

Hybrid Warfare: Danchuana Scenario (2016–2018)

Setting: present-day Middle East
Type: fictional country; open scenario
Focus: refugees; disease outbreak; terrorism; energy export politics

The Danchuana scenario was originally designed in 2016 as part of the European Union Jean Monnet program to Ukraine, and was first tested in Odessa in September of that year. It was also used as an online teaching simulation for Johns Hopkins University, before being given an unusual twelve-week run with students and Kosovo Security Force cadets at RIT Kosovo. The Danchuana scenario was a small, fictional Middle Eastern country set on the coast between Syria and Turkey, and a crossroads for energy exports, refugee flows from Syria to Greece, and contested political space between Western Europe and Russia. The teams included a local government, an insurgent group, EU and NATO teams, and by the second run, the simulation also included a separate Russian team. The scenario had an obvious lineage to Bechauna and Aybilistan, but placed more focus on the interaction of information and hybrid warfare with EES risks. It required participants to keep close tabs on events in the Syrian civil war, Turkish movements into Kurdish territories, refugee politics, and EU-Russian politics. The Syrian civil war spilled over into the scenario, and the news feeds were kept "open" to keep pace with changing conditions in the conflict itself.

The simulation opened without any "trigger" events to set things in motion, relying instead on participants to choose actions and set the tone and focus of the simulation. With large numbers of refugees moving into the country, local teams had to choose whether to ally with the EU, NATO, or Russia for assistance. Local politics – and specifically the split along party lines – made

---

[14] Aybilistan was tied to the Russian invasion of Crimea. However, the map used for the scenario was a modified version of Lesbos island in Greece, where Tracy and I (Briggs) had visited in 2004. In 2013, the refugee crisis that was to hit the island of Lesbos by 2015–16 was not well anticipated, and we ended up volunteering to help refugees on Lesvos and in Idomeni near the Macedonian border in 2016.

these choices difficult. This setup allowed exploration of the energy and environmental aspects of pipeline politics, refugees, public health, and other issues. In addition, it also allowed analysis of hybrid war actions where disasters were sparked intentionally, refugees were used as pawns, and misinformation was an effective weapon.

The simulation posed many of the same questions about the ways in which outside countries can deal with violence and corruption during disaster relief and stabilization, with the added ingredient of "active measures" in cyberspace by Russian groups.[15] Unlike the US students, who typically wanted to avoid corruption and were often paralyzed during planning when allegations of corruption appeared, the Kosovo participants turned the questions of corruption around in remarkably creative ways. Two students took the initiative to plant themselves as spies in other groups, creating unanticipated dynamics. For example, one student from the Kurdish team inserted herself as a police official in the home government, but after weeks of working with the green cell, felt the need to protect them, and passed along information they learned about potential US actions as a way to save Russian-leaning members of her team. The information warfare (even carried out over open Twitter accounts) became highly personal, and employed students' multimedia and filmmaking skills.

Contrasted with the US run of the same scenario, the simulation was a demonstration of cultural and political differences, particularly in making decisions and coming to agreements. It should be noted that with both graduate students at Johns Hopkins and undergraduates at RIT Kosovo, participants reported a strong motivation to study not only the class material, but, in an open scenario, to follow current events, read technical reports on issues such as protection of gas pipelines, and generally move beyond the normal curriculum into related fields. As an instructional tool, wargames are very difficult to create, but once used, they can provide a striking impression on participants and a deeper understanding of disaster risks and response.

Lessons learned. Danchuana was primarily intended as an instructional aid, giving participants a sense of the complexity of energy and environmental risks, and how easily assessing and responding to the risks can be disrupted by outside forces. While the previous wargames provided opportunity for participants to understand the complexity of issues beyond traditional risk assessments, the Danchuana wargame added elements of both current events and an outside actor (Russia) who had an interest in using disasters to destabilize the government, economy, and security environment – largely through

---

[15] These are described in more detail in Chapter 7.

cyberwarfare. While there may be ethical questions about teaching cyberwarfare techniques, NATO experts have repeatedly written that effective defense against information or hybrid warfare cannot be created passively. Effective defense requires experiential learning, not only for cyber experts but for those in related energy, environment, and disaster risk fields who may find themselves directly in the crosshairs of *resilience targeting* strategies.[16]

The wargame also showed how an open scenario, influenced by outside news and current events, may provide added realism but at times also overwhelm the simulation itself. The Johns Hopkins run of the simulation in October to November 2016 was partly overwhelmed by the US presidential election. The election results, which came as a surprise to many participants, injected intense uncertainty into the Middle Eastern politics, complicating the simulation so much that participants were asked to ignore US politics as much as possible. When the simulation was run in Kosovo in early 2017, a newly created US team experienced disagreement between White House appointees and the intelligence community, which seemingly mirrored the real-world events. We were reminded that the real world can easily outpace even intentionally designed catastrophes, and that too much detail and too many events can overwhelm the simulation's design and objectives.

While classroom or boardroom wargames can be valuable instructional tools for highlighting complexity and testing strategies, there is also a need to translate these simulations to inform risk planning and response capabilities. The wargame scenarios described above were snapshots into potential challenges faced by policy makers, military officers, and humanitarian responders, but taken alone they do not reflect the value of such simulations in preparing for emerging hazards and risks. When institutionalized, the use of wargames and simulations allows for scenarios to be "made real," and the vulnerabilities of systems and responses can be identified in advance of actual disasters. Discussing the work of the US military in the Pacific and especially the US Pacific Command in Hawaii, we present such institutionalization of wargames below.

Exercises and Disaster Risks: Wargaming the Pacific

Wargames are not only limited to the tabletop but also exist as live-action exercises. Live operations are essential. Whether one considers medical or

---

[16] Keir Giles, "The Next Phase of Russian Information Warfare," NATO Strategic Communications Centre of Excellence (2016), www.stratcomcoe.org/next-phase-russian-infor mation-warfare-keir-giles.

flight training, emergency responders or complex military operations, preparing on paper is never the same as the feel, stress, and logistics of live exercises. While both types of simulations are training tools for decision-making, they serve different purposes. In part because of their cost, live exercises are generally oriented toward practicing what would be considered routine or most likely operations. Pilots practice takeoffs, landings, and navigation. Soldiers participate in run-through exercises that are intended to simulate, as closely as possible, the combat conditions they are most likely to encounter. In contrast, tabletop exercises, much like electronic flight simulators, can be oriented toward unique or "low-probability" events that one hopes will never occur.

This type of simulation, more appropriately referred to as a military exercise, has been used by the US military for disaster response purposes in the Pacific. The two types of approaches – hypothetical simulations and live exercises – work in combination with one another, though they have somewhat different emphases. Each year, the US military carries out multinational live exercises, known as Cobra Gold, in Thailand and the surrounding region. Cobra Gold, initiated in 1982, provides an opportunity for the US and Asian militaries to conduct live operations and to practice the complex coordination necessary for movement, communication, and command-and-control in the region. Undoubtedly, these and other similar exercises provided essential training for multinational disaster relief operations, such as those following tsunamis in 2004 and 2011, and Typhoon Haiyan in the Philippines in 2013. Cobra Gold operations involve as many as thirty-five countries, the US military contributing thousands of troops each year.[17] Live exercises, however, must be largely scripted in advance, both for logistical and safety reasons. They are intended to help train for events that are known to have a good chance of occurring, not to explore new potential events except in rare cases. Exercises such as Cobra Gold are extremely valuable for joint training and communication, but in order to develop them over time and not simply replay the same scenario over and over again, a parallel program of scenario development needs to be in place.

At the US Pacific Command at Camp Smith in Hawaii, there is a small office that carries out a much quieter and yet essential strategic planning and simulation function. The Multinational Planning Augmentation Team (MPAT) was established around the year 2000 to provide coordination and support for Pacific Rim countries, with some thirty-three countries participating from the

---

[17] Diplomat, "What Will the 2018 Cobra Gold Military Exercises in Thailand Look Like?" January 31, 2018, https://thediplomat.com/2018/01/what-will-the-2018-cobra-gold-military-exercises-in-thailand-look-like/.

east coast of Africa through Asia to the Americas.[18] The philosophy behind MPAT was that emerging security risks and disasters would require a coordinated response from countries that otherwise may not cooperate with one another, or be able to do so. Every year, MPAT helps design and coordinate two simulations named Tempest Express, which are essentially tabletop wargames containing scenarios that address risks from pandemic disease outbreaks to terrorist attacks on oil infrastructure in the South China Sea.[19]

While MPAT is part of the US Pacific Command, the Tempest Express wargames are officially hosted and run by other member countries. This gives them ownership of the process and allows for greater investment from countries with less strategic planning capability. Tempest Express 24, for example, was held in 2014 in Colombo, Sri Lanka, where in addition to local officials and officers, the exercise included participants from Vietnam, Canada, Bangladesh, Australia, Philippines, New Zealand, Nepal, Maldives, Cambodia, Indonesia, Malaysia, Mongolia, Singapore, Thailand, the United States, and Japan.[20] Working with scenarios that include disaster response has allowed MPAT and its members to develop hundreds of pages of communication and response protocols, so that when countries have to cooperate in response to a major disaster, the relevant officials have already worked with one another and have a basic common understanding of how to operate and communicate. The standard operating procedures have been in development since 2002 – nearly one thousand pages are constantly updated and discussed by member states. These wargames also allow participants to explore scenarios of relevant emerging risks well in advance, and in a more applied setting than hypothetical reports of emerging risk trends. The simulations also open participation to nonmilitary and nongovernmental organizations, allowing a whole-of-government approach.

This approach to international cooperation and disaster planning has sometimes been criticized as "paper pushing" by those not familiar with the programs and the need to maintain international networks.[21] These programs,

---

[18] US Pacific Command, "PH, US Concluded Participation in Tempest Express-27 Multinational Staff Planning Workshop," PACOM press release, August 5, 2015, www.pacom.mil/Media/News/Article/612322/ph-us-concluded-participation-in-tempest-express-27-multinational-staff-plannin/.

[19] Rita Boland, "Forces Take Pre-emptive Measures to Improve Response," *AFCEA Signal*, October 2008, www.afcea.org/content/?q=forces-take-pre-emptive-measures-improve-response.

[20] *News.LK*, "'Tempest Express – 24' Concludes," www.news.lk/news/sri-lanka/item/297-tempest-express-24-concludes.

[21] Adam Weinstein and William M. Arkin, "The US Is Going to War Tomorrow at This Fancy Pacific Beach Resort," *Gawker*, April 1, 2015, http://phasezero.gawker.com/the-u-s-is-going-to-war-tomorrow-at-this-fancy-pacific-1691769286.

which by their nature and intention are also not highly visible, can at times be at risk for budget cuts despite their small size. Networks are difficult to create and require constant maintenance, particularly over large geographic areas with many countries. In working environments where experts are often rotated out to different assignments, personal connections are often lost within a year or two if not maintained. Having a "living network" of experts allows community knowledge to be passed along to new members, so that the focus can remain on emerging risks and responses (rather than people having to constantly relearn how to work with one another in a multilateral environment). MPAT is an example of a highly valuable disaster risk program that uses wargames as a central communicating and training tool. Our USAF Minerva team put considerable effort into highlighting their importance to Pentagon officials. Although the Minerva team did not work with MPAT (Colonel Robyn Read had done so in the past), our approaches did overlap. MPAT, by its design, focused on creation and maintenance of a response network within the Pacific Rim. What was lacking was the ability to develop and test coherent strategies for long-term, emerging disaster risks.

Beyond MPAT: Net Assessment in Disaster Planning

The Pacific theater needed something similar to MPAT but with more technically complex and formalized scenarios to be used in wargames. It also needed a system for analyzing responses to take account of the potential environmental hazards, disaster response decisions, available resources, and detailed knowledge of the overlapping environmental, energy, security, and other systems. The Minerva team looked to the Pentagon's Office of Net Assessment, and in particular the strategic planning work of Andrew Marshall. Marshall, who established the Office of Net Assessment during the Nixon administration, served as its director from 1973 to 2015. Coming from the generation of defense specialists described by Fred Kaplan's *Wizards of Armageddon*, he was also given the nickname Yoda as the center for wisdom and strategic thinking at the Pentagon.[22] Perhaps not coincidentally, his office was also responsible for the first abrupt climate change and security report by DOD in 2003.[23]

The origins of net assessment at the Pentagon partly stemmed from the need to provide a more accurate assessment of Soviet military capability, and to treat the USSR and Warsaw Pact as organizations rather than singular entities. It was

---

[22] Fred Kaplan, *The Wizards of Armageddon* (Palo Alto, CA: Stanford University Press, 1991).
[23] Schwartz and Randall, *An Abrupt Climate Change Scenario*.

common for US planners to overestimate Soviet capabilities, because they looked at the USSR as a single, rational actor. An alternative was to see it as a complex system of often poorly functioning bureaucracies and communist ministries who used military equipment that was often faulty or in poor repair. Therefore, Andrew Marshall developed a system whereby the "red" team would interact with US planning and provide a more comprehensive (or net) assessment of both sides' strategies, capabilities, and intentions. The aim of such net assessments has been to "illuminate emerging problems and strategic opportunities far enough in advance for senior leaders to have time to make decisions that will either mitigate the former or exploit the latter."[24]

Similar approaches may be needed for the vast complex array of newly emerging hazards and risks that are associated with climate change. Like US defense planners of the 1950s, too often we conceive of and portray climate-related disaster risks in simplistic and linear ways. Government officials (those who do not deny climate change) point to the IPCC reports that show linear graph lines of gradually increasing air temperature. The concepts of abrupt climate change, let alone environmental hazards that interact to create overwhelming disaster risks, are more difficult to conceive and often dismissed as being "low-probability" events. This is deeply problematic in disaster risk assessment. The history of aircraft safety, for example, has shown that a focus on singular and "normal" risks grossly underestimates overall risks from interactions of factors that can overwhelm mechanical systems or human judgment.[25]

With respect to the Pacific theater, faced with the complex array of climate-related hazards, we needed broader strategies for taking the high resolution of disaster scenarios such as the work on Oahu, and for piecing them together into a larger picture of the region's potential futures. What we had hoped to accomplish, but were unable to before the Minerva funding ended, were two projects nicknamed *Bishop North* and *Scattered Lantern*. The projects, discussed below, were based on the Pentagon concept of net assessment – instead of looking at security only in terms of armed forces arrayed against allies, the idea was to undertake a more comprehensive assessment of risks and vulnerabilities. The intention was to take data from the scenarios, apply wargame and simulation methodologies to test responses, and then use defense planning concepts to create a larger narrative of disaster constellations across large

---

[24] Andrew F. Krepinevich and Barry D. Watts, *The Last Warrior: Andrew Marshall and the Shaping of Modern American Defense Strategy* (New York: Basic Books, 2015), 226.

[25] Nancy Leveson, Nicolas Dulac, Karen Marais, and John Carroll, "Moving beyond Normal Accidents and High Reliability Organizations: A Systems Approach to Safety in Complex Systems," *Organization Studies* 30, No. 2–3 (2009): 227–49.

geographic regions. Instead of taking the more traditional approach of breaking down the potential disaster risks piecemeal (e.g., assessing the 2050 sea level rise risks to Jakartan transport infrastructure), the more ambitious idea was to develop a series of scenarios and coordinate them in order to identify the points of interactions: where disaster risks highlighted key vulnerabilities, where response capabilities were lacking or were counterproductive, and where more research or monitoring was needed.

The Bishop and the Wizard

The concept for Bishop North originated at a French business school (HEC) conference outside Paris in late 2010. Discussing risk regulation surrounding the Icelandic volcanic eruptions of earlier that year, volcanologist Dave Pieri emphasized the need for decision frameworks on how to respond to catastrophic risks. These discussions led to the wargame layer used with USAF the following spring as well as to a proposal, generated in cooperation with GlobalInt, on creating formal decision frameworks for emerging disaster risks. The use of tailored scenarios for wargames was only applicable to select groups of participants, and the results were often not easily exportable. We believed that better systematic integration of expert contributions from scientific, engineering, professional, and local/indigenous knowledge would avoid the somewhat haphazard nature of wargame scenario development.[26] The idea behind Bishop North was to formalize training for decision-making for situations in which participants face decision uncertainty (e.g., what alternatives exist and which should be chosen), and when the disaster risks and hazards are also highly uncertain (e.g., what physical conditions will exist).[27] Such decision analysis is common in risk assessment (including business), but the hope was to combine them with region-specific assessments of emerging hazards.

The Oahu scenario (see Chapter 5) clearly demonstrated the salience of this issue. In the event of a large-scale emergency, the first priority for the state of Hawaii would be to remove hundreds of thousands of tourists from hotels in

[26] Jessica Mercer, Ilan Kelman, Lorin Taranis, and Sandie Suchet-Pearson, "Framework for Integrating Indigenous and Scientific Knowledge for Disaster Risk Reduction," *Disasters* 34, No. 1 (2010): 214–39; J. Richard Eiser, Ann Bostrom, Ian Burton, David M. Johnston, John McClure, Douglas Paton, Joop Van Der Pligt, and Mathew P. White, "Risk Interpretation and Action: A Conceptual Framework for Responses to Natural Hazards," *International Journal of Disaster Risk Reduction* 1 (2012): 5–16; Mauro Falasca, Christopher W. Zobel, and Deborah Cook, "A Decision Support Framework to Assess Supply Chain Resilience," *Proceedings of the 5th International ISCRAM Conference* (2008): 596–605.

[27] "Bishop" was an inside nickname for Pieri, a reference to the brilliant and eccentric Walter Bishop character from the TV series *Fringe*.

Waikiki, partly for safety reasons and partly to provide housing for emergency responders. Yet, it was unclear how this would be possible if the airports were not in operation. Few people knew what contingency plans the airlines or the hotels had in place. While tsunami warning systems are set up across the state of Hawaii, false alarms and lack of clear contingency plans make the public response highly uncertain. The false nuclear alert of January 13, 2018, issued by the state's Emergency Alert System and Commercial Mobile Alert System, was an example of the disconnect between disaster warning and public knowledge of response.[28] The false alert, interpreted by most as an impending nuclear attack from North Korea, triggered both panic and paralysis, even among first responders. While simulation training and decision matrices are not themselves sufficient, increasing attention to so-called outlier events and disaster risks is warranted.

Bishop North was therefore intended to identify decision-making systems and their vulnerability under different disaster scenarios, beginning with decisions necessary for flight operations and then moving to include the logistics units, support companies, commercial passengers as well as cargo carriers and companies dependent on them. Aircraft were a good place to start, being themselves highly sensitive to certain hazards like volcanic ash, and highly vulnerable to changing environmental conditions. The poor response of most airline companies to the 2010 Icelandic volcano eruptions demonstrated how avoiding one form of disaster can spark cascading impacts across highly globalized systems. And while such decision-support systems exist in many areas, we felt it would complement the scenario work the team was conducting for the Pentagon.[29]

Scattered Lantern grew from the same idea, and while it was never a formal project or proposal, it was intended as a larger structure within which to fit different scenarios, wargames, and disaster response decision-making across the vast geographic area of the US Pacific Command. The idea was to weave together scenarios from across the Pacific, starting in Hawaii and then moving

[28] Alia Wong, "Pandemonium and Rage in Hawaii: A False Alert of an Impending Missile Attack Highlights Just How Unprepared the Country Is for Nuclear Disaster," *Atlantic*, January 14, 2018, www.theatlantic.com/international/archive/2018/01/pandemonium-and-rage-in-hawaii/550529/. Cynthia Lazaroff, "Dawn of a New Armageddon," *Bulletin of the Atomic Scientists*, August 6, 2018, https://thebulletin.org/2018/08/dawn-of-a-new-armageddon/.
[29] Mario Mazzocchi, Francesca Hansstein, and Maddalena Ragona, "The 2010 Volcanic Ash Cloud and Its Financial Impact on the European Airline Industry," *CESifo Forum* 11, No. 2 (2010): 92–100; Sigudur R. Gislason, Tue Hassenkam, Sorin Nedel, N. Bovet, Eydis S. Eiriksdottir, Helgi A. Alfredsson, Caroline P. Hem, Z. I. Balogh, K. Dideriksen, N. Oskarsson, B. Sigfusson, G. Larsen, and S. L. S. Stipp, "Characterization of Eyjafjallajokull Volcanic Ash Particles and a Protocol for Rapid Risk Assessment," *Proceedings of the National Academy of Sciences* 108, No. 18 (2011): 7307–12.

west across the Pacific island states to Oceana and the Indonesian islands to Singapore and Malaysia. In meetings in Canberra and Singapore, I (Briggs) described this concept of a grand archipelago, where disaster risk scenario and planning capabilities could be seeded across these countries, and perhaps coordinated by institutions such as the newly created ASEAN disaster coordination office in Jakarta.[30] Although the project only went through initial stages in cooperation with Australia and Singapore, similar pushes for regional net assessments have been made by various disaster risk and climate security communities across the globe. More such efforts are necessary to gain clarity and resolution on potential future risks.[31]

Conclusion

Wargames and simulations provide lessons applicable to disaster risks, help train those tasked with assessing and responding to such risks, and aid new developments in risk assessment methodologies. As noted in Chapter 3, the business literature on scenario creation refers to "wind tunneling" or validation stage for potential futures.[32] For complex energy and environmental risks, the validation stage requires much more detail than simply suggesting that facts will be double checked. The use of wargames and simulations is by no means a replacement for traditional validation, nor is it appropriate in all contexts or a cure-all for intractable environmental conflicts. Wargames, however, help scenarios evolve over time, and can become something more than a one-time tabletop exercise.

The wargame scenarios described in this chapter provide some lessons for disaster risk assessment and planning. A crucial role of the simulations is to illustrate how a seemingly simple solution can severely complicate situations on the ground, worsening insecurity and increasing environmental risks. Often, intervening without a strategy is itself a setup for disaster. The Aybilistan wargame in Ukraine ended with an EU military intervention to the island, which in the "hotwash" assessment was described as a significant mistake, owing to a lack of clear strategy and rules of engagement. Immediately after the simulation, David Galbreath, professor of international security at the

[30] Formally, the ASEAN Coordinating Centre for Humanitarian Assistance on Disaster Management.
[31] See the Planetary Security Initiative, "The Hague Declaration on Planetary Security," www.planetarysecurityinitiative.org/declaration.
[32] Thomas J. Chermack, Susan A. Lynham, and Wendy E. A. Ruona. "A Review of Scenario Planning Literature," *Futures Research Quarterly* 17, No. 2 (2001): 7–32.

University of Bath, gave a talk in which he argued that intervention without strategy had become too common, driven by politics rather than sober realizations of how difficult it is to become involved in a disaster or complex emergency. Across the scenarios, corruption also became a salient problem. Corruption undermined trust within and between governments, prevented effective outside assistance during emergencies, and was a key vulnerability in hybrid conflict/disaster environments where an outside adversary sought to increase instability. Although the topic has long been discussed in reference to food aid and security, it needs to be emphasized more in reference to emerging hazards and risks.[33]

In this chapter, we also discussed the need for an environmental concept of net assessment. Energy and environmental systems often lack intentionality, but disasters are rarely purely "natural." The associated risks and impacts are heavily conditioned by human behavior. The need for environmental net assessment has become obvious not only due to the complexity of emerging hazards and risks, but also because of the ability of human actors to influence energy and environmental systems to create instability. Many disasters are triggered by the intersection of natural hazards and human created vulnerabilities. Increasingly, however, we find cases in which disaster risks and insecurity are intentional, with actors targeting the vulnerabilities of systems that underlie the ability of societies to sustain themselves.[34] It is to these cases of "hybrid disasters" that we now turn.

---

[33] Penny Green, "Disaster by Design: Corruption, Construction and Catastrophe," *British Journal of Criminology* 45, No. 4 (2005): 528–46; Graham Hancock, *Lords of Poverty: The Power, Prestige, and Corruption of the International Aid Business* (New York: Atlantic Monthly Press, 1992).

[34] Chad Briggs and Inka Weissbecker, "Salting the Earth: Environmental Health Challenges in Post-conflict Reconstruction," in *Assessing and Restoring Natural Resources in Post-conflict Peacebuilding*, ed. David Jensen and Steve Lonergan (New York: Earthscan, 2012), 111–34; David E. Mosher, Beth E. Lachman, Michael D. Greenberg, Tiffany Nichols, Brian Rosen, and Henry H. Willis, *Green Warriors: Environmental Considerations for Army Contingency Operations from Planning through Post-conflict* (Santa Monica, CA: RAND Corporation, 2008).

7

Hybrid Disasters and Security

A hybrid disaster is a manmade one, when forces of nature are unleashed
as a result of technical failure or sabotage.
  – Igor Boyarsky and Amiram Shneiderman, "Natural and Hybrid
Disasters – Causes, Effects, and Management"

Disasters are never purely natural. There are always human components to the nature or perception of risk – from social and technical resilience to political valuation of ecosystems at risk. As we discussed in earlier chapters, the security aspects of disasters are generally interpreted in terms of direct or cascading impacts, such as Hawaii hurricanes affecting readiness of military forces on Oahu. Hazards by themselves do not equal risks – those depend on human institutions and decisions. Yet, disasters are not merely passive hazards waiting to be translated into risks. Disasters can also be created by human actions, and particularly deliberate interventions with natural or human systems.[1]

In the broadest scale, even the good intentions of urban planners have often resulted in horrific consequences for the well-being of cities and their residents.[2] The ultramodernism of architects and designers like Le Corbusier, for example, left cities far less resilient, both structurally and socially. This is one definition of hybrid disasters – they are cases where human actions have left populations more vulnerable to risks, resulting in a hybrid condition between natural and unnatural disasters. We have already discussed such cases in previous scenarios from Peru to Hawaii, and in many ways, that definition is so broad it encompasses most disaster risks. Hybrid disasters can be also viewed from a different perspective; they occur due to sabotage or when natural forces are used deliberately against humans. Ilan Kelman provides a

---

[1] See Ilan Kelman, "Hybrid Disasters or Usual Disasters?" *Disaster and Social Crisis Research Network Electronic Newsletter*, No. 41 (2010): 9.
[2] James Scott, *Seeing Like a State* (New Haven, CT: Yale University Press, 2002).

number of historical examples – from the Russian strategic use of winter against its opponents to the intentional breaching of dikes by the Dutch Army.[3] The Royal Air Force over Germany in World War II and the US Air Force during the Korean War both targeted dams as a way to slow industrial production and movement of enemy forces. During the Vietnam War, the US military used various herbicide-spraying operations and deliberate forest fires to reduce the enemy's "natural" advantage.[4] They also employed cloud-seeding techniques to prolong the monsoon season and block enemy supply routes along the Ho Chi Minh Trail.[5] The use of environment as a weapon is not at all uncommon throughout history, nor are environmental consequences of war or preparation for war. What may be different now are the ways in which environmental and energy systems can be manipulated and the enormous consequences these changes have for both disaster and security risks.

This chapter discusses two new forms of hybrid disasters. Recent developments in hybrid warfare in conflicts such as Ukraine since 2014 illustrate a shift in the relationship between disaster risks and security. Energy and environmental systems are used not as a secondary weapon during an open conflict but instead are integral to a spectrum of tools used to destabilize countries and regions. These are approaches that Western countries are ill equipped to address. The other aspect of hybrid disasters that requires discussion is the development and use of geoengineering technologies. Geoengineering technologies hold some promise but also pose enormous risks. Again, we find that Western institutions are not designed to assess or address the hazards associated with these technologies. While a growing literature has attempted to discuss some of the security implications of geoengineering, militaries (and in particular the US Department of Defense) have been reticent to engage in these assessments.

With respect to both hybrid warfare and geoengineering, the lack of institutional capacity to assess emerging risks represents a significant challenge, and requires new risk assessment methods. In the case of hybrid warfare, the strategies themselves depend on the inability to anticipate and assess risks associated with this form of warfare. In the case of geoengineering, there may be no intention to work around existing institutions, but the ability to employ

---

[3] Ilan Kelman, "Acting on Disaster Diplomacy," *Journal of International Affairs* 59, No. 2 (2006): 215–40. Between 1500 and 2001, one-third of all major floods in the Netherlands were caused intentionally. See Christina Reed, "Floods Fail in War, Win as Weapon against Sea Level Rise," *Earth and Space Science News,* June 29, 2015, https://eos.org/articles/floods-fail-in-war-win-as-weapon-against-sea-level-rise.

[4] Joseph Trevithick, "Firestorm: Forest Fires as a Weapon in Vietnam," *Armchair General,* June 13, 2012, http://armchairgeneral.com/firestorm-forest-fires-as-a-weapon-in-vietnam.htm.

[5] Michel Chossudovsky, "The Ultimate Weapon of Mass Destruction: 'Owning the Weather' for Military Use," *Global Research,* September 9, 2017, www.globalresearch.ca/the-ultimate-weapon-of-mass-destruction-owning-the-weather-for-military-use-2/5306386.

technologies that alter global climate systems carries risks and potential widespread consequences that have already found their way into the genre of Hollywood disaster films.[6] In both cases, we found that scenario planning is one of the few techniques available for attempting to anticipate potential risks associated with these forms of hybrid disasters.

The challenges associated with these scenarios are perhaps greater than what we have seen in previous examples, and both (for different reasons) fell outside the scope of scenario development during the DOE and USAF Minerva projects. This chapter therefore discusses attempts by other organizations (projects with which I (Briggs) was involved) to create scenarios on hybrid warfare and geoengineering, and to lay out steps for future efforts. We first provide some theoretical background on hybrid warfare and its applications in the context of energy and environmental security. We focus on the concepts of resilience targeting and hybrid warfare, including various types of cyberoperations. The first scenario discussed in this chapter – a wargame run in 2017 in Kyiv, Ukraine – shows how cyberoperations could be used by state or nonstate actors to create hybrid disasters. The second scenario, developed at Yale University in September 2011, highlights some disaster risks of geoengineering, and particularly those linked to the solar radiation management.

Hybrid Warfare and Resilience Targeting

In some ways, research on hybrid warfare and the use of environment as a weapon bookends all the projects and scenarios described in this book. Many of the original vulnerability concepts and research methodologies developed for DOE's abrupt climate change team were created not for climate-related risks but as a way to assess postconflict environmental health risks. In 2006, I (Briggs) returned to the United States from a Fulbright professorship in Hungary, a country in which I had studied and worked since the early 1990s. I took on a new post in which I was asked to square the circle of combining topics central to international relations, environmental risks, and a regional focus that included East-Central Europe and the Balkans. In October 2006, the University of Iowa's School of Public Health hosted a conference on medicine, conflict, and disasters, and it is engagement with this community that provided a crucial foundation for understanding how to integrate traditional studies of conflict with environmental and disaster risks.[7]

---

[6] See *Geostorm* (2017).
[7] In this context, a particular thank-you goes to Tara Smith, Paul Greenough, Maureen McCue, Gina Clarke, and Jennifer Kasper.

The challenges associated with assessing environmental health risks in the Balkans were daunting. In a meeting with experts from the European Union Mission in Sarajevo in 2007, they pointed out that the government of Bosnia-Herzegovina did not even have accurate figures on its own population size – its estimate and that of the CIA differed by hundreds of thousands of residents in a country of some 3 million. When asked what the primary environmental risks were for the country, one doctor shrugged, explaining that the government kept no statistics on causes of death and health risks. He simply said, "We think lots of people die in car accidents."

While the European Union and other governments were investing money in reconstruction of the country, they were doing so without knowledge of the consequences of investing in specific priorities. An official at the EU Directorate for Enlargement in Brussels admitted as much, noting they had few good data sources but had to make decisions anyway.

In some ways, the concerns over Bosnia fit the broader definition of hybrid disasters. If the EU invested heavily in steel refineries in the city of Zenica, for example, by some indicators, the national economic output would increase, but there was no monitoring or assessment of environmental risks associated with the projects. Some areas of Bosnia-Herzegovina would still be suffering environmental consequences from the war in the 1990s, particularly the existence of millions of land mines that cut off access to forests and agricultural lands across the country. By some rather coldhearted calculations, projects like landmine clearance were not economically justifiable because the residents of Bosnia who were injured or killed by land mines did not earn enough money to offset the costs of clearance.[8] What was needed was a way to help identify potential hotspots in vulnerable populations within the country, places where more attention could be directed to ways of improving resilience and ensuring that outside investment helped the country to recover from conflict.

The project on vulnerability assessments in Bosnia-Herzegovina and Serbia throughout 2007 came to the attention of the US Department of Energy in November of that year. There is a direct line between the postconflict assessments and abrupt climate change scenarios described earlier. It was not simply the need to use bottom-up methodologies to gather data and identify hotspots (an approach taken from field epidemiology), nor the need to develop scenarios to anticipate potential futures. The other commonality between environmental security and postconflict assessments was a concept we termed *resilience targeting*. Rather than simply the environment being used as a weapon during

---

[8] Shannon K. Mitchell, "Death, Disability, Displaced Persons and Development: The Case of Landmines in Bosnia and Herzegovina," *World Development* 32, No. 12 (2004): 2105–20.

war, resilience targeting refers to an adversary undermining the resilience of the society, causing instability and reducing the likelihood that the society or community will be able to recover once the conflict is over.

Many of the examples we uncovered from studying the Balkans, as well as Lebanon and Sri Lanka, were environmental in nature. However, relying on public health methodologies, our focus on resilience targeting identified several weapons that could be used to undermine society.[9] In Bosnia-Herzegovina, for example, the use of land mines during the conflict in the 1990s was rarely intended to harm military forces. The widespread pattern of use instead seems to suggest attempts to deny access – the cutting off the ability of farmers to use agricultural land, villagers to collect firewood, or civilians to use rural roads. Patterns of violence in Bosnia-Herzegovina were also not simply intended to kill but to humiliate. Widespread sexual violence and rape fractured communities after the war, inflicting traumas that were culturally taboo to discuss or seek assistance for. Resilience targeting can also be used to weaken infrastructure (a tactic by the US Air Force vs. Serbia in 1999[10]), destroy natural resources, or use other methods to undermine livelihoods, particularly those linked to food production. What we were describing and identifying, perhaps without knowing at the time, was the concept of hybrid warfare.

Hybrid Warfare and Energy and Environment Security Risks

The concept of hybrid warfare is surrounded by an enormously complex debate over its exact meaning, and we will not be able to do justice to all the nuances in this chapter. For our purposes, it is important to identify security concepts that contribute to its meaning and justify the need for a new term. There are three main aspects of hybrid warfare. The first is *irregularity*. In this sense, a hybrid war is conflict that is carried out by forces that are not always in uniform. This condition is quite common, and it runs against traditional notions of the armed forces and international law as understood by The Hague Conventions. The second component is that of *unconventional warfare*, which refers to the means through which conflict plays out. Poisoning of water reservoir, for example, is an unconventional method of warfare and, if carried out by terrorists, is also considered irregular. The third component is *disaster*

---

[9] Briggs et al., (2009) 122–33.
[10] Ward Thomas, "Victory by Duress: Civilian Infrastructure as a Target in Air Campaigns," *Security Studies* 15, No. 1 (2006): 1–33.

risks themselves, which need not be linked to warfare or security but can be a result of some successful actions. The attempted terrorist poisoning of Batllave Reservoir in Kosovo in 2015 was both unconventional and irregular.[11] Had it been successful, it would have also proven to be a disaster for the capital city of Pristina.

It was not a coincidence that the USAF Minerva team contained an irregular warfare specialist (Col. Read), nor that the military and intelligence experts we worked with were specialists in counterinsurgency strategies (COIN) or other aspects of irregular/unconventional security.[12] Two of the other Minerva chairs included John Nagl and Montgomery McFate, both COIN specialists.[13] With US forces engaged in Afghanistan and Iraq, in the mid-2000s, there was an increased push for "full spectrum analyses" that covered the broad range of potential security risks as well as the ways in which those risk were interrelated.[14] While EES is not always at the center of discussions, fighting the insurgency in Iraq required a consideration of factors such as energy infrastructure.[15] Yet, a focus on hybrid warfare did not simply mean considering the combination of other factors. Hybrid warfare refers to intentional conflict incorporating a broad strategy of various military and nonmilitary tools, from planting anonymous disinformation on Facebook sites to conventional warfare using uniformed troops. Used strategically, hybrid warfare can help destabilize a conventionally stronger opponent by exploiting vulnerabilities, masking responsibility for actions, and, in many cases, avoiding serious retaliation.

If we define a disaster as a disruption in the ability of a society or community to operate, then in many ways, hybrid warfare is a suitable strategy for creating disasters and sustaining instability. For example, in the case of Russian use of hybrid warfare in Ukraine, the goal of Russian strategy is not the conquering of territory (beyond Crimea) or the defeat of Ukrainian military forces in the field.

---

[11] *Guardian*, "Kosovo Cuts Pristina Water Supply over Alleged Isis Plot to Poison Reservoir," July 11, 2015, www.theguardian.com/world/2015/jul/11/kosovo-cuts-pristina-water-supply-over-alleged-isis-plot-to-poison-reservoir.

[12] Robert Wilkie, "Hybrid Warfare Something Old, Not Something New," *Air and Space Power Journal* 23, No. 4 (2009): 13.

[13] Montgomery McFate and Andrea V. Jackson. *The Object beyond War: Counterinsurgency and the Four Tools of Political Competition* (Alexandria, VA: Institute for Defense Analysis, 2006); John A. Nagl, James F. Amos, Sarah Sewall, and David H. Petraeus. *The US Army/Marine Corps Counterinsurgency Field Manual* (Chicago: University of Chicago Press, 2008); John A. Nagl, *Learning to Eat Soup with a Knife: Counterinsurgency Lessons from Malaya and Vietnam* (Chicago: University of Chicago Press, 2009).

[14] Adrian Wolfberg, "Full-Spectrum Analysis: A New Way of Thinking for a New World," *Military Review* 86, No. 4 (2006): 35.

[15] Michael Ruhle and Julijus Grubliauskas, "Energy as a Tool of Hybrid Warfare," NATO Research Paper No. 113 (April 2015).

Rather, an unstable Ukraine helps prevent Kyiv from moving toward the west or from allowing the European Union or NATO to trust the Ukrainian government. As has been argued before, continued instability in Ukraine works to the advantage of the Kremlin, and particularly as long as Moscow denies involvement in the Donetsk and Lugansk separatist governments/militias and other actions aimed at destabilizing the functioning of communities.[16] Ukraine has in many ways become a testing ground for new aspects of hybrid warfare, particularly in the use of cyberweapons to affect energy infrastructure and create environmental risks. It is worth exploring these new aspects of cyber-related energy and environmental risks, as they flow into the use of new technologies (e.g., geoengineering) discussed later in the chapter.

Cyberweapons and Operations in the EES Context

While there is a debate among military theorists on the proper definition of *hybrid warfare*, with some arguing that the concept of hybridity is nothing new under the sun, the introduction of new technologies has changed the nature of intentional disaster risks in their ability to undermine resilience from a distance.[17] As societies become more dependent on information technologies and infrastructure, we create vulnerabilities when such systems are disrupted or damaged. Global systems of trade and information rely on "just-in-time" deliveries of goods and services, and disruption at one point in the system creates cascading effects and impacts elsewhere. When severe floods hit Thailand in 2011, they prevented delivery of key components of computer hard drives across the globe, resulting in a sharp spike in computer prices in the United States and Europe.[18] A USAF scenario developed in the summer of 2011 (coincidentally, just weeks before the Thailand floods) describes a geophysical disaster that was made worse by cyberattacks on critical infrastructure.[19] Climate change and other geophysical disaster risks cannot be taken in isolation. These shocks to the system can be exploited through new technologies and hybrid disaster strategies. Below we discuss four: cyberoperations (cyber-ops), cyberaggression, sock-puppeting, and astroturfing.

---

[16] Lawrence Freedman, "Ukraine and the Art of Limited War," *Survival* 56, No. 6 (2014): 7–38.

[17] James K. Wither, "Making Sense of Hybrid Warfare," *Connections* 15, No. 2 (2016): 73–87.

[18] Thomas Fuller, "Thailand Flooding Cripples Hard-Drive Suppliers," *New York Times*, November 5, 2011, www.nytimes.com/2011/11/07/business/global/07iht-floods07.html.

[19] Colonel Mark Read (US Army) and a group of experts developed the "California Screaming" scenario as part of the USAF Minerva Symposium at Maxwell AFB in August 2011. Read's own work on scenario planning is worthwhile: Mark R. Read, "Planning through Complexity: Employing Scenario Analysis to Facilitate Climate Change Adaptation in Fragile States," *Climate Change and Fragile States: Rethinking Adaptation* 16 (2012): 110–14.

Cyber-ops refer to the use of information technologies to carry out attacks on an adversary. Rather than information warfare, these attacks are often directed toward infrastructure, computer data, or other valuable assets.[20] One of the most famous attacks in recent years was the use of Stuxnet worm to disable uranium centrifuges in the Iranian nuclear facilities. The Stuxnet attack, which was only unofficially linked to the US and Israeli governments, was a sophisticated cyber-op that physically damaged valuable equipment from a distance and without official accountability.[21] Less sophisticated methods are also in use; they are effective tools for countries like North Korea to leverage otherwise weaker military assets. For example, rather than keeping most of its expertise within agencies like the Federal Security Service, Russia relies on many independent computer hackers who are largely allowed to carry out all manner of criminal activities as long as these are not directed against the Russian state or Russian banks. Occasionally, they are called upon to carry out activities at the request of the Russian government. In this way, Russian cyber-ops utilize a large number of so-called mercenaries and privateers who cannot be directly linked to the Russian government or security services.[22] Such methods were used in 2007 during widespread denial of service (DDoS) attacks against the Estonian government, which resulted in a large disruption of government and economic activity for several days.[23] The following year, similar DDoS attacks were used against the Georgian state and its communication networks, in advance of Russian military operations.[24]

More recently, Russian cyber-ops were linked to power outages across parts of Ukraine in December 2015. While the Ukrainian attacks were not well publicized, they were very worrying for infrastructure experts as a demonstration of both how well prepared Russian cyber-ops could be (the attack required some six months of preparation) and how vulnerable Western and American utilities could be to energy security disruption.[25] This was not exactly news in theory, as in 2007, the US Department of Energy during Project Aurora demonstrated the ability to not only disable but destroy electrical generators

---

[20] Patrick Duggan, "Strategic Development of Special Warfare in Cyberspace," *Joint Forces Quarterly* 79 (2015): 46–53.

[21] P. W. Singer, "Stuxnet and Its Hidden Lessons on the Ethics of Cyberweapons," *Case Western Reserve Journal of International Law* 47 (2015): 79.

[22] Andrei Soldatov and I. Borogan, *Red Web: The Struggle between Russia's Digital Dictators and the New Online Revolutionaries* (New York: Public Affairs, 2015).

[23] Scott Shackelford, "Estonia Three Years Later: A Progress Report on Combating Cyber Attacks," *Journal of Internet Law* 13, No. 8 (2010): 22–29.

[24] Paulo Shakarian, "The 2008 Russian Cyber Campaign against Georgia," *Military Review* 91, No. 6 (2011): 63.

[25] Kim Zetter, "Inside the Cunning, Unprecedented Hack of Ukraine's Power Grid," *Wired,* March 3, 2016, www.wired.com/2016/03/inside-cunning-unprecedented-hack-ukraines-power-grid/.

through internet hacks.[26] Yet, this was one of the first times that an international actor had demonstrated both the capability and willingness to do so. The lesson here is that remote locations are no defense against security breaches and that new energy operations – such as those in the Arctic – are entirely vulnerable to similar attacks. If opposition, for example, to Shell Oil drilling operations in northern Alaska is based on environmental concerns, it would only take a relatively simple cyberoperation to trigger an oil spill or gas explosion and therefore force Western companies out of the region.

The second category of new tactics involves refinements of the traditional information warfare and is collectively known as *cyberaggression.* Cyberaggression may be thought of as a more advanced and coordinated version of cyberbullying and is defined as "electronic or online behavior intended to harm another person psychologically or damage his or her reputation," by using a wide array of internet services, social media, websites, mobile phone technologies, and other platforms.[27] Cyberaggression can be used not only to discredit key figures but to disrupt the behavior and operation of crucial mid-level officials who are normally protected from political attacks. If used properly, cyberaggression can disrupt negotiations, amplify uncertainty on key issues, or force key experts to withdraw from discussions. Although cyberaggression campaigns are well coordinated in advance, in order to be most effective, they are made to look as if they are spontaneous reactions to a (often fabricated) scandal by an outraged public.

An example cyberaggression may well have been the so-called Climategate emails released in late 2009 in the lead up to the climate change negotiations in Copenhagen. A large number of emails were stolen from a remote server in Tomsk, Russia, and released to coordinated allegations that key scientists in the United States and the United Kingdom had been fabricating climate change data.[28] The Russian state was never officially linked to this campaign nor were the Russian or Western oil companies, but it was believed in some circles that a collusion between certain countries and certain multinational corporations was intended to amplify uncertainty around climate change and thus prevent international agreements that would reduce demand for oil and gas.[29]

---

[26] Wayne Harrop and Ashley Matteson, "Cyber Resilience: A Review of Critical National Infrastructure and Cyber Security Protection Measures Applied in the UK and USA," *Journal of Business Continuity and Emergency Planning* 7, No. 2 (2013): 149–62.

[27] Duggan, 52.

[28] Anthony A. Leiserowitz, Edward W. Maibach, Connie Roser-Renouf, Nicholas Smith, and Erica Dawson, "Climategate, Public Opinion, and the Loss of Trust," *American Behavioral Scientist* 57, No. 6 (2013): 818–37.

[29] See Shanta Barley, "Climategate: Russian Secret Service Blamed for hack," *New Scientist,* December 7, 2009, www.newscientist.com/blogs/shortsharpscience/2009/12/since-over-1000-confidential-e.html.

A third category of cybertactics, and often related to cyberaggression, is the use of *sock-puppeting*, the creation and use of online accounts to pose as disinterested or expert concerned citizens (also known more colloquially as concern trolls). A state can pay netizens to handle multiple online accounts on news sites, discussion boards, and other online forums. The technique is used, for example, by climate deniers in spreading uncertainty concerning the science of climate change.[30] One account may post comments critical of new climate data, and the same user may then switch to an alternative account to write comments in support of the criticism. While not normally thought of as a military tactic, it has been discussed in the context of cyber-pseudo-operations, where governments can act as dissidents or guerillas online in order to spread disinformation.[31] It is worth noting that the more complicated and remote the topic is, the more susceptible it is to disinformation, uncertainty amplification, and conspiracy theories.[32]

If applied to a larger scale, promoting false identities can be used for *astroturfing*, which is the technique of creating the illusion of grassroots support/opposition, while in fact the "support" is closely orchestrated by another power.[33] Although an American term to refer to artificial grassroots movements, online, it has been used to considerable effect by Russia in Crimea and Donbas in Ukraine where territorial expansion was justified as a demand by those being invaded.[34] Highly successful astroturf campaigns may eventually create the very movement they pretend to represent – although, when this occurs, the original creators may no longer be in control of the situation.[35] Astroturfing has also been applied to climate change discussions, though often in the context of larger oppositional movements.[36]

When taken together, cyber and IT technologies allow for destabilization of communities without clear attribution of intent or responsibility. The Russian concept of *maskirovka*, for example, refers to masking states behind certain

---

[30] Steven Kolmes, "Climate Change: A Disinformation Campaign," *Environment* 53, No. 4 (2011): 33.

[31] Duggan, 51.

[32] Joseph Uscinski, Casey Klofstad, and Matthew D. Atkinson, "What Drives Conspiratorial Beliefs? The Role of Informational Cues and Predispositions," *Political Research Quarterly* 69, No. 1 (2016): 57–71.

[33] Duggan.

[34] Kristiina Muur, Holger Molder, Vladimir Sazonov, and Pille Pruulmann-Vengerfeldt, "Russian Information Operations against the Ukrainian State and Defence Forces: April–December 2014 in Online News," *Journal on Baltic Security* 2, No. 1 (2016): 28–71.

[35] There are many arguments that creation of the Tea Party movement in the United States by Koch Industries represents such momentum, which most recently has resulted in the emergence of Donald Trump.

[36] Peter Frumhoff, Richard Heede, and Naomi Oreskes, "The Climate Responsibilities of Industrial Carbon Producers," *Climatic Change* 132, No. 2 (2015): 157–71.

actions, by using proxies and claiming grassroots movements in other countries. The strategy relies on exploiting the Western notion of "peace-war-peace," where a country or organization like NATO is normally considered to be at peace, and plans for actions it would take if war was declared, after which a condition of peace would exist again. If a country's defense strategies do not draw this clear line between peace and war, political actors can use a wide spectrum of available tools to achieve their security objectives – whether to destabilize a region or undermine the collective trust of members in their institutions.

An effective way of disrupting resilience is to create a series of disasters. Without clear evidence of who is accountable, the political and psychological tendency is to blame the government responsible for the maintenance of energy, safety, or security. While in the past, such sabotage would have been enormously difficult, today, extensive damage (in some cases, psychological) can be carried out effectively and remotely. NATO troops on maneuver in eastern Poland in recent years have found information lifted from social media accounts linked to their mobile phones, with soldiers receiving warning messages containing photos of their homes and family.[37] Cyberaggression techniques can be used against high-ranking military officers or members of government, undercutting trust and morale – such tactics were witnessed in Ukraine throughout 2014, prior to the invasion of Crimea and the eruption of violence in Donetsk.[38]

Creating Disasters in Ukraine

Although media reports on the conflict have ceased outside of Ukraine itself, the conflict continues, and the Minsk cease-fire agreement is regularly broken (see Figure 7.1). Since the start of post-Maidan violence in 2014, more than ten thousand people have been killed and more than twenty thousand have been wounded, many of them civilians, including 298 killed when Malaysian Airlines Flight 17 was shot down over Donbass.[39] More than 1 million people have been displaced from the conflict zone, although many (especially older

[37] Teri Schultz, "Russia Is Hacking and Harassing NATO Soldiers, Report Says," *DW*, October 6, 2017, www.dw.com/en/russia-is-hacking-and-harassing-nato-soldiers-report-says/a-40827197.

[38] Yuriy Danyk, Tamara Maliarchuk, and Chad Briggs, "Hybrid War: High-Tech, Information and Cyber Conflicts," *Connections* 16, No. 2 (2017); Nolan Peterson, "In Ukraine, Russia Weaponizes Fake News to Fight a Real War," *Daily Signal*, March 30, 2017, www.dailysignal.com/2017/03/30/in-ukraine-russia-weaponizes-fake-news-to-fight-a-real-war/.

[39] Julian Coman, "On the Frontline of Europe's Forgotten War in Ukraine," *Guardian*, November 12, 2017, www.theguardian.com/world/2017/nov/12/ukraine-on-the-front-line-of-europes-forgotten-war.

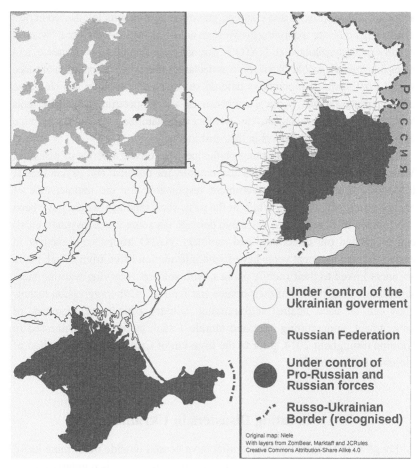

Figure 7.1 Conflict in Ukraine.
Source: Nielle (2016)

families) have returned over time, after spending years away in other cities. Across the "contact zone" between Ukrainian and separatist forces, some one hundred thousand professional and volunteer soldiers are engaged in direct or supporting roles.[40] In Ukraine, cyberaggression targets civilians and soldiers, and targeted assassinations of Russian dissidents are reported to be common in Kyiv.[41]

[40] Interfax-Ukraine, "Defense Ministry Says over 100,000 Military Volunteers Join Ukrainian Army," *Kyiv Post*, March 14, 2017, www.kyivpost.com/ukraine-politics/defense-ministry-says-100000-military-volunteers-join-ukrainian-army.html.

[41] Joshua Hammer, "The Killers of Kiev: How Putin Created an Assassin's Metropolis," *GK*, March 6, 2018, www.gq.com/story/killers-of-kiev-putin-assassins; Scott Stewart, "The Dirty

Events in Ukraine since 2013 have left the country more vulnerable, both from outside pressures and intervention and the effects of internal corruption and political distrust. An exercise in the spring of 2017, written by GlobalInt in cooperation with the EU Jean Monnet program, set out to test how much further these vulnerabilities could be pushed. This wargame scenario was developed around political and military factors rather than energy and environmental disaster risks. However, its use allowed local and international experts to test the boundaries of resilience in Ukraine, including the ways in which an outside adversary could create new disasters within the country. The Kyiv wargame was an example of the scenario created to test potential disaster risks, without the scenario explicitly outlining such hazards and risks in the first place. The role of participants was to role-play leaders of different country organizations, including Ukraine, Russia, the European Union, and NATO. If constructed properly, wargame scenarios can test conditions and responses, and, in this case, assessed the resilience of Ukraine in the face of active intervention from an adversary.

Kyiv Wargame, April 2017

Timeline: August to September 2017

Geographical scope: the country of Ukraine

Drivers: active measures against Ukrainian and NATO vulnerabilities; further invasion of Ukrainian territory by Russian armed forces

Security frame: traditional military security, with an emphasis on political vulnerabilities

Assumed vulnerabilities: no support from the United States; infrastructure vulnerabilities; corruption

Intervention points: unknown

Critical uncertainties: reaction from European Union members; US and French politics

---

The European Union and NATO had sponsored wargame training in Ukraine since shortly after the Maidan revolution and violence in the spring of 2014. The Aybilistan scenario (discussed in Chapter 6) was created for a wargame in Kyiv in 2014, and the Danchuana scenario (also in Chapter 6) was created in 2016 originally for use in Odessa. These two scenarios involved fictional

Work of Russian Assassins," *Stratfor Worldview*, September 14, 2017, https://worldview.strat for.com/article/dirty-work-russian-assassins.

countries to help diffuse potential political tripwires. Consequently, wargame participants were to pay attention to energy and environmental disaster risks and responses. By 2017, a final wargame was conducted with the support of the EU Jean Monnet program. This time, however, we decided that outside conditions (and particularly the UK Brexit vote and the US election of Donald Trump) had introduced so much uncertainty that the wargame was to be focused on potentially real conditions in Ukraine.

The scenario was created around events described in the book *War with Russia* by the former NATO Deputy Supreme Allied Commander Richard Shirreff.[42] The book, first published in May 2016, was itself based on NATO wargames that portrayed the invasion of Baltic states by the Russian military. The idea was to highlight how relatively unprepared NATO had become to defending its collective security. Reading the book in January 2017, one was struck by a glaring assumption embedded within the described scenario – that Hillary Clinton would win the 2016 US presidential election. Although not mentioned by name, the US president in the book was a woman, one who did not hesitate to invoke NATO's Article 5 collective security mechanism. The actual administration in Washington, DC, by that time had been avoiding any mention of NATO's Article 5, and security discussions in Europe through February 2017 were dominated by questions of how the United States would respond if NATO members were threatened by Russia. The June 2016 "Brexit" vote in the United Kingdom had also introduced uncertainty into the cohesiveness of the European Union, and the outcome of the April/May 2017 French presidential election had the potential to result in a further weakening of the EU.

The Kyiv wargame therefore set out to test not only the resilience of Ukrainian systems but whether outside assistance from the EU and NATO would even be possible given the new political realities of 2017. The wargame, which was also conducted in Pristina, Kosovo, in April/May 2017, established the following teams: Ukraine, Russia (red cell), the European Union (absent the United Kingdom), and NATO (absent the United States). The Russian team was tasked with "softening up" critical Ukrainian social, political, economic, energy, and military systems, in preparation for Russian military incursions into the cities of Mariupol, Kharkiv, and Odessa. As with most military-related wargames, the scenario was not based on assumptions that such events would occur or were even probable. They were, however, useful as tests of potential weaknesses within existing security structures and strategies.

---

[42] Richard Shirreff, *War with Russia* (London: Coronet, 2017).

Table 7.1: *Russian Strategies during the Kyiv Wargame in Kyiv, Ukraine*

Cyber-ops: Denial of service (DDoS) to banking, electricity, water, telecommunications, sewage, and other critical infrastructure systems, timed to create cascading impacts across systems.

Cyberaggression: Calculated cyberattacks were carried out against key deputies and the government and military, alleging corruption and other crimes, with the hope that such individuals would be less able to respond once the cyber-ops attacks began. Cyberaggression against key EU officials would also disrupt political discussions on how to respond to Ukrainian crisis.

Sock-puppeting: Social media used to spread rumors and false news articles describing the spread of disease outbreaks and food poisoning in Ukraine, as well as false reports concerning Middle Eastern refugees and violent attacks by Islamic extremists. False warnings of radiation leaks from nuclear plants, masked to appear as if such warnings were coming from official Ukrainian and European sources. Radiation warnings had a particular resonance in a country where a nuclear disaster had occurred some thirty years earlier.

Astroturfing: The creation of false peace groups and opposition to any forceful response against Russian actions, both in Ukraine and across European capitals.

The Russian team set out a series of coordinated cyber and information attacks primarily against Ukraine but also targeted key European policies and actors to prevent them from responding. This red team, consisting of experts with deep background knowledge of Russian strategies, information warfare, and European defense policies, understood well the weak points in Ukrainian resilience as well as potential European responses. Focusing on the cyber aspects of hybrid warfare and disasters described above, the Russian team in the wargame carried out a variety of actions (see Table 7.1) that both reduced resilience and increased the risk of hybrid disasters.

These coordinated actions were intended to undercut the resilience of the Ukrainian state and its communities, both by actively disrupting underlying support systems and by creating distrust in an already fragile political environment. The NATO players, lacking any formal defense agreement with Ukraine or support from the United States, were unable to intervene save for some covert attempts at bolstering cyberdefense of Ukrainian energy infrastructure. The European Union, itself divided internally over how to approach Russia, was likewise unable to do anything other than express concern over the developing situation. The Ukraine team in Kosovo made a positive effort to address allegations of corruption and therefore bolster its legitimacy internationally, but the Ukraine team in Kyiv was largely paralyzed by Russian actions and unable to respond.

Overall, participants described the wargame as highly frustrating, judging that the situation was highly asymmetric. The intention of the simulation, however, was not to find a solution to the scenario or to the current security situation in Ukraine, but instead to highlight the highly vulnerable nature of security risks and how easily a country's resilience could be undermined through cybertechnologies and other actions at a distance. While the actions taken by the Russian players in the wargame were not intended to spark disasters, they effectively pushed various underlying systems within the country to the breaking point, denying effective response capabilities or the ability to coordinate with outside actors who wished to provide assistance.

Although the Kyiv wargame was designed as a closed scenario, events in the real world soon caught up to the simulation. A large-scale cyberattack against Ukrainian systems, with cascading impacts across the globe, did in fact occur two months after the wargame.[43] Seemingly, the intent was not the defeat and collapse of the Ukrainian government but rather just enough destabilization that foreign governments and Western private investors would not have confidence in Ukrainian stability. All of this can be accomplished without foreign occupation or admittance of responsibility. Changes in technology have allowed warfare to take place below the normal threshold of what defense planners consider *proportionate response*, creating disasters or allowing them to occur where they would not have happened otherwise. Likewise, new technological developments can create new disaster risks and vulnerabilities due to intentional alterations of the climate and environment itself.

Geoengineering and Global Disaster Security

The concept of geoengineering dates back to the nineteenth century, when scientists first hypothesized the ability to control weather and prevent drought by cloud seeding and other techniques.[44] The concept of the greenhouse effect, of certain chemicals warming the atmosphere by trapping heat, has also been well understood since the nineteenth century, with the first warnings of human effects on the climate emerging in the early twentieth century.[45] Ideas of countering this effect, of using reflective particles or aerosols to artificially

---

[43] Andy Greenberg, "How an Entire Nation Became Russia's Test Lab for Cyberwar," *Wired*, June 20, 2017, www.wired.com/story/russian-hackers-attack-ukraine/.

[44] David W. Keith, "Geoengineering the Climate: History and Prospect," *Annual Review of Energy and the Environment* 25, No. 1 (2000): 245–84.

[45] Spencer R. Weart, *The Discovery of Global Warming* (Cambridge, MA: Harvard University Press, 2008).

cool the planet, have always been controversial and were first popularized in the context of nuclear war. In 1983, Carl Sagan and others calculated that an outbreak of nuclear war would not only cause unimaginable deaths from the warheads themselves but that dust raised in the air would spark a "nuclear winter" of freezing temperatures that would lay destruction on even the most remote parts of the earth.[46] Geoengineering, the concept of using technology to control climate or counteract global warming, has therefore always been wrapped in both a national security frame, as well as deep concerns over the wisdom, ethics, and controllability of such efforts.[47]

The atmospheric greenhouse effect warms the earth and atmospheric temperatures, resulting in averages that are higher than would be absent greenhouse gases like carbon dioxide and methane. Geoengineering is the use of technology to alter global or regional climate systems, either through a process of carbon dioxide removal (CDR) or solar radiation management (SRM). Carbon dioxide removal technologies have some analog with traditional environmental policies such as reforestation. The idea behind CDR technologies is that greenhouse gas mitigation may not be sufficient to prevent significantly negative climatic changes, which means that carbon dioxide already in the atmosphere must be removed and secured elsewhere. Some tested approaches to CDR include iron seeding of oceans.[48] The additional nutrients are meant to promote algae growth, which then removes carbon dioxide from the atmosphere and cycles it into the ocean. More advanced technologies involve carbon sequestration and removal, but these have mostly involved high energy input costs. Carbon dioxide removal policies may have some political impacts and shift the focus away from greenhouse gas mitigation policies, but otherwise the risks that their deployment presents are relatively localized.

Most security discussions of geoengineering have centered more on the solar radiation management technologies. SRM technologies range from deliberate injection of sulfates into the atmosphere to high-tech deployment of reflective materials into the stratosphere or low earth orbit. At a very local level, SRM can be used and is highly successful in lowering urban heat island effects, by painting roads or roof surfaces white or by increasing green spaces in cities. At a global level, SRM technologies are far more problematic. Deployment of geoengineering technologies may be highly unpredictable, with unintended

---

[46] Richard P. Turco, Owen B. Toon, Thomas P. Ackerman, James B. Pollack, and Carl Sagan, "Nuclear Winter: Global Consequences of Multiple Nuclear Explosions," *Science* 222, No. 4630 (1983): 1283–92.

[47] The 1964 Stanley Kubrick film *Dr. Strangelove* gave a somewhat parallel concept of intentionally shrouding the earth in radiation. Although not climate related, it did anchor many perceptions of nuclear winter two decades later.

[48] Quirin Schiermeier, "Dumping Iron at Sea Does Sink Carbon," *Nature*, July 18, 2012, www .nature.com/news/dumping-iron-at-sea-does-sink-carbon-1.11028.

consequences that may not be considered without effective governance structures. Even discussing these technologies is highly problematic, and creates
political concerns over their deliberate use in creating disasters.

As the USAF Minerva project had a remit to cover any number of energy and
environmental security risks, some researchers approached us to ask for help in
discussing potential security risks of geoengineering technologies. While the
US Department of Defense gave us wide latitude in determining which research
areas were relevant for our assessments, geoengineering was a bridge too far.
While I (Briggs) did participate in some discussions and scenarios around
geoengineering, and wrote one of the first pieces on its potential security
risks,[49] the Pentagon was very clear that any such discussions or research
were *not* to be done using any DOD time, money, or resources.[50] The
Department simply refused to discuss the issue, and certainly did not want
the Air Force research funds to be linked to these risky technologies.

The US Air Force did conduct research into weather modification technologies in the 1950s and 1960s, and was central to research into environmental
impacts of atmospheric nuclear testing. During the Vietnam War, two USAF
squadrons sprayed defoliants (e.g., Agent Orange) to help track Viet Cong
insurgents.[51] People tend to remember these projects and their environmental
and health consequences. The US military's use of Agent Orange and its health
effects on returning veterans led to the signing and ratification of the
Environmental Modification Convention (ENMOD) in 1976, with both the
United States and the Soviet Union "prohibiting the use of any environmental
or geophysical modification activity as a weapon of war."[52] DOD was therefore
legally prohibited from using or contributing to geoengineering technologies.
Even the most innocuous research into the topic could set off conspiracy
theories about military control of climate systems. The discussions presented
in this book therefore do not reflect the US DOD or USAF views in any way.

Many of the technologies developed have been done so by private companies, with corporations such as Google, Microsoft, and SpaceX expressing
interest in geoengineering applications.[53] The concept and applications therefore lack any clear governance mechanisms, being both outside of most state

---

[49] Chad M. Briggs, "Is Geoengineering a National Security Risk?" *Policy* 109 (2010): 85–96.
[50] They were, instead, facilitated by our company, GlobalInt.
[51] James Rodger Fleming, "The Pathological History of Weather and Climate Modification: Three
Cycles of Promise and Hype," *Historical Studies in the Physical and Biological Sciences* 37,
No. 1 (2006): 3–25; Herbert S. Appleman, "An Introduction to Weather Modification," No.
AWS-TR-177-REV, Air Weather Service (1969).
[52] Convention on the Prohibition of Military or Any Other Hostile Use of Environmental
Modification Techniques, available at www.un-documents.net/enmod.htm.
[53] Jeremy Hsu, "Bill Gates's Hidden Dreams of Geoengineering Revealed," *Popular Science*,
January 27, 2010, www.popsci.com/science/article/2010–01/bill-gates-geoengineering-pas
sion-revealed.

actions and raising difficult legal questions concerning cause and effect, intention, and loss/damage.[54] For some, geoengineering has become an alternative to climate mitigation policies, either for those who lack faith in state policies to reduce greenhouse gas emissions or for those who are skeptical of climate change theories in the first place.[55]

Solar Radiation Management

While CDR technologies attempt to slow down climate change by mitigating the greenhouse effect, solar radiation management (SRM) technologies focus more on incoming solar radiation. On average, 30 percent of radiation from the sun is reflected back into space, with reflectivity (also known as albedo) varying according to specific surfaces.[56] Ice and snow, for example, are highly reflective and absorb very little solar radiation, while black matte surfaces absorb a very high proportion. Some terrestrial ecosystems, such as the Arctic, can experience an abrupt shift in albedo conditions when surfaces change from highly reflective ice to much more absorbent open seawater.[57] SRM technologies are intended to deliberately shift the amount of solar radiation absorbed in earth systems, thereby creating cooling effects.

Changes in solar radiation may result from cooling processes such as those that follow large volcanic eruptions. The Mount Pinatubo eruption in 1991 ejected some 20 million tons of sulfur dioxide into the atmosphere, lowering global average air temperatures by nearly half a degree Celsius over the course of two years.[58] The Tambora eruption in 1815 led to significant regional drops in temperatures across Europe and subsequent loss of agricultural productivity and widespread food shortages.[59] Some researchers have argued that a series of four volcanic eruptions in tropical areas between 1275 and 1300 AD led to the so-called

[54] Adam Corner and Nick Pidgeon, "Geoengineering the Climate: The Social and Ethical Implications," *Environment: Science and Policy for Sustainable Development* 52, No. 1 (2010): 24–37.

[55] Katherine Ellison, "Why Climate Change Skeptics Are Backing Geoengineering," *Wired*, March 28, 2018, www.wired.com/story/why-climate-change-skeptics-are-backing-geoengineering/.

[56] Donald K. Perovich, Bonnie Light, Hajo Eicken, Kathleen F. Jones, Kay Runciman, and Son V. Nghiem, "Increasing Solar Heating of the Arctic Ocean and Adjacent Seas, 1979–2005: Attribution and Role in the Ice-Albedo Feedback," *Geophysical Research Letters* 34, No. 19 (2007).

[57] Michael Winton, "Amplified Arctic Climate Change: What Does Surface Albedo Feedback Have to Do with It?" *Geophysical Research Letters* 33, No. 3 (2006).

[58] P. Minnis, E. F. Harrison, L. L. Stowe, G. G. Gibson, F. M. Denn, D. R. Doelling, and W. L. Smith, "Radiative Climate Forcing by the Mount Pinatubo Eruption," *Science* 259, No. 5100 (1993): 1411–15.

[59] Davide Zanchettin, Oliver Bothe, Hans F. Graf, Stephan J. Lorenz, Juerg Luterbacher, Claudia Timmreck, and Johann H. Jungclaus, "Background Conditions Influence the Decadal Climate

Little Ice Age that lasted from the thirteenth to the sixteenth century.[60] Volcanic eruptions entail a combination of volcanic ash blocking the sunlight and the release of sulfur dioxide, which reflects certain wavelengths of radiation into the stratosphere. Shifts in the overall solar radiance balance then lead to changes in global climatic systems.

The logic behind the SRM technologies is to use science to shift global climatic systems back to early or preindustrial levels. A massive injection of sulfates into the atmosphere is one idea, but one which is problematic due to its severe environmental effects (i.e., creation of acid rain). More advanced SRM technologies use mirrored or reflective surfaces, which can often be controlled to allow precise amounts of solar radiation into the lower atmosphere. Science fiction movies tend to portray such technologies as large mirror arrays in outer space, but SRM can also involve injection of small reflected particles into the boundary layer between the troposphere and the stratosphere. These reflective nanoparticles are controllable and regionally specific, meaning they can be deployed in the upper atmosphere over a specific country or geographic region.[61] Far from being science fiction, technologies to create SRM nanoparticles already exist – but should they be used? Security and disaster risks associated with SRM geoengineering can be broken down into three interrelated factors: lack of governance, unpredictable side effects, and intended negative effects. These are discussed in detail in Table 7.2.

Governing geoengineering is complicated by the framing of associated security risks, the cost-benefit structure of geoengineering efforts, and the availability to redress if engineering actions by one actor harm another. Most states refrain from discussing these issues. This has created a gap in potential governance of norms, rules, and agreements for geoengineering, leaving such considerations to global corporations, such as Google, that fall outside of traditional security definitions.[62] If, for example, Microsoft deploys SRM

Response to Strong Volcanic Eruptions," *Journal of Geophysical Research: Atmospheres* 118, No. 10 (2013): 4090–106.

[60] Gifford H. Miller, Aslaug Geirsdottir, Yafang Zhong, Darren J. Larsen, Bette L. Otto-Bliesner, Marika M. Holland, David A. Bailey, Kurt A. Refsnider, Scott J. Lehman, John R. Southon, Chance Anderson, Helgi Bjornsson, and Thorvaldur Thordarson, "Abrupt Onset of the Little Ice Age Triggered by Volcanism and Sustained by Sea-Ice/Ocean Feedbacks," *Geophysical Research Letters* 39, No. 2 (2012).

[61] David W. Keith, "Photophoretic Levitation of Engineered Aerosols for Geoengineering," *Proceedings of the National Academy of Sciences* 107, No. 38 (2010): 16428–31; Bengt Fadeel, Hanna L. Karlsson, and Kunal Bhattacharya, "Geoengineering: Perilous Particles," *Science* 340, No. 6132 (2013): 548–49; Peter J. Irvine, Stefan Schäfer, and Mark G. Lawrence, "Solar Radiation Management Could Be a Game Changer," *Nature Climate Change* 4, No. 10 (2014): 842.

[62] Some reports suggest that this lack of global governance may be intentional on the part of some governments who wish to see these decisions left to commercial enterprises. See Martin Lukacs, "Trump Presidency 'Opens Door' to Planet-Hacking Geoengineer Experiments," *Guardian*,

Table 7.2: *Security and Disaster Risks Stemming from SRM Geoengineering*

Lack of governance: SRM technologies far outstrip any existing legal agreements or governance, save for ENMOD. If the Indian space agency (ISRO), for example, decided to deploy nanoparticles to control the onset of the Indian monsoon, could anyone legally object? More worrying are considerations that these technologies would not be deployed by governments but by corporations, in which case legal responsibility would be even more difficult to establish.[a]

Unpredictable side effects: Climatic systems are highly complex, and intervention in solar radiation is likely to have unintended consequences. Reestablishing cooler temperatures over the Arctic in order to promote the growth of sea ice, for example, may alter rainfall in the temperate areas of the Northern Hemisphere. The resulting floods or droughts would be difficult to ascribe to geoengineering efforts, especially if those operating the technologies are unwilling to share data. Significant environmental disasters could be triggered outside of the "controlled" area.[b]

Intended negative effects: Beyond the unintended consequences of using geoengineering, it would also be possible for the technology to be used against either states or specific populations within the state. For example, sudden warming of areas covered in permafrost would damage and disrupt oil and gas pipelines. Extreme heat events could be directed against particular cities, or rainfall could be directed to one agricultural region and denied to another.

[a] Bidisha Banerjee, "The Limitations of Geoengineering Governance in a World of Uncertainty," *Stanford Journal of Law, Science, and Policy* 4, No. 1 (2011).
[b] Jason J. Blackstock and Jane C. S. Long, "The Politics of Geoengineering," *Science* 327, No. 5965 (2010): 527.

technologies in Canada to help cool permafrost formations and, soon after, shifts in the polar vortex lead to deadly floods in China, who is to blame?

The unintended side effects of geoengineering likewise prevent traditional legal structures from attributing responsibility. As most climate systems are highly complex, interrelated, and nonlinear, it would be extremely difficult to attribute blame to a specific loss or damage (e.g., drought in northern Europe) as a result of engineering actions in another part of the globe. The existence of such technologies would, however, open the door for some leaders to attribute blame for environmental disasters, even in the absence of scientific causality. An important aspect of the geoengineering debate is the pervasive existence of conspiracy theories surrounding their use, from chemtrails to Alaskan radar facilities. It would be easy for cyberoperators to produce false information concerning the causes behind environmental disasters such as droughts and floods, including the formation of false social and political movements on both sides of the issue. Given the highly uncertain nature of the technological

March 27, 2017, www.theguardian.com/environment/true-north/2017/mar/27/trump-presidency-opens-door-to-planet-hacking-geoengineer-experiments.

impacts, and the high prevalence of conspiracy thinking surrounding these technologies, a security frame could easily be inserted at any time these technologies were deployed.

It may well be possible to use (or threaten to use) solar radiation technologies as potential weapons. The associated security risks depend in part on the ways they are framed. A deliberate use of SRM to melt Arctic ice and allow year-round shipping from Europe to Asia via the Northern Passage may be viewed as a benign economic benefit to Russia, but other states may interpret environmental impacts of the melting ice as highly negative and threatening. Such interpretations are likely to complicate political relations or fuel preexisting conflicts.

The complexity of intentional versus unintentional actions, direct impacts and indirect, cascading impacts, scaling from local action to global effect and back to local impact – all these considerations are difficult to take into account at once when discussing geoengineering hypothetically. While the science behind the greenhouse effect may be well established, changing the global climate to produce a desired effect will likely never be simple. Increasing rainfall in one region may reduce it in another, or the rainfall may come so suddenly that a drought is broken by the appearance of sudden and deadly floods. Even when specific impacts are identified, the human and political reactions to such events may not be known in advance. Scenarios and simulations are therefore useful tools for assessing security risks linked to geoengineering. The scenario described below was meant to be a first step to understanding such risks. However, in face of the complexity of geoengineering security implications, it did not fare well.

The Yale University Scenario (2011)

Timeline: present day to five years in the future

Geographical scope: global

Drivers: deployment of SRM technologies for regional changes in weather; corporate adoption of SRM technologies; accelerated melting of Arctic ice

Security frame: environmental and ecological security; parallel disaster frame

Assumed vulnerabilities: no governance of geoengineering technologies; imperfect information on effects

Intervention points: unknown

Critical uncertainties: reaction from affected countries; uncertain security frames; attribution of intent

In 2011, the Yale University Climate and Energy Institute and the Centre for International Governance Innovation in Canada jointly ran a scenario workshop on geoengineering.[63] The workshop used the more traditional two-axis method for scenario formation, with the axes representing either/or formulations of technology being controllable versus uncontrollable, with impacts understood as collective or individual. The approach produced six scenarios, which the participants then attempted to expand upon with detailed narratives concerning probable events in the future. Despite a follow-up event on the subject in Ottawa, Canada, in 2012 and Potsdam, Germany, in subsequent years, the security risks of geoengineering (or climate engineering, as the alternative term is sometimes used) have not received as comprehensive an assessment process as they deserve.

The Yale scenarios touched upon several aspects of the intersection between climate change and security noted in Table 7.2. For example, the lack of governance structures for discussing, adjudicating, and resolving security risks was threaded throughout the scenarios and mostly represented by the axis between self-interest and the common good. The basic setup of the scenario creation process, however, prevented an in-depth discussion or exploration of the security risks. During the discussions, many participants made simplistic assumptions. For example, one participant stated that after a drought in China, the Chinese government would respond with a nuclear attack on the city of San Francisco. Both scenario and simulation processes require input from a range of experts as well as a bounded narrative methodology that can validate the identified risks, ensuring they retain their plausibility and complexity.

Overall, the Yale workshop illustrated the shortcomings of traditional scenario methods. The scenarios required greater detail in terms of scientific, engineering, and political dynamics. They also needed to be followed by simulations that would cover the hybrid and nonstate aspects of disaster and security risks that potentially stem from geoengineering efforts. For example, in situations where disasters are (or are viewed to be) deliberate, both state and nonstate actors may respond with an array of actions – from cyber-ops and sabotage of remote systems to the manipulation of social media and news to inflict economic or political damage on opponent. It is not only the environmental impacts from geoengineering-related disasters that are of concern but also the ways in which these are perceived, interpreted, and manipulated to spark or worsen larger conflicts.

[63] Bidisha Banerjee, George Collins, Sean Low, and Jason J. Blackstock, *Scenario Planning for Solar Radiation Management* (New Haven, CT: Yale Climate and Energy Institute, 2013). The workshop facilitator was Jay Ogilvy of the Global Business Network (GBN).

Conclusion

The extensive work done on disaster risk mitigation and resilience building tends to view the "adversary" in terms of natural hazards. The aim of this chapter was to show how environmental disasters, and specifically those often labeled as "natural," not only contain a human element but can be intentionally created by humans. These so-called hybrid disasters have security implications in both war and during peacetime. Various types of cyberoperations, for example, are effective and increasingly used strategies of hybrid warfare, capable of creating hybrid disasters. In this chapter, a wargame applied on the Ukrainian political situation served as an illustrative example of the current and potential risks that hybrid disasters pose. In conflict situations, even when the conflict is not openly violent as is often the case in Ukraine, for some actors, disaster risks and vulnerabilities become both tools and targets. As perhaps the ultimate form of hybridization of the environment and technology, geoengineering represents these risks and disaster potential at a much larger and much more uncertain scale.

We are likely to see increased incidences of both hybrid disasters with security implications and hybrid wars that affect energy and environmental systems.[64] The very nature of these hybrid risks prevents easy attribution or early warning. Deadly floods occur not only because of changes in precipitation but also due to numerous previous decisions concerning land use, urban planning, transport infrastructure, and insurance, among others. Different cyberoperations could worsen such disasters, for example, by preventing or undermining warning systems, spreading false information during a disaster, or claiming the disaster did not exist. Political actors may take advantage of the impacts for political purposes, for example, to consolidate government and police control following a disaster. Attacks on critical infrastructure can also be carried out in such ways that the events look "natural." This turns the environment into a potentially powerful weapon. Whether it is the development of new technologies, the shifting nature of warfare, or changing boundary conditions of environmental systems because of climate change, these new challenges require new forms of thinking. New approaches are not particularly time or resource intensive but need political will and the overcoming of traditional obstacles that have kept our perceptions of these risks notably blinkered. It is to these obstacles that we turn next.

---

[64] Patrick Cullen, "Hybrid Threats as a New 'Wicked Problem' for Early Warning," *Hybrid COE Strategic Analysis*, May 25, 2018, www.hybridcoe.fi/wp-content/uploads/2018/06/Strategic-Analysis-2018-5-Cullen.pdf.

8

Obstacles and Opportunities

In the spring of 2009, the Organization for Security and Cooperation in Europe (OSCE) held a meeting at a resort on the outskirts of Athens, Greece. Representatives of the fifty-six members from most countries of Europe, Central Asia, and North America sat in a large banquet hall and, over several days, discussed existing and emerging security risks to regions that encompassed much of the Northern Hemisphere. The ministerial forum, focused on economic and environmental issues, raised the question of environmental causes of forced migration, including what the future of migration into Europe might look like given the changing climate. Outside experts explained the close links between environmental factors and migrants/refugees. There was, however, reluctance on the part of some ministers and ambassadors to accept that climatic changes might significantly affect the numbers of people attempting to leave places like Africa for Europe. At one point, a seemingly exasperated ambassador from Ireland broke into the discussion, exclaiming, "Why is this so difficult to believe? My country's history is dominated by an environmental disaster that forced half the population to leave. And we think it won't happen here?"

Six years later, in 2015, the numbers of migrants and refugees crossing into the European Union skyrocketed, most of them making illegal and risky crossing by sea from Turkey to Greece. Small islands like Lesvos and Chios were overwhelmed with hundreds of thousands of people, who then fled to mainland Greece, and from there into Macedonia, Serbia, and EU countries.[1] The increase was caused by a number of factors, including the Syrian civil war, the ISIS campaign in Iraq, and a resurgence of Taliban warlord violence in Afghanistan and Pakistan. The large numbers of people claiming refugee status

[1] Eleni Andreouli, Lia Figgou, Irini Kadianaki, Antonis Sapountzis, and Maria Xenitidou, "'Europe' in Greece: Lay Constructions of Europe in the Context of Greek Immigration Debates," *Journal of Community and Applied Social Psychology* 27, No. 2 (2017): 158–68.

sparked political crises in Europe, starting in Hungary in early 2015, and shifted the political climate in countries like Austria, Slovenia, and Italy. While Germany, Sweden, and some other EU members accepted large numbers of these refugees, what quickly became apparent was an inability of EU institutions and political culture to deal with the growing numbers. Hungarian prime minister Orban described the movement of migrants as a crisis and threat to "Christian civilization," while others pointed out that as most European countries had falling population levels, immigration was the only solution to impending economic risks.[2]

By March 2016, the "Balkan route" from Greece into Macedonia was cut off, first to everyone except Syrians, then shortly afterward to all those claiming refugee status. Hundreds of thousands were forced to remain in Greece, a country that was experiencing its own financial crisis prior to the influx of migrants.[3] Many were trapped near the Greek–Macedonian border in the small village of Idomeni. There was no formal camp at Idomeni – barely any United Nations presence – just mud and rain and thousands of people living in tents, most of them women and children. The images from the camp were horrific, the actual conditions even worse, with quickly spreading disease and lack of food and supplies.[4] For many people who saw Idomeni on the news, it was hard to believe that what they were seeing was in the European Union. Many did not want to believe what they were seeing, wanted to think it had been overblown or that someone else would take care of the issue. Political leaders blamed each other for the emerging disaster, blamed migrants for having left their homes or having left Turkey, blamed the EU for having "manufactured" the crisis, or wanted to ignore the issue entirely.[5] Many local Greeks who were witnessing the conditions, despite their own financial troubles, on the islands and in Idomeni tried to help. New organizations emerged to fill in the gaps left by the EU or UN, and individuals donated food, clothing, or firewood. The response of people on the ground and their perception of the situation were far different from how the disaster was framed and discussed from far away. One Slovak volunteer at the

---

[2] Miklos Haraszti, "Behind Viktor Orban's War on Refugees in Hungary," *New Perspectives Quarterly* 32, No. 4 (2015): 37–40; Massimo Livi Bacci, "Does Europe Need Mass Immigration?" *Journal of Economic Geography* 18, No. 4 (2017): 695–703.

[3] Bodo Weber, "The EU-Turkey Refugee Deal and the Not Quite Closed Balkan Route," Friedrich Ebert Stiftung, Dialogue Southeast Europe, June 2017; Mariya Ilcheva, "Traveling along the Balkan Route One Year On," *Deutsche Welle*, August 26, 2016, www.dw.com/en/traveling-along-the-balkan-route-one-year-on/a-19506005.

[4] Tracy and I (Briggs) worked with the organization Lighthouse Relief on the island of Levos in 2016. In March of that year, we organized a small relief effort to Idomeni, focused on women and children. The observations here refer to our firsthand experiences.

[5] Pablo Gorondi, "Hungary's Orban: EU Leaders Don't Want to Stop the Migrants," Associated Press, February 29, 2016, www.samoaobserver.ws/en/29_02_2016/world/3091/Hungary's-Orban-EU-leaders-don't-want-to-stop-the-migrants.htm.

Idomeni camp remarked, "If the European leaders were forced to come here, walk in this mud, talk to these people, they would see it differently."[6]

Much of the discussion in this book has centered on the needs of those who are already undertaking disaster risk assessments or are interested in how climate change affects international security or defense. One of the enduring lessons since the Peruvian scenario (Chapter 4), however, has been the difficulty in convincing others – and particularly at the organizational level – of the importance of the identified emerging risks. During the past decade, we have given numerous briefings on the potential impacts of climate change, associated emerging hazards, and the ways in which these will affect different elements in society, from migration patterns to the flooding of coastal infrastructure. The receivers of such briefings would often nod in agreement, compliment us on the importance of our work, and then return to their organizations or agencies as per business as usual.

While the planning scenarios and wargames described in this book were developed within a select network of experts, the overriding purpose of such efforts was to translate the findings and make them both accessible and believable to policy makers and the public. We were not always successful in doing so. At the time of writing this chapter, heat waves are sweeping the Arctic, and there are devastating floods in Japan. Yet, media attention has been largely focused elsewhere, international climate agreements are in jeopardy, and "getting the message out" competes both with short-term security concerns and continued refusals to accept established scientific research. The purpose of this chapter is to draw attention to these potential obstacles, both as an admission that not all working environments are conducive to effective risk assessments and as an opportunity to suggest ways to mitigate the problems. The chapter addresses several prevailing obstacles to translating, assessing, and communicating complex EES risks: anti-science attitudes and climate change denial, uncertainty assessment, and communication as well as bureaucratic stovepiping and secrecy.

Anti-science Attitudes and Climate Change Denial

Many established scientific theories have their detractors. Some insist that the earth is flat, that biological evolution does not exist, that the germ theory of

---

[6] In 2015, migrants were largely from Middle Eastern countries, such as Syria and Iraq, fleeing violence. By 2018, the Lake Chad region in Africa become a key source of instability, environmental stress, and migrants. See Chitra Nagarajan, Benjamin Pohl, Lukas Ruttinger, Florence Sylvestre, Janani Vivekananda, Martin Wall, and Susanne Wolfmaier, *Climate-Fragility Profile: Lake Chad Basin* (Berlin: Adelphi Research, 2018).

disease is a hoax, and that Einstein's general theory of relativity was a Jewish conspiracy.[7] Anti-science rhetoric in politics is not new. We have seen it before – from the warnings of anti-intellectualism of H. L. Mencken to the more overt politics against science described in the writings of George Orwell. Recent books have decried loss of faith in expertise, threats against the intelligence and law enforcement communities in the United States, and violence and harassment against journalists and scientists in discussions about the rise of "fake news."[8] While it is beyond the scope of this book to discuss the general background of anti-science attitudes in society, given our focus on climate change as a source of disaster risks, we cannot overlook one important and related phenomenon – climate change denial.

Denial of anthropogenic climate change is perhaps not as extreme as other anti-science attitudes.[9] Climate denialists are not a fringe group of eccentrics like "flat-earthers." There are both political and psychological reasons why the belief persists, and people who attacked the scientific consensus on climate change hold considerable political power in countries such as the United States, Canada, Australia, and Russia. In these countries, political elites have been influenced by oil and gas industries into hampering climate change mitigation policies, and at times silencing government scientific research into climate-related fields.[10] In countries like Canada and Australia, however, these efforts have not had as much an impact on larger public trust in science and the evidence concerning climate change. Among Western countries, the United States is fairly unique in the widespread and perhaps growing distrust of science and scientific evidence.[11]

Climate change denial in some countries has a distinct ideological component, often related to distrust in central authorities and mistrust of official experts. Even as people and organizations come to accept potential disaster

---

[7] Thomas Powers, *Heisenberg's War: The Secret History of the German Bomb* (New York: Alfred A. Knopf, 1993).

[8] Tom Nichols, *The Death of Expertise: The Campaign against Established Knowledge and Why It Matters* (New York: Oxford University Press, 2017); Michael Hayden, *Playing to the Edge: American Intelligence in the Age of Terror* (New York: Penguin, 2018); David M. J. Lazer, Matthew A. Baum, Yochai Benkler, Adam J. Berinsky, Kelly M. Greenhill, Filippo Menczer, Miriam J. Metzger, Brendan Nyhan, Gordon Pennycook, David Rothschild, Michael Schudson, Steven A. Sloman, Cass R. Sunstein, Emily A. Thorson, Duncan J. Watts, and Jonathan L. Zittrain, "The Science of Fake News," *Science* 359, No. 6380 (2018): 1094–96.

[9] While some authors prefer to use the term *climate skeptics, skepticism* is a normal and healthy condition within scientific methodology. More troubling are people and organizations who refuse to accept evidence of climate change, regardless of scientific data and the potential consequences of ignoring such risks.

[10] Justin Farrell, "Corporate Funding and Ideological Polarization about Climate Change," *Proceedings of the National Academy of Sciences* 113, No. 1 (2016): 92–97.

[11] Jean-Daniel Collomb, "The Ideology of Climate Change Denial in the United States," *European Journal of American Studies* 9, No. 9–1 (2014).

risks from climate change, it is not an easy political decision how to focus resources in areas of greenhouse gas mitigation, disaster risk mitigation, or disaster response policies. Economic costs associated with climate-related mitigation or adaptation policies are difficult to calculate, with short-term costs appearing to outweigh long-term risks, if uncertainty is amplified enough. This uncertainty amplification has been the deliberate strategy of some industries and has spilled over into some countries' domestic politics.[12] The uncertainty is amplified through both regular media reporting and social media activities. Media representation of climate-related risks has very often given equal weight to skeptics and deniers, creating a false sense of uncertainty over available scientific evidence. Social media have further allowed amplification of conspiracy theories and false information concerning climate-related disaster risks, from the UN Agenda 21 takeovers of the US government to claims that US geoengineering technology has created disasters such as earthquakes and hurricanes.[13] The role of communicating climate-related disaster risks has often fallen to scientists, who are not only often untrained in media relations but also have professional obligations not to overstate conclusions from available research.

As with any risk issue, the way in which a particular risk is framed largely predetermines how it will be discussed politically, including the level of evidence necessary for a risk to be considered "substantive." Climate change risks in many countries have been framed in terms of livelihoods, food security, and migration, meaning that climate-related hazards are perceived as risks to basic needs.[14] The United States, in contrast, has often seen climate change defined in terms of long-term economic costs, drawing upon widely held earlier assumptions that climate change impacts would most seriously affect less developed countries.[15] This American framing, while shifting in recent years, allows greater amplification of uncertainty in the perception that short-term costs outweigh long-term benefits. Part of this American exceptionalism to

---

[12] Robert J. Brulle, "Institutionalizing Delay: Foundation Funding and the Creation of US Climate Change Counter-Movement Organizations," *Climatic Change* 122, No. 4 (2014): 681–94.

[13] I (Briggs) was personally accused of hiding information on the ability of the US Air Force to influence weather and climate. As the head of environmental and energy research for USAF/AU, people believed I had firsthand knowledge and control of facilities such as HAARP, and my denials were interpreted as proof that secrets were being kept. See Linley Sanders, "'Geostorm' Hurricane Conspiracy Theory Claims the US Government Controls Weather," *Newsweek*, October 24, 2017, www.newsweek.com/government-not-controlling-hurricanes-despite-con spiracy-theory-692252.

[14] Janani Vivekananda, "How Are Climate Change and Human Security Interrelated," in *Implications of Climate Change and Disasters on Military Activities*, ed. Nikolov Orlin and Veeravalli Swathi (Dordrecht, Netherlands: Springer, 2017), 87–90.

[15] E.g., Trevor Houser, Solomon Hsiang, Robert Kopp, and Kate Larsen, *Economic Risks of Climate Change: An American Prospectus* (New York: Columbia University Press, 2015).

climate change perception may be rooted in the nature of education and religion in the United States, but another important factor is the institutionalization of uncertainty and doubt surrounding climate change risks in the United States and other countries.[16]

Naomi Oreskes has documented how a combination of scientific uncertainty and distrust in authority can be exploited to increase the effects of climate denial in the population.[17] Just as industry campaigns worked to deny the connection between cigarette smoking and health risks, many of the same lobbyists shifted work to casting doubt on climate change research and associated risks.[18] While in the past, such efforts may have been centralized in certain public relations campaigns and industry-funded think tanks, today, such disinformation can be spread much more quickly and personally via social media platforms. The hybrid warfare strategies (discussed in Chapter 7) apply not only to creating disasters but also to preventing communities and states from properly assessing these risks in the first place. Russian disinformation campaigns have worked to spread climate change denial methods in the United States, and have been active in attempting to disrupt greenhouse gas mitigation policies and renewable energy investments in Europe.[19] While climate change denial and the related resistance to change may partly be an issue of psychological barriers to climate change–related information, more commonly, it stems from the nature of organizational and administrative structures.

Since 2017, the US presidential administration has systematically removed references to climate change and access to climate-related data across the federal government.[20] Government cabinet positions have been held by vocal

---

[16] Stephen C. Zehr, "Public Representations of Scientific Uncertainty about Global Climate Change," *Public Understanding of Science* 9, No. 2 (2016): 85–103.

[17] Naomi Oreskes and Erik M. Conway, "Defeating the Merchants of Doubt," *Nature* 465, No. 7299 (2010): 686.

[18] Naomi Oreskes, *Merchants of Doubt: How a Handful of Scientists Have Obscured the Truth on Issues from Tobacco Smoke to Climate Change* (London: Bloomsbury Press, 2015).

[19] US House of Representatives Committee on Science, Space, and Technology, "Russian Attempts to Influence US Domestic Energy Markets by Exploiting Social Media," March 1, 2018, https://science.house.gov/sites/republicans.science.house.gov/files/documents/SST% 20Staff%20Report%20-%20Russian%20Attempts%20to%20Influence%20U.S.%20Domestic %20Energy%20Markets%20by%20Exploiting%20Social%20Media%2003.01.18.pdf; Claire Dupont, "When Decarbonisation Meets Disinformation: EU-Russia Energy Relations," IES Policy Brief No. 15 (June 2016).

[20] Kari De Pryck and François Gemenne, "The Denier-in-Chief: Climate Change, Science and the Election of Donald J. Trump," *Law and Critique* 28, No. 2 (2017): 119–26; Victoria Herrmann, "I Am an Arctic Researcher: Donald Trump Is Deleting My Citations," *Guardian*, March 28, 2017, www.theguardian.com/commentisfree/2017/mar/28/arctic-researcher-donald-trump-deleting-my-citations; Umair Irfan, "'Climate Change' and 'Global Warming' Are Disappearing from Government Websites," *Vox*, January 11, 2018, www.vox.com/energy-and-environment/2017/11/9/16619120/trump-administration-removing-climate-change-epa-online-website.

critics of climate science and research, with the US Department of Defense remaining an outlier in taking climate change risks and associated disaster hazards seriously. Yet, even at the Pentagon, the first update to the US National Security Strategy in 2017 removed all references to climate change, despite Secretary Mattis and various service chiefs testifying to Congress on the real risks associated with future climate change.[21] References to climate change risks have also been removed from environmental departments at the state level in Florida and Wisconsin, with North Carolina prohibiting climate change data from being used in coastal planning assessments.[22] These policy moves are not merely top-down impositions by elites but also illustrate widespread and growing disbelief among Republicans in the United States and intense polarization of the issue between parties.[23]

The securitization of the climate change debate has been described as an important counterweight to climate skepticism and denial in the United States, as the authority of the military may be trusted more by some people than that of academics and scientists.[24] It was not the intention of the Department of Defense to insert itself or take sides in such a highly charged issue, and senior Pentagon officials often privately expressed unease at how their department was seemingly leading ahead of the Environmental Protection Agency (EPA). US military officers, trained to avoid political disputes, were at best agnostic on climate change issues at first and only reluctantly accepted the importance of integrating environmental factors into their operational and strategic planning. This reluctance may have earned them an even greater amount of trust from otherwise skeptical Americans, but it is important to note that military-civilian relations are very different in each country. In Canada, for example, between 2006 and 2015, the government of Stephen Harper restricted many discussions of climate change and energy security issues, including concerns of Canadian Defense officers who were

[21] *Yale Environment 360*, "Trump Removes Climate Change as Threat to US in New Security Strategy," Yale School of Forestry and Environmental Studies, December 18, 2017, https://e360 .yale.edu/digest/trump-removes-climate-change-as-threat-to-u-s-in-new-security-strategy.

[22] Ian Johnston, "Officials in US Replace Science with Climate Change Denial Days after Donald Trump's Election Victory," *Independent*, January 3, 2017, www.independent.co.uk/news/ world/americas/climate-change-denial-us-officials-wisconsin-donald-trump-presidential-elec tion-victory-global-a7506831.html; Chris Toumey, "Science Policy in the Days of Trump," *Nature Nanotechnology* 12, No. 10 (2017): 934.

[23] Riley E. Dunlap, Aaron M. McCright, and Jerrod H. Yarosh, "The Political Divide on Climate Change: Partisan Polarization Widens in the US," *Environment: Science and Policy for Sustainable Development* 58, No. 5 (2016): 4–23.

[24] See discussion of the role of elites in Robert J. Brulle, Jason Carmichael, and J. Craig Jenkins, "Shifting Public Opinion on Climate Change: An Empirical Assessment of Factors Influencing Concern over Climate Change in the US, 2002–2010," *Climatic Change* 114, No. 2 (2012): 169–88.

worried about accelerating changes in the Arctic.[25] In Germany, the Ministry of Defense has routinely deferred to the Foreign Ministry on climate issues, as those are deemed too political (as per German historical legacy, the military should not be seen as involved in politics).[26] In other words, while the US military had a positive role to play in overcoming climate skepticism in the United States, military involvement in climate issues may have the opposite effect in other countries.

Yet, for both civilian and military communities, disaster and public health risks provided some of the most useful frameworks for describing and assessing the interaction between climate change and security. People tend to be most persuaded when they can see concrete ways in which environmental changes affect what they value. As noted earlier, discussions of 2°C average air temperatures and impacts on people in far-off lands only provide openings for those who would seek to delay necessary action in mitigation or adaptation. How environmental changes translate into value risks varies greatly according to the communities, societies, religions, geographies, professions, and many other variables. No one story will get everyone's attention. The intention behind using scenarios to describe various disasters related to energy and environmental changes was to provide a flexible framework where multiple narratives and stories could be told. Presentation of numbers and facts does not translate well to most communities, and the conclusion that nothing can be done might nudge people into paralysis or passivity. The best approach appears to be one in which people can become participants in the assessment and planning process, one that gives them tools to deal with uncertainty.

Uncertainty: Assessment, Amplification, Communication

In summer 2009, at a meeting of the Center for Strategic and International Studies in Washington, DC, the Department of Energy team attempted to explain how previous approaches to environmental security had been too simplified and unworkable for policy making. Among the experts in the room, a scientist from the NASA Goddard Space Center in Maryland raised her hand and asked, "But how do you deal with all the multiplying uncertainties created by having so many variables?" The ensuing discussion involved long explanation of the role that early warning plays in security risks and highlighted the very diverse ways in which different communities (in this case, scientific

---

[25] Sarah Zhang, "Looking Back at Canada's Political Fight over Science," *Atlantic*, January 26, 2017, www.theatlantic.com/science/archive/2017/01/canada-war-on-science/514322/.

[26] Personal communication with German Foreign Ministry officials, October 2010.

and intelligence communities) deal with uncertainties in their work. In this section, we briefly discuss the role of uncertainty in science, cognition, and policy making to show how uncertainty shapes risk assessment attitudes and policies.

Most people – whether in politics, science, or everyday life – try to minimize uncertainties as much as possible. The reasons vary. Scientists, for example, have a professional obligation to reduce uncertainties (particularly in methodologies), so that they do not fall prey to producing false positives (i.e., claiming that chemical A leads to disease X without very high confidence that such a causal relationship exists). Scientific methodologies, including methods of peer review and informal acceptance of new ideas, are designed in a very conservative manner meant to tamp down on fringe theories, ungrounded speculations, methodological errors, sampling problems, and other seemingly esoteric issues such as bio-extrapolation. In the context of emerging hazards and risks, when faced with uncertainty, we do not always make what might be considered the most rational decisions, given scientific evidence. This is because we use heuristics, or cognitive shortcuts, to make decisions based on past choices and values. These shortcuts rely on the most readily available information placed into the most easily accessible frameworks according to past experiences, even if the phenomenon is new and does not fit easily into established categories.[27] For example, in light of growing reports that incidences of autism in young children have been rapidly increasing in the United States, many have turned to an easily understandable (if scientifically incorrect) explanation that vaccines were the cause of autism.[28] Even if it was well established that exposure to mercury leads to a rise in risk of autism, there is no easy course of action for escaping the exposure to methylmercury (such as from the burning of coal in power plants).[29]

Appropriate policies to mitigate or adapt to disaster risks often rely on government action, but here, too, we find that approaches to uncertainty

---

[27] Nick Pidgeon, Roger E. Kasperson, and Paul Slovic, eds., *The Social Amplification of Risk* (Cambridge: Cambridge University Press, 2003).

[28] Peter Bearman, "Just-So Stories: Vaccines, Autism, and the Single-Bullet Disorder," *Social Psychology Quarterly* 73, No. 2 (2010): 112–15.

[29] Philip Holmes, K. A. F. James, and Len S. Levy, "Is Low-Level Environmental Mercury Exposure of Concern to Human Health?" *Science of the Total Environment* 408, No. 2 (2009): 171–82. In fact, antivaccine myths were a key weapon of Russian misinformation campaigns in US politics. See David A. Broniatowski, Amelia M. Jamison, SiHua Qi, Lulwah AlKulaib, Tao Chen, Adrian Benton, Sandra C. Quinn, and Mark Dredze, "Weaponized Health Communication: Twitter Bots and Russian Trolls Amplify the Vaccine Debate," *American Journal of Public Health*, August 23, 2018, https://ajph.aphapublications.org/doi/10.2105/AJPH.2018.304567.

complicate the problem and can provide considerable obstacles to effective risk assessment and management. Political responses to scientific uncertainty can run in one of two ways. The first approach is known as *uncertainty absorption*, where policy makers justify their decisions to act or not act based upon incontrovertible scientific evidence.[30] The dilemma posed to modern governments is that they are expected to act rationally and to delegate authority to bureaucracies, expecting that administrative agencies possess expertise and knowledge suitable to the task. When the US Congress passes laws stating that drinking water should be kept to "safe" levels, it is left to the EPA to translate available scientific evidence into concrete regulations. In the case of arsenic, for example, this means drinking water should contain no more than ten parts per billion of the substance.

Yet, scientific data do not always provide easily translatable information, even in controlled laboratory studies such as ecotoxicology. When asked to translate scientific research on newly emerging risks and hazards in complex, nonlinear systems, policy makers must make clear political judgments on the need for action. This may lead some to overstate the amount of certainty associated with future projections or what is considered safe.[31] Referring to "science," politicians can strip away the uncertainty surrounding scientific evidence and cherry-pick data points or ignore data that are inconvenient. This process of absorbing uncertainty is not merely a deliberate decision on the part of politicians, but it is often built into the process of bureaucratic decision-making. Accepting new information may put past decisions into question. When faced with increasingly bad news about the state of an organization, for example, some managers may absorb uncertainty by refusing to consider new information.[32]

This leads to the second approach policy makers can take with respect to uncertainty, which is to amplify it. If a policy maker has already decided that she does not want to take new action, she can choose to highlight the uncertainty surrounding a question and claim that new decisions cannot be made until all available information is collected. At times, a decision not to act may not be entirely deliberate but rather may come from a misunderstanding about the nature of policy making. A decision not to act is still a policy action. Policy makers or managers may also amplify uncertainty as a form of dishonesty,

[30] Gordon Tullock, *The Politics of Bureaucracy* (New York: Public Affairs Press, 1965).
[31] Vincent T. Covello, Detlof von Winterfeldt, and Paul Slovic, "Communicating Scientific Information about Health and Environmental Risks: Problems and Opportunities from a Social and Behavioral Perspective," in *Uncertainty in Risk Assessment, Risk Management, and Decision Making* (Boston, MA: Springer, 1987), 221–39.
[32] Chad M. Briggs, "Damming Science: Problems of Scientific Research in Environmental Administration," PhD diss., Carleton University, Ottawa, ON, 2001.

attempting to hide their true intentions or goals under a veil of rationality. This process is also known as *goal displacement*, or the act of hiding a political goal "under a veneer of neutral or technical competence."[33] For example, politicians supporting the oil and gas industries may argue that it is "premature" to design greenhouse gas mitigation policies until all uncertainty in the climate sciences have been dispelled, or energy regulators, intent on saving money from avoiding infrastructural improvements, may ignore geologic data on historic risks from tsunamis, claiming that the data are "outliers" and not definitive enough to justify action.[34]

Research into tsunami databases, for example, revealed that in the mid-1960s, when the Japanese power company Tepco began construction of the Fukushima Daiichi nuclear power station, engineers designed the plant for a maximum potential 3.1-meter tsunami – despite the fact that five historical events were known to have exceeded that height in the region.[35] Tepco upgraded the design tsunami to a maximum of 5.7 meters in 2002. Still, four historical tsunamis exhibited run-up values in the region that exceeded the upgraded design. In 2009, Yukinobu Okamuru, a senior geologist with a government-affiliated research laboratory, warned about the tsunami risk in the Tohoku area based on the finding made by Abe et al. about the 869 AD Jogan tsunami.[36] The tsunami represented concrete physical evidence of a large tsunami on the Sendai Plain and the Tohoku area. The fact that it was not taken into account by Tepco in the hazard assessment for the Fukushima Daiichi plant not only demonstrates how solid quantitative geologic evidence was badly ignored but also constitutes a violation of risk guidelines defined by the International Atomic Energy Agency (IAEA).[37] The discovery of the Jogan tsunami clearly proved that tsunamis producing very large run-up values occur in the Tohoku area more frequently than once

---

[33] Michael Harmon, "The Responsible Actor as 'Tortured Soul': The Case of Horatio Hornblower," *Administration and Society* 21, No. 3 (November 1989): 283–312.

[34] See, e.g., Johannis Noegerath, Robert J. Geller, and Viacheslav K. Gusiakov, "Fukushima: The Myth of Safety, the Reality of Geoscience," *Bulletin of the Atomic Scientists* 67, No. 5 (2011): 37–46.

[35] Noegerath et al.

[36] Hisashi Abe, Yoshisada Sugeno, and Akira Chigama, "Estimation of the Height of the Sanriku Jogan 11 Earthquake-Tsunami (A.D. 869) in the Sendai Plain," *Journal of the Seismological Society of Japan* 43 (1990): 513–25. See also Koji Minoura and S. Nakaya, "Traces of Tsunami Preserved in the Inter-tidal Lacustrine and Marsh Deposits: Some Example from Northeast Japan," *Journal of Geology* 99, No. 2 (1991): 265–87; Koji Minoura, Fumihiko Imamura, D. Sugawara, Y. Kono, and T. Iwashita, "The 869 Jogan Tsunami Deposit and Recurrence Interval of Large Scale Tsunami on the Pacific Coast of Northeastern Japan," *Journal of Natural Disaster Science* 23 (2011): 83–88.

[37] Noegerath et al.

every ten thousand years, which defined the IAEA threshold recurrence for a postulated initiating event (PIE).[38]

Uncertainty and complexity are not challenges that would simply disappear by ignoring them; they have to be addressed head-on. Some professions must address uncertainty daily. The aviation industry, for example, is one in which environmental factors have always played a major role. While aircraft systems are extremely safe and technological development, such as computerized navigation, have made pilots' tasks easier, recognition of uncertainty, nonlinear risks, and comprehensive risk assessment of systems are still integral to pilots' training.[39] The same goes for identifying and assessing climate-related disaster risks. As with aircraft disasters, the consequences are too extreme and unacceptable to think in terms of single-variable, median trend line assumptions about what the world will look like in the future. Accurate prediction of complex, nonlinear systems will be extremely difficult, but we can train people to be more aware of potential risks and vulnerabilities.

Institutional Rationality and Mission

Over time, executive and policy decisions made in pursuit of particular goals or frameworks become codified in institutions and standard operating procedures. It can be difficult to move away from the original goals of the institution and, as Wack's experience with Shell Oil illustrated, to consider evidence and perspectives that question the conventional wisdom of the organization. Whether this is described in terms of Simon's concept of bounded rationality or the more dysfunctional "garbage can" theories of March and Olsen, organizational theorists have long argued that institutional rules and pressures remain significant obstacles to effective integration of information, particularly when it counteracts or contradicts received wisdom.[40] For purposes of our discussion on disaster planning and assessment, two particular challenges need to be highlighted: organizational mission and stovepiping.

---

[38] This is an "event identified during design as capable of leading to anticipated operational occurrences or accident conditions." See IAEA glossary available at www.iaea.org/ns/tutorials/ regcontrol/intro/glossaryi.htm#I14.

[39] David R. Hunter, "Risk Perception and Risk Tolerance in Aircraft Pilots," No. DOT/FAA/AM-02/17 (Washington, DC: Federal Aviation Administration, Office of Aviation Medicine, 2002).

[40] Michael D. Cohen, James G. March, and Johan P. Olsen, "A Garbage Can Model of Organizational Choice," *Administrative Science Quarterly* 17, No. 1 (1972): 1–25; Herbert A. Simon, "Theories of Bounded Rationality," *Decision and Organization* 1, No. 1 (1972): 161–76.

Organizational mission refers to the overarching goals an institution seeks to achieve, and the formal and informal rules and pressures instituted to achieve those goals. Organizations also develop standard operating procedures to operate most efficiently. These are common ways of responding to common situations, to which employees are trained and expected to take on the rationality associated with these procedures. The public administration and political science literature has, since the late nineteenth century, described organizations and bureaucracies as taking on lives of their own.[41] Organizations, whether businesses, nonprofits, or government bureaucracies, take on particular characteristics, depending on the reasons for their founding, the conditions under which they have grown, the sources of their funding or revenue, and the personalities of influential leaders. Government organizations are often defined by missions, whether that mission is to educate children, protect a country's borders, or provide cities with sustainable energy technologies. Some organizations have multiple and overlapping responsibilities. The US Coast Guard, for example, has multiple missions of providing search and rescue, maintaining navigation, preventing drug smuggling, responding to environmental disasters, and patrolling Arctic waters, among others.[42] The missions of some other organizations may be less well defined, conditioned by politics or perhaps working with standard operating procedures that have not kept pace with the outside world. How do organizational missions and standard operating procedures affect assessments of complex EES risks?

A recurring lesson of scenario planning and wargaming for disaster risks has been that organizations with clearly defined missions are best able to identify how emerging hazards pose a risk to them, even if dealing with disasters is not an explicit goal. If a government agency or business does not possess a clear idea of why it exists and what its members are meant to accomplish, risks of climate change or other environmental factors will seem nebulous, uncertain, and not an issue that needs to be addressed at present. This does not mean that an organization must identify climate change adaptation as part of its mission. On the contrary, some organizations with the clearest idea of how climate change poses potential disaster risks are those that want nothing to do with it. The best example of this has been the US military.

---

[41] These "lives," of course, may be complex, involving subcultures and resistance against official missions. See Neil R. Britton, "Constraint or Effectiveness in Disaster Management? The Bureaucratic Imperative versus Organizational Mission," in *Seminar on New Directions in Understanding Civil Disaster Management* (Sydney: University of Sydney, Department of Government and Public Administration, 1989).

[42] Thomas H. Collins, "Change and Continuity: The US Coast Guard Today," *Naval War College Review* 57, No. 2 (2004): 7.

The US military defines its members as *warfighters*, meaning men and women who are trained for combat or to support those in combat.[43] The common (dark) joke in the air force was that it trained airmen to "kill people and break things," so while it may have the capacity to undertake operations like disaster relief, these detract from its primary missions.[44] At first glance, this made the military seem an unlikely candidate for accepting the importance of climate-related disaster risks. However, in the last few years, the US military has become one of the most outspoken proponents for taking climate security seriously.[45] The reason for this is quite simple. US military planners know what they want to accomplish and, for this purpose, how many men and women need to be moved to which locations with what materiel. US military officers train on how to prioritize different threats and how to develop long-term strategies for keeping certain adversaries in check. Climate change risks themselves never rise to the top of the priority list, but they are so pervasive, so potentially widespread and disruptive, that they threaten military missions in a variety of ways.[46]

Like the spring 2011 USAF wargame, while a volcanic eruption in Alaska in itself is not a major threat, when it disrupts the ability to move vital resources toward a real military crisis, the environment needs to be taken seriously. After the wargame, we asked one of the participating pilots why he was completely unwilling to risk flying through volcanic ash cloud when he would be willing to risk or give up his life in a fight with the Chinese Air Force (PLAAF). He replied, "Because it's not my job to risk my aircraft before I get to the fight." Contrast this with Ryanair CEO Michael O'Leary, who in 2010 argued that it was "perfectly safe" for commercial aircraft to fly through volcanic ash clouds.[47] His organizational mission differed greatly from that of USAF.

---

[43] Not all militaries are the same. Many militaries in places like Europe or Japan, for example, see themselves as peacekeepers and are trained more to act as police forces. See Tom Woodhouse, "The Gentle Hand of Peace? British Peacekeeping and Conflict Resolution in Complex Political Emergencies," *International Peacekeeping* 6, No. 2 (1999): 24–37.

[44] Robert Munson, "Do We Want to 'Kill People and Break Things' in Africa?" *ASPJ Africa and Francophonie*, 4th Quarter (2009), www.airuniversity.af.mil/Portals/10/ASPJ_French/ journals_E/Volume-01_Issue-1/Munson_e.pdf. Munson's argument about AFRICOM was that its mission was not entirely clear, which made some issues (especially those related to the environment) a higher priority and yet less crystalized.

[45] Damian Carrington, "Climate Change Will Stir 'Unimaginable' Refugee Crisis, Says Military," *Guardian*, December 1, 2016, www.theguardian.com/environment/2016/dec/01/climate-change-trigger-unimaginable-refugee-crisis-senior-military.

[46] Chad M. Briggs, "Climate Security, Risk Assessment and Military Planning," *International Affairs* 88, No. 5 (2012): 1049–64.

[47] *Telegraph*, "Volcanic Ash: Ryanair Boss Michael O'Leary in Withering Attack on Met Office," June 1, 2010, www.telegraph.co.uk/travel/travelnews/7794331/Volcanic-ash-Ryanair-boss-Michael-OLeary-in-withering-attack-on-Met-Office.html.

Other organizations find it more difficult to determine why new and emerging disaster risks might affect their mission. Organizational missions are not always set in stone. The way in which members of an organization are meant to behave are conditioned by their coworkers, the stories they are told, and both the written and unwritten understandings of what constitutes proper behavior. Businesses may continue selling products or providing services that are no longer needed. Government agencies may continue to follow standard operating procedures without realizing that they have not adjusted properly to new environments.[48] Much like individuals, many organizations will be constrained by their past actions and the definitions that they had been given in terms of their mission. Sometimes this is the lack of ability to innovate, where newcomers or outsiders with new ideas are silenced simply because of the weight of tradition. With other organizations, there are political or legal constraints to their jurisdictions, where they recognize emerging risks but are unable to address them outside of boundaries that were set for previous missions.

For example, NATO Headquarters in Brussels has an Emerging Security Challenges Division and various Centers of Excellence, which conduct valuable research on areas such as cybersecurity or hybrid warfare. Yet, organizationally, NATO was designed and structured during the Cold War to address a conventional military threat from the Soviet Union and Warsaw Pact. NATO, historically speaking, has only responded to direct military threats against its members and has only ever once (following September 11, 2001) invoked its collective security response under Article V of its charter. Consequently, many experts in NATO are able to recognize emerging risks that can spill over into its member states, but the organization itself lacks many of the tools and mechanisms to respond.[49] NATO is generally restricted from acting outside of NATO member states. If a security risk were to originate within one of those states, addressing it may be too politically dangerous. In a 2012 scenario workshop for NATO Headquarters in Brussels, one NATO official explained why political constraints made addressing emerging risks such as climate change particularly difficult: "Look, you US Air Force guys have it easy. You can look at the map and point your finger at any spot on the globe, saying 'we need to do something about this place and this event.' And then you go do it if the president says so.

---

[48] Moshe Farjoun, "Organizational Learning and Action in the Midst of Safety Drift: Revisiting the Space Shuttle Program's Recent History," in *Organization at the Limit: Lessons from the Columbia Disaster* (London: Wiley-Blackwell, 2005), 60–80.

[49] Tyler Lippert, "NATO, Climate Change, and International Security: A Risk Governance Approach," PhD diss., RAND, 2016; Matthew Kroenig, "Facing Reality: Getting NATO Ready for a New Cold War," *Survival* 57, No. 1 (2015): 49–70.

At NATO, we have to wait for everyone to agree that something is a crisis, and in the right place."

For most organizations, whether it is the city council of Pueblo, Colorado, or the Swedish Civil Contingencies Agency (MSB), the focus, assessments, and response capabilities will be limited. These organizations may not be able to respond to risks that originate from far outside their borders. Historically, this made sense. Most disaster risks originated locally, and in cases where they did not (such as river or air pollution), laws and governance structures evolved over time so that risk mitigation policies could be put into place.[50] The globalized nature of disaster risks these days, however, will force businesses and governments to look beyond their traditional boundaries. This will not be easy. Scenario planning and simulations can be very useful when applied to organizations with clear missions, but such risks can seem ephemeral to others. Psychological studies have shown that people in North America and Europe tend to believe that climate change impacts will most affect people far away and that the most probable risks will be the least damaging.[51] Accepting new risks can be difficult at the individual level, and it is even more challenging for organizations to adapt to new realities.

A related challenge for organizations is how well they can share information and coordinate assessments and responses both within and between different institutions. This is the challenge of *stovepiping* – departments (even within the same organization) can be functionally different from one another, working within different rules and procedures and having overlapping responsibilities with other departments, or not coordinating with others at all.[52] Universities represent a common example of this institutional challenge, where different colleges and departments are so organizationally and intellectually segregated from one another that attempts to address multidisciplinary or interdisciplinary topics (such as environmental studies) is extremely difficult.[53] Stovepiping is also famously present in large bureaucracies, such as the US Department of Defense, where multitudes of civilian offices, defense contractors, and various

---

[50] Of course, there are various exceptions to this. If a multinational corporation operating a gold mine in Romania spills cyanide into a river in Hungary, the downstream country is bound to suffer a disproportionate risk without any clear legal recourse when things go wrong. See Claudia Kraft, Wolf von Tumpling, and Dieter W. Zachmann, "The Effects of Mining in Northern Romania on the Heavy Metal Distribution in Sediments of the Rivers Szamos and Tisza (Hungary)," *CLEAN – Soil, Air, Water* 34, No. 3 (2006): 257–64.

[51] Alexa Spence, Wouter Poortinga, and Nick Pidgeon, "The Psychological Distance of Climate Change," *Risk Analysis: An International Journal* 32, No. 6 (2012): 957–72.

[52] William J. Lahneman, "Outsourcing the IC's Stovepipes?" *International Journal of Intelligence and Counterintelligence* 16, No. 4 (2003): 573–93.

[53] Lance J. Hoffman, Diana Burley, and Costis Toregas, "Thinking across Stovepipes: Using a Holistic Development Strategy to Build the Cybersecurity Workforce," *IEEE Security and Privacy* 1 (2011): 1–11.

military branches may work on similar issues at the same time, potentially at cross purposes to each other.[54] When the USAF Minerva project started in 2010, one of the biggest and most immediate challenges was determining who in the Department of Defense was already working on energy and environmental security issues or related topics, such as base infrastructure, energy efficiency, and cybersecurity.[55] Even in a nascent field such as EES, a great amount of time is spent on simply trying to identify colleagues, reach out to them, and ensure that we are not duplicating efforts.

Another downside of bureaucratic specialization is the idea of object fixation. Organizational missions and standard operating procedures can create a culture in which only certain goals are emphasized and only certain perspectives are accepted, at the expense of alternative assessments and policies. Both in downhill skiing and cycling, instructors will often say, "If you want to avoid hitting something, stop looking at it." In a counterintuitive way, this can be true of risk assessments and associated policies, as well. For example, the US Department of Defense prioritizes war-fighting missions. At first glance, this focus is in line with many academic studies of climate security and risk that attempt to link environmental changes with the onset of violent conflict. From a Pentagon perspective, however, such linkages are potentially dangerous. Focusing on violent conflict as the outcome could become a self-fulfilling prophecy by shutting out perspectives that emphasize human security and alternate pathways to avoiding conflict.

A related, cautionary note should be made on "securitization" or "militarization" of concepts like climate security or disaster risk. From the beginning of environmental security debates in the late 1980s, critics and cautionary voices have noted that placing environmental risks in the context of military security can lead to blind spots or counterproductive strategies.[56] While the point of this book is to describe military and intelligence tools that can be used to help assess environmental and disaster risks, this should not be confused with the idea that these communities are suitable for solving these issues. Militaries are themselves some of the world's largest polluters and users of energy, and while the US military may have remarkable capabilities for responding quickly to disasters, it does not see such responses as its primary mission. Most military

---

[54] Perry M. Smith and Daniel M. Gerstein, *Assignment: Pentagon: How to Excel in a Bureaucracy* (Washington, DC: Potomac Books, 2007).

[55] S. H. Ali, A. Zia, and Rebecca Pincus, *Strategic Response to Energy-Related Security Threats in the US Department of Defense* (Burlington: University of Vermont, 2014).

[56] Daniel Deudney, "Muddled Thinking," *Bulletin of the Atomic Scientists* 47, No. 3 (1991): 22–28; Betsy Hartmann, "Rethinking Climate Refugees and Climate Conflict: Rhetoric, Reality and the Politics of Policy Discourse," *Journal of International Development* 22, No. 2 (2010): 233–46; Barnett, "Security and Climate Change."

planners and strategists in the United States would prefer that someone else mitigate disaster risks so that continued (and increasing) responses are not necessary.[57]

Secrecy as an Obstacle to Communicating Complex EES Risks

While the US military (and, to a lesser extent, intelligence agencies) had an advantage in identifying how climate change and disaster risks would affect their organizational mission, the secretive nature of military and security agencies poses problems to communicating EES risks. Throughout this book, we have emphasized the need for information sharing and engaging with a broad network of experts. Information sharing is not something at which militaries excel. Military and security organizations are dominated by the need for secrecy and compartmentalization of information. Employees and service members are expected to obtain security clearances so they can handle classified information. Once information becomes classified, releasing it to the public becomes a very complex process.

Whether there is an overclassification of information for traditional security issues is a matter for others to debate. The Department of Energy, an agency dominated by the need to protect nuclear secrets, has a strong organizational ethos of maintaining secrets concerning technology, and its intelligence functions lean more heavily toward counterintelligence and the protection of information. Yet, for environmental risks, most of the relevant data on emerging hazards and risks already exist in the public realm. Much of the relevant information remains open source but not easily accessible. As one senior intelligence official has noted, these are "secrets in the open" that require approaches that do not fit with organizational models of military or intelligence organizations.[58]

Open source refers to information that has not been classified, meaning it is not officially secret. The standard approach to collecting open-source information on

---

[57] See Betsy Hartmann, "Population, Environment and Security: A New Trinity," *Environment and Urbanization* 10, No. 2 (1998): 113–28. Hartmann's argument was that the Pentagon had an interest in environmental security as a way of expanding its bureaucratic footprint. But since 2001, much of the military has felt overstretched, and energy-environmental-disaster issues were treated with dismissal or resignation without clear examples of how the risks affected operational or strategic missions. Still, Hartmann's article is worth reading, especially as it relates to refugees and the population debate.

[58] Carol Dumaine, "On a Global Foresight Commons," *SEED Magazine*, November 23, 2010, http://seedmagazine.com/content/article/on_a_global_foresight_commons/.

emerging environmental and disaster risks has been to harvest data from published research articles. Scholarly research articles are, by definition, not secret, but this does not mean they are "open access." Most academic journals lie behind digital paywalls, which tend to be very expensive, and many universities can only afford to subscribe to a certain number of electronic databases.

DOE's 2007 GlobalEESE project attempted to address this problem by creating an electronic network of experts to share information in an unclassified space. In the age of Wikileaks, military organizations have refused to consider any unclassified online network and often rely on outside organizations to provide discussion forums.[59] In Washington, DC, such discussions would often be organized by think tanks such as the CNA Corporation, the New America Foundation, or the Center for Climate and Security. In Europe, climate security discussions tended to take place in Brussels beginning in the mid-2000s. Since 2015, the government of the Netherlands has sponsored the Planetary Security Conference each winter in The Hague. While these efforts are highly important, there is still an information gulf between military and intelligence agencies and the public that might benefit from their experience. In addition, many countries severely restrict the type of environmental research that can be undertaken, and in some states, environmental scientists and activists are often targeted.[60]

In countries that encourage environmental research, some of the most promising open sources of information – graduate students and junior faculty – need better institutional backing. Researchers who are early in their academic careers often suffer from a combination of brilliance, ambition, frustration, and awareness of career risks. Graduate students and young professors must commit to long hours and hard work for little pay, with no guarantee of a job or tenure. Scientists take these risks because they are passionate about the subjects they study, and they also tend to be most aware of new developments in their respective fields. Younger scientists are often motivated to have their research known and to be recognized by others as contributors. Yet, they are vulnerable to punishment, if they are too outspoken. Either public engagement can be viewed as unprofessional and unproductive, or, if they are successful, older

---

[59] Our USAF Minerva team, specifically Tracy and Chad Briggs, had to refuse security clearances in order to operate effectively. One senior Pentagon official joked that we had "reverse-compartmentalized" ourselves, and the Air Force was initially not at all happy about the request. However, in practice, we could obtain more data and work with more scientists that way. This was unusual and only possible because the work was done as an academic subcontract and nothing we produced reflected government or military policy.

[60] Miriam Matejova, Stefan Parker, and Peter Dauvergne, "The Politics of Repressing Environmentalists as Agents of Foreign Influence," *Australian Journal of International Affairs* 72, No. 2 (2018): 1–18.

faculty may become resentful. Graduate students, postdoctoral researchers, and junior faculty are often the best sources for finding new information. They can be easier to approach than senior professors but at the same time must be protected (professionally speaking), and their engagement must be credited as being valuable. Again, the scenario processes, provided they remain unclassified and accessible to these researchers and experts, remain a promising venue for people to contribute their expertise. Local and indigenous expertise is also highly valuable, provided that political environments do not target such experts for sharing information with outsiders.

Conclusion

In this chapter, our intent was to draw attention to some of the key obstacles in communicating EES risks to policy makers and the public. We argued that in some instances, complex scenarios and the often compelling narratives they provide may help in this process. For example, we noted that one of the main reasons for climate change denial, at least in the United States, is the framing of climate change that allows amplification of uncertainty. Misinformation can spread through social media as well as purposefully by political actors. From a planning perspective, climate change denial is a problem, since unconcerned citizens fail to demand better policies from their government representatives and unconcerned planners fail to explore and implement better practices. Drawing attention to disaster and public health risks from climate change may be one of the most useful ways to counter climate change denial. The scenario planning process we describe in this book can present such risks in an understandable format, taking into account cultural, social, political, and other conditions.

In this chapter, we also returned to the issue of uncertainty, which is a topic we discuss in several previous chapters. Here we specifically focused on the institutionalization of uncertainty in scientific and policy circles and the ways in which such institutionalization hinders effective disaster planning. For example, the two most common political responses to scientific uncertainty – absorption and amplification – may lead to cherry-picking of evidence or delaying of action, among other things. A delay in planning for unknown disasters, in particular, may be costly in face of emerging disaster risks. Although complex scenarios do not offer direct solutions to this problem of institutionalized uncertainty, they do allow for space where uncertainty is at least preserved and explained quite deliberately, rather than being secreted away or ignored.

We further identified organizational mission, stovepiping, and secrecy as obstacles to effective communication of EES risks. One of our conclusions is that organizations with clearly defined missions are better able to identify emerging risks, whether or not such organizations focus on climate change or disasters. Adjusting to new environments is difficult due to the constraints of standard operating procedures, previous mission standards, or tradition. The globalized nature of disaster risks, however, may leave governments and businesses with no other choice but look beyond traditional boundaries and missions and share information within and between different institutions, organizations, and countries.

9

Planning for the Uncertain Future

A common refrain in politics is that the world is becoming more complex and interconnected and that we are often unprepared for globalized risks such as those stemming from climate change, refugee flows, or hybrid warfare. Traditional methods to assess such risks often fall short, resulting in frequent surprises as extreme events expose critical vulnerabilities in our systems. New methods are, however, available to assess these complex risks and vulnerabilities. This book focused on one: military and intelligence scenario planning developed through an adaptation of wargaming on energy and environmental security risks.

Our motivation was to assist the public and policy makers in grasping potential impacts of long-term, highly uncertain risks – whether in understanding environmental impacts of postwar reconstruction investments in the Balkans or assessing public health risks from climate change in the Arctic. A crucial aspect of the multifaceted approach to disaster risk assessment and planning is the need for communication across disciplines, departments, and countries. Translating scientific data from climatology to operational military planning and then back to political scientists studying regional impacts has been a constant challenge – one addressed through presenting scenarios and wargames as effective approaches in planning for complex disasters.

Disasters occur when changes overwhelm a system. These changes can be (and often are) combinations of human actions and environmental factors, creating crises from refugee camps in Greece to hurricanes in Hawaii. Isolating "natural" causes in a disaster risk assessment is increasingly difficult and misleading. This has been one of the most important lessons of the energy and environmental security since the mid-2000s – unlike earlier work focusing on "vulnerability hotspots" in places like Africa, new combinations of hazards are creating disaster risks all over the globe, from London to Dakar. For example, climate change affecting agriculture in the Lake Chad region of

182

Africa may have significant impacts on economic development of rural towns in Italy – these impacts cascade across traditional boundaries.[1] Older assumptions about how climate change will affect people in far-off lands do not hold true, yet our institutions and risk frames remain rooted in the past.

Our work on scenarios and wargames has also revealed that understanding uncertainty and "preserving" it in assessments is a necessary step for preventing poor estimations of risk. Too often, when we seek to reduce uncertainty, we either dismiss a risk until more information is available, or mistakenly project confidence on what the future will hold, citing solid predictions. The intelligence community's concept of warnings is a better approach. While it is less solid in its ability to predict just one, linear future, it provides a scope wherein risks can be found, discussed, and understood. The scenarios for New York and Hawaii could not predict when, how, and why hurricanes might threaten these regions, but enough was understood to identify vulnerabilities and make risk mitigation and adaptation plans for when Sandy and Lane did occur. When critical vulnerabilities (nodes) are present, scenarios and simulations can help identify the multiple pathways by which emerging risks can overwhelm existing resilience. Traditional assessments and wisdom told us ten years ago that hurricanes in New York or Hawaii were simply too improbable to consider realistically. Unfortunately, times and the environment have changed, and in abrupt ways.

Agencies from FEMA to the European Environment Agency are already adapting to these new realities. However, we cannot and should not limit disaster assessments to specialty teams and agencies, whose bandwidth is always limited and where politics can prevent discussion of sensitive topics. One purpose of this book is to reach audiences beyond those already dealing with disaster planning full-time and illustrate that effective discussion of possible futures can take place – and in fact needs to occur – across different levels and jurisdictions. Universities, state and local governments, and regional and international associations have the capacity and expertise to participate in such assessments and foster dialogue. Such varied, international expertise is necessary for security risk resolution at varying scales.

Below, we discuss what we currently see as the two most pressing EES challenges for the future: abrupt climatic changes and their effects on the water, energy, and food production systems. We then focus on three regions that we believe would most benefit from future complex scenarios to tackle their own complex EES challenges: Canada, the Arctic region, and Antarctica.

---

[1] Lorenzo Tondo, "'They Are Our Salvation': The Sicilian Town Revived by Refugees," *Guardian*, March 19, 2018, www.theguardian.com/world/2018/mar/19/sutera-italy-the-sicilian-town-revived-by-refugees.

Looking into the Future: Abrupt Changes and the Energy-Water Nexus

The state of climate science is now far more advanced than work published in the Fifth IPCC Assessment would indicate. The collective assessment of many scientists who specialize in abrupt change is that changes will occur more quickly and in places that already exhibit other forms of instability. Both scientific and archeological records indicate that numerous abrupt climatic changes have already occurred at various times during human history (the Holocene), affecting wide areas of southern latitudes.[2] Large areas of what is now the Sahara Desert in Africa was once forested, and monsoon rains feeding the Nile and western India have been disrupted in the past.[3] The Akkadian Empire in northern Mesopotamia experienced large-scale migration from the region and a collapse of regional kingdoms.[4] More recent human history has unfolded at a time of relative stability in global temperatures, but these are conditions that cannot easily be taken for granted.

Very often, climate change has been portrayed as a gradual, long-term shift in average air temperatures. Subsequently, media discussions regarding climate change and climate negotiations tend to focus on the 2°C goal for mitigation. Unfortunately, these portrayals are misleading. Climate change does not merely affect air temperatures, nor do disasters deal in averages. Instead, climate change represents an increase in greenhouse gases trapping heat energy from the sun, which otherwise would be radiated back into space. This greenhouse effect has been understood for centuries, but we tend to focus on what is most visible and most easily measurable – air temperature readings in the troposphere. The energy absorbed from the sun only partly goes into the atmosphere, with most being absorbed into the oceans (hydrosphere), some into the earth and vegetation (lithosphere), and other heat affecting large ice formations

---

[2] Arash Sharifi, Ali Pourmand, Elizabeth Canuel, Erin Ferer-Tyler, Larry C. Peterson, Bernhard Aichner, Sarah J. Feakins, Touraj Daryaee, Morteza Djamali, Abdolmajid Naderi Beni, Hamid Lahijani, and Peter Schwart, "Abrupt Climate Variability since the Last Deglaciation Based on a High-Resolution, Multi-proxy Peat Record from NW Iran: The Hand That Rocked the Cradle of Civilization?" *Quaternary Science Reviews* 123 (2015): 215–30.

[3] Peter de Menocal, "Palaeoclimate: End of the African Humid Period," *Nature Geoscience* 8 (2015): 86–87; Yen Yi Looa, Lawal Billab, and Ajit Singha, "Effect of Climate Change on Seasonal Monsoon in Asia and Its Impact on the Variability of Monsoon Rainfall in Southeast Asia," *Geoscience Frontiers* 6, No. 6 (2015): 817–23.

[4] Heidi Cullen, Peter B. Demenocal, Silke Hemming, G. Hemming, Francis H. Brown, Tom Guilderson, and Frank Sirocko, "Climate Change and the Collapse of the Akkadian Empire: Evidence from the Deep Sea," *Geology* 28, No. 4 (2000): 379–82; Harvey Weiss, "Late Third Millennium Abrupt Climate Change and Social Collapse in West Asia and Egypt," in *Third Millennium* BC *Climate Change and Old World Collapse*, ed. H Nuzhet Dalfes, George Kukla, and Harvey Weiss (Berlin: Springer, 1997), 711–23.

(cryosphere).[5] The additional energy in the earth's system not only expresses itself in terms of daytime high temperatures but also affects everything from ocean currents to melting Arctic ice. Changes in precipitation are far more likely to be noticed, and very few societies have the capacity to withstand acute flooding or prolonged drought. Australia has already been experiencing such changes (due to shifts in Indian Ocean currents) for over a decade, affecting both its food and energy production capabilities.[6] The 2010 flooding in Pakistan, caused by variability in the West Indian Monsoon, and extreme heat around Moscow were perhaps examples of what may become more common in the future.[7]

Yet, there is disagreement among climate scientists as to how accurately predictions can be made. Some claim that probabilities simply cannot be assigned, because we are forcing the climate into a unique combination of conditions. For these researchers, the best that we can hope for is to better understand the tipping mechanisms and possible scenarios, but that it is perhaps misleading to claim that we have "covered the gaps."[8] There will undoubtedly be continued surprises, but how, when, and where these changes will be felt cannot well be predicted in advance. If anything, the pervasive uncertainty in abrupt climate science makes the risk assessment outcomes more dangerous, in the sense that the climate system is known to be quite sensitive and already shifting. Without better knowledge, humans are less in control of mitigating specific risks.

More important for intelligence analyses and policy translation, however, is that a focus on what *is* known can be exploited. Highlighting and amplifying uncertainty are effective actions for those who wish to stall policy by sowing doubt among actors, particularly in systems that pride themselves on evidence-based policy making (see Chapters 7 and 8). By claiming that the science is "not certain," opponents to action can falsely claim that no action should be taken at this time. Legal cases have brought to light that companies like Exxon-Mobil knew about the risks of climate change decades ago, yet denied such knowledge and funded institutions to sow doubt on the issue, which helped them gain unimpeded access to fossil fuel reserves and market sales.[9]

[5] Kevin E. Trenberth, John T. Fasullo, and Jeffrey Kiehl, "Earth's Global Energy Budget," American Meteorological Society (March 2009).

[6] Earth Observatory, "World of Change: Drought Cycles in Australia," NASA, https://earthobservatory.nasa.gov/WorldOfChange/AustraliaNDVI.

[7] Michon Scott, "Heavy Rains and Dry Lands Don't Mix: Reflections on the 2010 Pakistan Flood," Earth Observatory, NASA, April 6, 2011, https://earthobservatory.nasa.gov/Features/PakistanFloods; *ABC News*, "Russian Heatwave Killed 11,000 People," September 17, 2010, www.abc.net.au/news/2010-09-18/russian-heatwave-killed-11000-people/2265184.

[8] Timothy Lenton and Juan-Carlos Ciscar, "Integrating Tipping Points into Climate Impact Assessments," *Climatic Change* 117, No. 3 (2013): 585–97.

[9] Peter Frumhoff, Richard Heede, and Naomi Oreskes, "The Climate Responsibilities of Industrial Carbon Producers," *Climatic Change* 132, No. 2 (2015): 157–71.

Yet it is not only the actions of greenhouse gas producers that have impacts on potential disaster risks. Climate-related hazards can shift environmental risks, but one reason why even marginal changes in energy and temperature can have such enormous effects is the vulnerability connecting water and energy (and closely related areas like food). As noted in various scenarios in earlier chapters, water reserves are especially vulnerable to abrupt climatic changes. We discuss this vulnerability and its implications for the future below, focusing on electricity generation (thermal plants and hydroelectric power generation plants) and food production (i.e., the energy-water nexus).

The Energy-Water Nexus

The energy-water nexus comprises complex networks held together by critical nodes in systems where the ability to provide energy, water, or food can easily be compromised by unanticipated shocks or long-term pressures. Expanding economies, growing populations, and development of infrastructure and governance systems have led to the intensified reliance on energy, water, and food production systems. In industrialized regions and economies, the relationship between water, energy, and food is highly complicated and interdependent. Water is no longer simply a local resource to be exploited but a commodity in high demand that is processed, transported, used, and reprocessed on vast geographical scales. Energy is needed at all stages of water-related activities. There is a positive feedback loop where more energy requires more water, and more water requires more energy.

Immense amounts of water are needed for electricity production depending on type, source, and production facility. The required water may be as little as one liter per kilowatt hour (kWh) (for dry cooled energy plants) to two hundred liters per kWh (hydropower) or six hundred liters per kWh for some biofuels.[10] Water transport and processing exact high energy demands, creating an embedded energy cost for water use through its life cycle. Converted to weight, a typical US household will directly use nearly 2.7 million pounds of water a year, most of which must be pumped, filtered, and cleaned.[11] In some countries, energy and water resources may not exist in the same regions as the population or industrial centers. Leveling out these disparities requires

---

[10] Dana Larson, Cheryl Lee, Stacy Tellinghuisen, and Arturo Keller, "California's Energy-Water Nexus: Water Use in Electricity Generation," Southwest Water, 2007, www.swhydro .arizona.edu/archive/V6_N5/feature3.pdf.

[11] Barbara Carney, Thomas Feeley, and Andrea McNemar, "Water Requirements for Thermoelectric Generation," NETL UNESCO Conference paper, US DOE, www.netl.doe.gov/ technologies/coalpower/ewr/water/pdfs/NETL%20Paper%20Unesco%20Conference.pdf.

extensive investments in infrastructure. Countries such as Norway or Canada, blessed with large amounts of both energy and water, face very different choices than countries where water outweighs energy (e.g., Bangladesh) or energy exists without water (e.g., Saudi Arabia).

Worldwide, most electricity is produced by burning fossil or nuclear fuels, and converting some of the heat into energy to spin turbines. Often, these power plants are "thermal" designs, meaning that approximately one-third of the heat is converted to energy, while the rest must be dissipated into the environment, usually through coolant water. Thermal power plants are designed to handle certain temperatures and require certain amounts (and quality) of coolant water, without which they must scale back production or shut down entirely.

Extreme heat events – whether from climate change or urban heat island effects – are indications of this vulnerability. In the summer of 2003, seventeen French nuclear power plants were taken offline when coolant water temperatures exceeded design limits, requiring massive electricity importation from German facilities. Certain US facilities have likewise been powered down during extreme heat events, which are also peak times for electrical demand.[12] Such events are now becoming common. Recent years have seen prosperous Asian cities such as Shanghai suffer from rolling blackouts and brownouts, often due to weather conditions that have restricted delivery of coal from domestic sources.[13] Yet, despite the obvious risks to sustained operation, most planned electrical capacity in South Asia relies on thermal plant designs, often in water scarce regions.[14]

Hydroelectric power generation plants, too, will likely face challenges due to the changing climate. These plants at times represent the difficult trade-offs faced by countries in providing either energy or water, particularly in at-capacity systems. As one example, the Toktogul Reservoir in Central Asia is highly sensitive to relatively small changes in snowpack. In recent years, shortfalls in electricity production have had severe cascading impacts on the economy and stability of Kyrgyzstan. The Kyrgyz government was faced with

[12] Cleo Paskal, *The Vulnerability of Energy Infrastructure to Environmental Change* (London: Chatham House, 2009).
[13] Christina Larson, "China's Looming Conflict netween Energy and Water," *Yale Environment 360*, April 10, 2012, http://e360.yale.edu/feature/chinas_looming_conflict_between_energy_and_water/2522/.
[14] The largest installed capacities of hydroelectricity are China with 200 GW, Canada with 89 GW, the United States with 80 GW, Brazil with 70 GW, Russia with 45 GW, India with 33 GW, Norway with 27 GW, Japan with 27 GW, and Venezuela with 15 GW. As a percentage of total electricity consumed, Norway, Venezuela, and Paraguay are nearly 100 percent dependency on hydroelectric sources. See "List of World's Largest Hydroelectricity Plants and Countries – China Leading in building Hydroelectric Stations," March 29, 2011, www.greenworldinvestor.com/2011/03/29/list-of-worlds-largest-hydroelectricity-plants-and-countries-china-leading-in-building-hydroelectric-stations/.

the dilemma to produce either winter electricity for the capital or summer irrigated crops for export. In choosing winter energy, the country's GDP dropped 6 percent the following year due to export losses. Downstream impacts on areas such as the Aral Sea continue to be incapacitating. With a breakdown in Soviet-era agreements on water-energy sharing between Kyrgyzstan and Uzbekistan, Bishkek struggles to find enough winter energy, while Tashkent (which has energy) finds itself short of water.[15]

Hydroelectric plants are also extremely important for Chinese and Indian electricity production, contributing some 20 percent and 16 percent, respectively, of total generation. Likewise, Russia gains some 17 percent of its power from hydroelectric plants.[16] These plants are (by definition) dependent on water availability with lower reservoir levels and river flows sharply reducing energy potential. Below a certain level, hydroelectric production ceases altogether. Dams in South and Southeast Asia are also at risk of siltation after construction is complete, with Chinese reservoirs losing around 3 percent capacity per year.[17] The Three Gorges Dam on the Yangtze River traps 172 million metric tons of sediment every year, which reduces power efficiency of the dam and greatly increases downstream erosion, leaving the dam more vulnerable to drought conditions.[18] Through their impacts on water availability, climatic changes are also likely to affect global food production.

Historically, energy security and water have been considered separately, though each is known to be closely related to food systems and production. The water-energy-food connection is often complex, but when water is scarce (or flooding extensive), energy and food prices rise in tandem. In nonindustrial regions, GDP growth is often directly proportional to available rainfall. Droughts, floods, and ill-timed precipitation directly affect food production and sales with widespread disruptions possible even in more advanced

---

[15] Adam Albion, "Winter of Discontent – Electricity Supply Problems in Central Asia," *Jane's Intelligence Review* 20, No. 12 (2008): 54–55; Katherine J. Bowen-Williams, "Tensions over Hydroelectric Developments in Central Asia: Regional Interdependence and Energy Security," *Asia Pacific Perspectives* 10, No. 2 (2011): 133–60.

[16] Abhishek Shah, "List of World's Largest Hydroelectricity Plants and Countries – China Leading in Building Hydroelectric Stations," *Green World Investor*, March 29, 2011, www .greenworldinvestor.com/2011/03/29/list-of-worlds-largest-hydroelectricity-plants-and-coun tries-china-leading-in-building-hydroelectric-stations/.

[17] Dams force rivers to drop their sediment loads in reservoirs, resulting in "hungry" downstream water that increases erosion. See S. L. Yang, J. Zhang, and X. J. Xu, "Influence of the Three Gorges Dam on Downstream Delivery of Sediment and Its Environmental Implications, Yangtze River," *Geophysical Research Letters* 34, No. 10 (2007).

[18] Zhongyuan Chen, Zhanghua Wang, Brian Finlayson, Jing Chen, and Daowei Yin, "Implications of Flow Control by the Three Gorges Dam on Sediment and Channel Dynamics of the Middle Yangtze (Changjiang) River, China," *Geology* 38, No. 11 (2010): 1043–46.

countries.[19] Extreme weather patterns in 2010, for example, led to extensive floods in Pakistan, resulting in food shortages that took time to be fully remedied, and which were made worse by the concurrent wildfires and grain embargo in Russia.[20] With food prices rising to record levels in recent years, lack of access to affordable foodstuffs can spark unrest and discontent. Such trends are made worse both by environmental changes and competing water/ land claims for energy production. Some analysts have argued that price spikes helped trigger the Arab Spring revolts across North Africa and the Middle East and that bread riots in Cairo in 2008 were an early warning signal.[21]

At the same time, food production involves significant energy inputs, whether in the form of manpower, fuel for mechanized production, transport, or fertilizer. Irrigation and pump systems draw heavily from energy grids, and in some areas, are the largest rural power consumers. The scarcer or more remote the water supply, the more energy is needed to transport irrigation waters. Yet, water is also needed to produce the energy in the first place. And with the rise in importance of biofuels, agriculture and energy are both invested to produce more energy. At times, vulnerability cycles are established where a breakdown in any one component can bring large energy-agricultural systems to a halt when community resilience has been compromised. Although these and other challenges are of global nature, we chose to focus on three of the world's regions to further explore these vulnerabilities and suggest how a complex scenario approach and particularly the development of new scenarios might help states identify complex EES challenges of national interest.

Developing New, Complex Scenarios

In the remaining sections of this chapter, we show how the focus on scientific knowledge and uncertainty, rather than probability, is needed for meeting planning needs for complex regions. Specifically, we discuss some environmental and political challenges in Canada (linked predominantly to the energy-water nexus) and in the Arctic and Antarctic regions (linked to abrupt climatic

---

[19] Environmental Leader, "Worst US Drought in 50 Years Drives Up Grain Prices, Ethanol under Pressure," August 13, 2012, www.environmentalleader.com/2012/08/13/worst-us-drought-in-50-years-drives-up-grain-prices-ethanol-under-pressure/.

[20] *National*, "Pakistan Flood Victims Face Food Shortages," August 4, 2010, www.thenational.ae/world/asia/pakistan-flood-victims-face-food-shortages-1.535351.

[21] Sarah Johnstone and Jeffrey Mazo, "Global Warming and the Arab Spring," *Survival: Global Politics and Strategy* 53, No. 2 (2011): 11–17; Liam Stack, "Food Crisis: A Daily Quest for Bread in Cairo," *Christian Science Monitor,* June 6, 2008, www.csmonitor.com/World/Middle-East/2008/0606/p04s05-wome.html.

changes), emphasizing the need for new strategic approaches to tackle uncertainty and misinformation.

Pivoting to the North: EES in Canada and the Arctic

Canada was once the center of environmental security research worldwide, playing a leading role in advancing discussions on human security and climate change. In the early 1990s, politically, the country was a global leader on environmental issues, as exemplified by its role in adoption and ratification of international treaties (and especially the Montreal Protocol) and the Canada–United States Air Quality Agreement.[22] Perhaps not surprisingly, the overwhelming focus of Canadian environmental security considerations is the warming Arctic. In the mid-1990s, Canada became the first chair of the Arctic Council (1996–98). By 2000, the country's Arctic foreign policy was geared toward protection of Canadian interests and cooperation with its northern neighbors; it identified transboundary environmental threats (e.g., climate change, nuclear waste, and persistent organic pollutants) as a crucial challenge for the circumpolar states.[23] However, the following discussions of energy and environmental security in Canada have been focused primarily on energy independence and the control of shipping routes in the warming Arctic.[24] Consequently, there are relatively few Canadian environmental security assessments linking issues such as climate change, energy security, biodiversity, and infrastructure.

With immense land and coastal areas, natural resources, and energy exports, with a warming Arctic and a potentially growing risk of disasters, Canada must be proactive in preparing for risk mitigation and adaptation. Absent dedicated and advanced horizon-scanning, Canada's Pacific and Arctic regions in particular are likely to experience overwhelming environmental security challenges, of which the struggle for shipping routes and the search for new energy sources may be only the most obvious ones. Environmental and energy security risks will not be limited to the Arctic, and many risks will cascade across both systems and geographical regions. Changes to Arctic sea ice, for example, force shifts in the polar vortex and Jetstream patterns both in North America and Europe, allowing winters where it is colder in Alabama than

---

[22] Robert Paehlke, "Environmentalism in One Country: Canadian Environmental Policy in an Era of Globalization," *Policy Studies Journal* 28, No. 1 (2000): 160–75.
[23] Department of Foreign Affairs and International Trade, Northern Dimension of Canada's Foreign Policy (2000), www.dfait-maeci.gc.ca/circumpolar/pdf/ndcfp-en.pdf.
[24] Andrea Olive, *Canadian Environment in Political Context* (Toronto, ON: University of Toronto Press, 2016).

northern British Columbia. Such unexpected shifts in climate can lead to increased risks of droughts and floods (e.g., the 2013 Alberta floods were linked to the Jetstream slowing)[25] with major implications for Canada's power generation as well as agricultural and food production.

Canada both relies on hydropower and exports a significant amount of electricity (net value of $2.8 billion in 2015),[26] mostly to the United States. Approximately 60 percent of Canada's electricity is from hydropower, with Quebec, British Columbia, Manitoba, Ontario, and Newfoundland and Labrador producing more than 95 percent of it.[27] A single power plant, like Quebec's Robert-Bourassa station, can service 1.4 million people.[28] Prolonged droughts, however, would reduce this energy production, affecting both domestic energy needs and Canada's national and provincial economies. In British Columbia, for example, almost 90 percent of electricity comes from hydropower generation.[29] The province relies on meltwater from the snowpack, which has been shrinking, with earlier springs and longer summers prolonging the dry season. Over the coming years, the snowline is expected to start retreating higher into the mountains, shrinking the winter snowpack even more.[30] The impact on hydropower generation will depend on specific conditions, and is likely to vary further into the future. A study of a water resource system in Quebec, for example, has concluded that the annual mean hydropower would decrease as a result of climate change in the coming decades, but by the middle of the twenty-first century, it would begin increasing.[31] The expected impacts of water strain on Canada's food production are similarly variable.

[25] Seth Borenstein, "Jet Stream Seen as a Culprit in Alberta Floods and Path of Superstorm Sandy," *Global News*, June 25, 2013, https://globalnews.ca/news/671326/jet-stream-seen-as-a-culprit-in-alberta-floods-and-path-of-superstorm-sandy/.

[26] National Energy Board, "2015 Electricity Exports and Imports Summary," www.neb-one.gc.ca/nrg/sttstc/lctrct/stt/lctrctysmmr/2015/smmry2015-eng.html.

[27] See Canadian Hydropower Association, available at https://canadahydro.ca/.

[28] Canadian Hydropower Association, *Hydropower in Canada: Past, Present and Future* (Ottawa, ON: Canadian Hydropower Association, 2008).

[29] Charlotte Helston and Andrew Farris, "Large Hydropower," Energy BC, http://energybc.ca/largehydro.html.

[30] Emily Chung, "Shrinking Mountain Snowpack, Drier Summers Spell Trouble for Vancouver Water Supply," *CBC News*, March 16, 2018, www.cbc.ca/news/technology/vancouver-water-shortage-climate-snowpack-conservation-1.4562900.

[31] Marie Minville, François Brissette, Stephane Krau, and Robert Leconte, "Adaptation to Climate Change in the Management of a Canadian Water-Resources System Exploited for Hydropower," *Water Resources Management* 23, No. 14 (2009): 2965–86. See also T. Wagner, M. Themeßl, A. Schuppel, H. Gobiet, H. Stigler, and S. Birk, "Impacts of Climate Change on Stream Flow and Hydro Power Generation in the Alpine Region," *Environmental Earth Sciences* 76, No. 4 (2017): 1–22.

Climate change can open new land for agriculture in Canada, with the possibility of growing new crops in the North. In some areas, the amount of arable land could rise by up to 40 percent by the middle of the twenty-first century.[32] However, these new areas will need infrastructure – roads and irrigation systems among other things. Furthermore, the potential lack of water would be a significant obstacle to expanding farmland. The Dust Bowl drought of the 1930s devastated Canada's prairies that contain about 80 percent of the country's farmland. Similar droughts may await in the future. Rising heat, water shortages, and crop failures are then likely to strain Canada's food production by the end of the century.

Canadian provinces – especially Alberta, Saskatchewan, and Manitoba – are vulnerable to droughts, which are expected to become more severe later in the century. In Alberta, for example, the melting glaciers in the Rocky Mountains will shrink a previously reliable source of water. Flooding may damage infrastructure, increase erosion, and contaminate groundwater. For example, in 2013, heavy rains contributed to the rupture of a dike near Bradford West Gwillimbury in Ontario, flooding more than 190 acres of farmland.[33] Droughts and floods would also reduce pasture availability, and potentially increase the weed growth (due to higher CO_2 levels) and the prevalence of pests, which would require higher energy use due to the manufacture, transportation, and application of pesticides. Heat waves would also increase livestock mortality, and reduce milk production in the dairy industry.[34] Variable weather patterns such as late frost can significantly reduce crops. For example, late frosts in 2012 led to a loss of 85 percent of the Ontario apple crop, resulting in a $60 million loss.[35]

In British Columbia, the Okanagan Valley is one of Canada's driest places, with agriculture already straining the water supplies. Climate change is expected to make the region even hotter. The higher frequency of droughts and extreme flood events will affect crops, potentially reducing them by up to 50 percent of the average yields.[36] Some areas of British Columbia have

---

[32] Chris Arsenault, "In Canada, Climate Change Could Open New Farmland to the Plow," Reuters, September 24, 2017, www.reuters.com/article/us-heatwave-canada-farming/in-canada-climate-change-could-open-new-farmland-to-the-plow-idUSKCN1BZ075.

[33] Roger Klein, "Bradford, Ont. Declares State of Emergency over Flooded Farms," CTV News, June 12, 2013, https://barrie.ctvnews.ca/bradford-ont-declares-state-of-emergency-over-flooded-farms-1.1322798.

[34] Agriculture and Agri-Food Canada, "Impact of Climate Change on Canadian Agriculture," www.agr.gc.ca/eng/science-and-innovation/agricultural-practices/agriculture-and-climate/future-outlook/impact-of-climate-change-on-canadian-agriculture/?id=1329321987305.

[35] City News, "Ontario Fruit Crops Decimated by Frost," May 9, 2012, http://toronto.citynews.ca/2012/05/09/ontario-fruit-crops-decimated-by-frost/.

[36] Agriculture and Agri-Food Canada, "Impact of Climate Change on Canadian Agriculture."

already been seeing less rain, pushing them to rely more on water reservoirs that are currently not adequate, given the water needs. For example, Vancouver – British Columbia's largest population center and traditionally an area with abundant rain – has began feeling the effects of water shortages due to climate change and population growth and has been imposing summer water restrictions since 2015.[37] Further up the Pacific coast, in Yukon, drier winters followed by hot summers could lead to droughts in regions formerly unaccustomed to such conditions.[38]

The use of scenarios, as discussed in this book, would assist Canada's federal and provincial governments in addressing emerging risks associated with climate security. In addition to exploring further impacts on hydropower generation and food production (and especially cascading effects from potential complex disasters), the assessments could answer other important questions: What are the most worrying and unrecognized risks from environmental factors to Canada? What are some major uncertainties surrounding these risks? Are there potential tipping points that would make risks nonlinear (i.e., abrupt)? What are the key vulnerabilities (i.e., critical nodes) in essential systems? What actions might increase resilience for these systems or dependent communities? Despite the rapidly emerging hazards from the Arctic to the Prairies, Canada has lagged in developing scenarios related to its own risk potential. Wildfires from the oil sands region of Alberta to the forests of British Columbia have burned out of control for consecutive summers, forcing mass evacuations and blanketing entire regions in smokes for months on end.[39] Linking these risks together, from energy security (including contentious pipeline policies) to environmental changes across regions, would provide a more coherent picture of potential futures that Canadians face.

Scenarios developed for the Pacific region may focus on risks such as energy exports and North Pacific Arctic climate, but these could also be coupled with earthquake/tsunami hazards and Canadian engagement in the wider Pacific. The Arctic scenarios could address specific Arctic risks, with an emphasis on aboriginal concerns and experiences, developing climatic changes, energy security opportunities and concerns, and impacts on military operations/strategy. Such a scenario could detail, for example, possible tsunami risks to Arctic coastal communities heightened by changes to sea and land ice, risks where

[37] *CBC News*, "Here Are the Places in Canada – Yes, Canada – Vulnerable to Drought," March 22, 2018, www.cbc.ca/news/technology/water-at-risk-canada-drought-1.4570333.

[38] *CBC News*, "Here Are the Places in Canada – Yes, Canada – Vulnerable to Drought."

[39] Such scenarios should not be limited to TV news. See Weather Network, "Canada in 2030: Frequent, More Intense Wildfires a Reality," August 11, 2018, www.theweathernetwork.com/news/articles/canada-in-2030-alberta-british-columbia-wildfires-heatwave-drought-lightning-climate-change/108193.

information is highly uncertain yet impacts are high. We discuss the Arctic theater below in more general terms.

EES Challenges in the Arctic Region

In many ways, the Arctic region is the most important for understanding the nature of climate change and the extent of its security impacts. Average air temperatures in the Arctic have shifted far more rapidly than in other parts of the globe, and the impacts on ice – be it land-based ice sheets and glaciers or floating sea ice – have been visible and dramatic over the past decade. Only seven years ago, the US Navy was predicting that the Arctic sea would not be navigable until well into the second half of the twenty-first century.[40] Rapid loss of sea ice in subsequent years, however, has forced revision of those planning expectations so that an ice-free Arctic may soon be a reality.

The loss of land-based ice sheets and melting permafrost have effects on infrastructure and transport. In some northern coastal towns of Alaska, for example, these factors all combine to increase erosion rates by as much as ten meters per year. With average air temperature changes approaching 10°C from historical norms, the climate change impacts on global weather systems, ecosystems, energy infrastructure, and local cultures can be profound.[41] In many ways, what happens in the Arctic does not stay in the Arctic, with cascading impacts flowing south to affect environmental risk and security policies to countries around the globe. For example, future changes in the Arctic systems may shape climate variability across Europe, including southern European nations.[42] Europe's severe winter storms have been in part attributed to changes in wind patterns in the Arctic climate.[43]

Many historical assumptions about stability in the Arctic can no longer be assumed, and the best-laid plans may suffer from the ground (quite literally) shifting underneath one's feet. As the region with the most rapid

---

[40] Tim Gallaudet, *The US Navy's Task Force Climate Change and the Navy's Arctic Roadmap* (Washington, DC: Office of the Oceanographer of the Navy, 2011).
[41] Edward Schuur, A. D. McGuire, Christina Schadel, Guido Grosse, J. W. Harden, D. J. Hayes, Gustaf Hugelius, Charles D. Koven, P. Kuhry, David Lawrence, Sue Natali, David Olefeldt, Vladimir E. Romanovsky, Kevin Schaefer, M. R. Turetsky, Claire C. Treat, and Jorien E. Vonk, "Climate Change and the Permafrost Carbon Feedback," *Nature* 520, No. 7546 (2015): 171–79; Timothy Lenton, "Arctic Climate Tipping Points," *Ambio* 41, No. 1 (2012): 10–22; Richard Alley, *The Two-Mile Time Machine: Ice Cores, Abrupt Climate Change, and Our Future* (Princeton, NJ: Princeton University Press, 2014).
[42] Gerald Herman and Winthrop Johnson, "The Sensitivity of the General Circulation to Arctic Sea Ice Boundaries: A Numerical Experiment," *Monthly Weather Review* 106 (1978): 1649–64.
[43] Jiping Liu, Judith A. Curry, Huijun Wang, Mirong Song, and Radley M. Horton, "Impact of Declining Arctic Sea Ice on Winter Snowfall," *Proceedings of the National Academy of Sciences* 109 (2012).

environmental changes, it has come under intense scrutiny from Arctic countries, energy companies, military planners, and even new players such as China and South Korea. The environmental and energy risk constellations are therefore diverse, at times overlapping, but rarely representing a unified perspective on what the future holds and what plans should be made to prepare for it. For example, opening of the summer sea ice in the Arctic will allow for increased tourism and the ability of cruise liners to navigate where it had previously been impossible. While this may prove an economic opportunity for some, such tourism also places increased responsibilities on militaries and coast guards to provide search-and-rescue capabilities that had previously been unneeded, in environments and over distances that pose serious logistical challenges.

The complexity of risk issues in the Arctic is potentially overwhelming. Historically, it is a region with acute environmental hazards; however, rapidly changing environmental conditions overlaid with complex geopolitical and energy dynamics will make the future of the region much less predictable. Traditional predictions for operational and strategic conditions may therefore be sorely inadequate in the Arctic. Prevailing security assessments attempt to ground analyses in terms of "most probable" geophysical changes, often based upon scientific summaries such as the IPCC. Analyses of possible developments in the Arctic region are simplistic on two counts. First, they tend to reduce the impacts of climate and other environmental changes to single, deterministic variables, rather than addressing them as complex, variable systems. Second, the idea of conflict is too often constricted to open warfare between states. While human security approaches can broaden these concepts, there is no need to step away completely from the methods and policies used by military and intelligence communities. On the contrary, as this book has sought to show, intelligence methods can provide frameworks for assessing Arctic environmental changes in ways that are neither simplistic nor blinkered.

Taken together, most security discussions concerning the Arctic region are overly conservative both in assumptions about the rate of environmental change and in the security strategies and tactics. With the rate of environmental changes in the Arctic shifting rapidly, countries in North America and Europe are already behind in adapting to a new physical environment and the significant logistical challenges presented by Arctic shipping, energy explorations, search and rescue, and other northern activities. NATO-operated ice breakers are relatively few, particularly compared to construction schedules for Russia, China, and even South Korea, leaving much of NATO naval patrol to US nuclear submarines. At the same time, while countries like Denmark argue for Arctic rights under the aegis of the UN and the Arctic Council,[44] others may turn to misinformation and even unconventional warfare.

Take, for example, the role of Denmark and Greenland, where Denmark held traditional sovereignty and is now in the process of devolving rights to the people of Greenland. Given traditional suspicions among Greenlanders of Danish policies, it may not be difficult for an outside effort to spread disinformation, create astroturf groups, and make negotiations between Denmark and Greenland over mineral rights much more difficult. In arenas of contentious politics, outside investors (such as Chinese state interest operating under the flag of a British corporation) can more easily make inroads and establish operations that are not in the security interests of Greenlanders, Danes, or NATO allies. At the International Polar Year Conference in Montreal in 2012, a US Air Force scenario workshop had three groups construct just such scenarios for Greenland – the convergence was striking, as the groups could have addressed any security issue in the Arctic and all independently settled on outside mineral investment in Greenland.[45]

Given the nature of uncertainty with climate change science, disinformation campaigns have already been largely successful in slowing effective discussion of the Arctic energy-environmental security landscape.[46] While anticlimate efforts are fueled by Western interests, as well, any spread of disinformation or uncertainty and attacks on key experts help destabilize any concerted action to address either climate security or the geophysical environments of the Arctic within which Western militaries must operate. Consequently, the Arctic states as well as those interested in the region need to turn to more pragmatic approaches, such as scenario planning and complex risk assessments, and away from the prevailing focus on state-centered security and predictive models.

Looking toward the South: EES in Antarctica

When the first scenario driver cards were written for the US Department of Energy's GlobalEESE program in the spring of 2009, one of the cards

---

[44] The United States, as it has not ratified the UN Convention on the Law of the Sea, is hampered in its adjudication efforts.

[45] The workshop was organized under the USAF Minerva project, chaired by Chad Briggs, and where Miriam Matejova, Tracy Briggs, Rebecca Ng, and Jennifer McKee were facilitators. The work groups comprised a mix of scientists, military experts, policy makers, and corporate executives.

[46] This was very much the case in Canada, where military and government scientist discussions of climate or energy security in the Arctic were all but prohibited under the Harper government from 2005 to 2015. See Jonathon Gatehouse, "When Science Goes Silent," *Maclean's* 126, No. 18 (2013): 1.

specifically detailed potential collapse of the West Antarctic ice sheet. This was before much of the recent scientific data were available, when movies such as *Day after Tomorrow*, and the dramatic breakup of the Larsen B ice shelf were the only signals, and when information about accelerating melt of Arctic sea ice and Greenland ice sheets was still relatively new. The Antarctic driver was partly included for the sake of completeness, with some expectation that it would only apply to long-range scenarios and that the probability of an accelerated breakup remained quite low. As mentioned earlier, probability estimates were removed from the original driver cards in order to help smoothen the scenario creation process. This allowed occasional consideration of an abrupt and possibly catastrophic climate change impacts in the Antarctic. The original card did describe potential outcomes of "abrupt sea level changes of 2–3 m occur[ing] by 2100," but during scenario workshops, most participants considered this to be wildly extreme.

Much more recent research now suggests that the melting of the Antarctic has been doubling every twenty years, potentially soon surpassing the melting of Greenland. Between 2010 and 2016, Antarctica has lost more than fourteen hundred square kilometers of its grounded-ice area (i.e., the ice near the ocean floor).[47] The speed and extent of this melt, and especially of the West Antarctic Ice Sheet (WAIS), is prompting scientists to revise the global sea level rise projects upward.[48] Most of WAIS is below sea level, with ice shelves at risk of disintegration due to warming ocean water or surface melting. Some scientists believe the melting thresholds for the major ice shelves are reachable within this century.[49] Acceleration of ice streams may trigger further separation from the bedrock, eventually leading to the WAIS collapse and global sea level rise. The East Antarctic Ice Sheet, previously considered stable and even increasing, is currently thinning at a rapid rate.[50]

Beyond the more visible environmental changes to the Antarctic, political winds are slowly shifting as well. The Antarctic region is governed by a treaty convention that dates back to the 1950s, with primary signatories limited to

---

[47] Hannes Konrad, Andrew Shepherd, Lin Gilbert, Anna E. Hogg, Malcolm McMillan, Alan Muir, and Thomas Slater, "Net Retreat of Antarctic Glacier Grounding Lines," *Nature Geoscience* 11 (2018): 258–62.

[48] Jonathan Watts, "Underwater Melting of Antarctic Ice Far Greater than Thought, Study Finds," *Guardian*, April 2, 2018, www.theguardian.com/environment/2018/apr/02/underwater-melting-of-antarctic-ice-far-greater-than-thought-study-finds.

[49] Surface atmospheric temperatures of about 5°C and 8°C would exceed the melting point in summer for the major ice shelves and the WAIS itself, respectively. See Timothy M. Lenton, Hermann Held, Elmar Kriegler, Jim W. Hall, Wolfgang Lucht, Stefan Rahmstorf, and Hans Joachim Schellnhuber, "Tipping Elements in the Earth's Climate System," *PNAS* 105, No. 6 (2008): 1786–93.

[50] Konrad et al.

those "conducting substantial research activity there."[51] While the original system attempts to prohibit development of the continent beyond that required for scientific research, certain countries are eying a combination of climate change and long-term political trends to destabilize those norms.[52] As one US Air Force major (O5) theorized, "China's behavior in the Arctic and South China Sea might have as much to do with asserting claims in Antarctica in the long run, as anything else."[53]

The "long game" – taking a different perspective on geopolitics and how others are planning for changes – requires stepping outside of one's usual thinking or the standard views of one's organization. As Cleo Paskal warns in her writings, we need to reconsider how climate change, international laws and norms, and shifting geopolitics affect our assumptions about how the world works.[54] If, like Richard Alley noted about Greenland, we make the mistake of assuming that Antarctica is a big, constant "ice cube," we miss the significance of how the world is changing and how others might perceive that change and take advantage of it better than we do.

Conclusion

In November 2009, a group of state and federal government officials from the United States were in the small agricultural community of Shepparton, Victoria, in the southeast of Australia. Outside the city, farmers working on an irrigation system of the Goulburn River were discussing their experiences with drought, expressing concern over how well they could adapt and feed their sheep and cattle if the climate continued to change. "The government did well with water trading," one explained, "though we went from dairy farms to wineries in some places, and I'm not sure we can survive too long on wine alone." The farmer looked out over a mostly dry creek bed and explained further, "We've been here for about 150 years, us meaning not the Aboriginals, of course. And we set up these sheep stations and farms expecting it would always be the same. But now that we have this community and families and

---

[51] See the Secretariat of the Antarctic Treaty, available at www.ats.aq/devAS/ats_parties.aspx?lang=e&lang=e.
[52] Julia Jabour, "China and the Rules of Engagement in Antarctica," *Maritime Issues*, April 25, 2017, www.maritimeissues.com/commentary/china-and-the-rules-of-engagement-in-antarctica.html.
[53] Personal communication at the Air Command and Staff College, 2011.
[54] Dhanasree Jayaram, "The 'Three Geos': A New Approach to Study Environmental Security Scenarios in the Asia-Pacific," *International Affairs Forum* 5, No. 2 (2014): 106–17.

markets, we're just trying to adapt, but no amount of technology can help us if the water just decides to stop coming."[55]

Nine years later, Australian politics is still grappling with ways to address risks from climate change, forcing changes in leadership while the country experiences a debilitating drought that has severely hurt farmers and rural communities.[56] Despite innovative policies and technologies that helped Australia navigate through previous droughts, the country is still struggling to set out a strategy for fighting the future. They are hardly alone. The challenges facing us not only threaten in the sense of the occasional storm or flood but also undermine some of the key elements at the core of our communities and societies. People at the local level often understand what these risks mean, but translating them into larger political strategies and policies remains an enormous challenge – one that is possible to address.

The approaches described in this book are not meant to provide predictive success in knowing what will happen but instead are meant to help prepare people for potential events and emerging risks, particularly those that run against our intuition and common sense for how the world should work. The political and legal institutions established during the Cold War, for example, were designed to address conventional conflicts as understood by Western Europeans and North Americans. At least in the Western world, disasters continue to be described as natural, the media attempt to find simple cause-and-effect relationships during disasters, and conflict is often seen in black-and-white terms (e.g., either one is at war, or one is not). However, experts such as Ilan Kelman have long argued that disasters are neither natural nor unknowable. The associated risks and impacts are heavily conditioned by human behavior. How those impacts play out depends largely on a combination of complex hazards, critical vulnerabilities, and available response. In order to identify disaster risks and responses in advance (and particularly when disaster risks intersect with security policies), more effort must be made to move beyond traditional categories of thought. We must become more familiar with emerging risks so that when we are confronted with them in the real world, we do not find ourselves paralyzed with indecision.

Larger governments, such as in the United States, already have dedicated facilities for creating simulated disasters and for helping other agencies to use

---

[55] Personal communication, November 2009. I (Briggs) was one of those delegates sent to learn from Australia about water security policies and technologies, a joint project between the state of California and the Australian Trade Commission.

[56] Greg Jericho, "If You're Talking about Drought but Not Climate Change, You're Not Doing Your Job, PM," *Guardian*, August 29, 2018, www.theguardian.com/business/grogonomics/2018/aug/30/if-youre-talking-about-drought-but-not-climate-change-youre-not-doing-your-job-pm.

the simulations in training. In particular, FEMA's Emergency Management Institute and National Exercise Simulation Center can provide extensive resources to organizations and agencies to test their disaster scenarios and response plans. These resources include the provision of virtual news, experts from across the Department of Homeland Security, and recommendations on how to improve responses. The US Department of Defense has programs such as the Navy's Task Force Energy and Task Force Climate Change, the army its Green Warriors program, and the various US Air Force projects on energy efficiency (in addition to the previously mentioned weather intelligence capabilities). In this book, we are not claiming that the military is the proper place for carrying out disaster security research. While the USAF Minerva program was successful, the program had to be aware of significant obstacles and challenges associated with working in a security organization. At the same time, the US Department of Defense was far more receptive to new ideas than many civilian university departments, where old paradigms die hard.

When planning for and responding to a disaster, it is understandable that the primary focus will be on the hazards and associated risks. The complexity of disasters and cascading impacts may be just as important but difficult to see through traditional risk assessment processes that can trace only first- and perhaps second-order impacts. As we strived to demonstrate in this book, the use of complex scenarios is a way to overcome this problem. Scenarios are useful in policy making, since they often reveal critical vulnerabilities in the existing systems. Existing policies then may be adjusted or new ones may be created to address the identified problems and, ultimately, to cope with the futures of which the scenarios are warning. Scenario planning therefore allows training for all types of events, including those we know would happen and those we may hope to never see. The emphasis is on the mitigation of impacts rather than events, since one cannot prevent volcanoes from erupting or earthquakes from striking.

The scenarios described in previous chapters avoided discussions of probability. Often, the literature on scenarios in decision-making focuses on the ability to predict future events accurately in order to address those situations that decision makers are most likely to face. *Black swan* events are often defined as high-impact, low-probability events. This can be highly misleading when we do not actually know the probabilities involved. These probabilistic judgments are also often made by small groups of people who, while experts in their own fields, may have a tendency to downplay information that they do not understand well and that falls outside of the respective fields. Plausibility should not be confused with probability or median projections. It is entirely possible, and at times necessary, for scenario components to be presented at the extreme end of a plausibility-possibility spectrum. When the first scenario driver cards were written in 2009–10, I (Briggs) wrote two cards largely in jest – one dealing with a massive solar storm (a Carrington Event), the other with a zombie outbreak.[57] One was an extreme disaster in itself with unknown probability, the other a fictional event. Workshop participants resisted my suggestion not to use them, with one Swedish defense colleague explaining, "We need to see how vulnerable we really are. We can always work backwards from there."[58]

In working with the scenarios presented in this book, we were not predicting (nor was it our responsibility to predict) what *would* happen. Rather, the role of intelligence in disaster risk was to help identify potentially catastrophic pathways well in advance of decisions that would make such outcomes a reality. Academic studies that attempted to show, for example, that climatic environmental changes would lead to violent conflict were not as useful as scenarios identifying alternate pathways that could avoid conflict. An admiral once remarked, "If we know 100 percent that conflict in say, Somalia, will erupt in five years because of climate change, that is saying there's nothing we can do. Our only option then is to try to keep it from spreading." In other words, uncertainty is necessary, because it allows for potential choices and alternatives. Waiting for full certainty means that those choices have already been lost.

The tools and approaches described here are neither expensive nor particularly difficult. Rather, they require political will and trust to operate, a recognition of the importance of both science and local expertise, and the ability of policy makers to question previously held beliefs and chart out a new (if somewhat difficult) future. Avoiding or minimizing disasters cannot be done without acknowledging the risks in the first place and learning how to accept the uncertainty that comes with those risks.

---

[57] The zombie card used data from Philip Munz, Ioan Hudea, Joe Imad, and Robert J. Smith, "When Zombies Attack! Mathematical Modelling of an Outbreak of Zombie Infection," *Infectious Disease Modelling Research Progress* 4 (2009): 133–50.

[58] Ernie Tretkoff, "Legislation Seeks to Protect Power Grid from Space Weather," *Space Weather* 8, No. 5 (2010). The solar storm impacts on energy grids were soon after highlighted by popular books warning of an electromagnetic pulse (EMP) bomb by North Korea. By our judgment, this was only a plausible risk to local installations. See Mark Schneider and Roscoe Bartlett, *The Emerging EMP Threat to the United States* (Fairfax, VA: National Institute Press, 2007), 3.

Bibliography

2011 Tohoku Earthquake Tsunami Joint Survey Group (TETJSG). "Nationwide Field Survey of the 2011 off the Pacific Coast of Tohoku Earthquake Tsunami." *Journal of Japan Society of Civil Engineers, Ser. B2* 67 (2011): 63–66.

ABC News. "Russian Heatwave Killed 11,000 People." September 17, 2010. www.abc .net.au/news/2010–09-18/russian-heatwave-killed-11000-people/2265184.

Abe, Hisashi, Yoshisada Sugeno, and Akira Chigama. "Estimation of the Height of the Sanriku Jogan 11 Earthquake-Tsunami (A.D. 869) in the Sendai Plain." *Journal of the Seismological Society of Japan* 43 (1990): 513–25.

Agriculture and Agri-Food Canada. "Impact of Climate Change on Canadian Agriculture." www.agr.gc.ca/eng/science-and-innovation/agricultural-practices/ agriculture-and-climate/future-outlook/impact-of-climate-change-on-canadian- agriculture/?id=1329321987305.

Aguirre, Monti. "Peru's Energy Future." *International Rivers*, June 9, 2016. www .internationalrivers.org/blogs/233/peru-s-energy-future.

Alagappa, Mutiah. "Rethinking Security: A Critical Review and Appraisal of the Debate." In *Asian Security Practice: Material and Ideational Influences*, edited by Mutiah Alagappa. Palo Alto, CA: Stanford University Press, 1998.

Albion, Adam. "Winter of Discontent – Electricity Supply Problems in Central Asia." *Jane's Intelligence Review* 20, No. 12 (2008): 54–55.

Ali, S. H., A. Zia, and Rebecca Pincus. *Strategic Response to Energy-Related Security Threats in the US Department of Defense*. Burlington: University of Vermont, 2014.

Alley, Richard. *The Two-Mile Time Machine: Ice Cores, Abrupt Climate Change, and Our Future*. Princeton, NJ: Princeton University Press, 2014.

American Physiological Society. "Army Study Improves Ability to Predict Drinking Water Needs." *ScienceDaily*, July 11, 2009. www.sciencedaily.com/releases/2009/ 07/090708073849.htm.

Andreouli, Eleni, Lia Figgou, Irini Kadianaki, Antonis Sapountzis, and Maria Xenitidou. "'Europe' in Greece: Lay Constructions of Europe in the Context of Greek Immigration Debates." *Journal of Community and Applied Social Psychology* 27, No. 2 (2017): 158–68.

Applegate, Patrick J., Nina Kirchner, Emma J. Stone, Klaus Keller, and Ralf Greve. "An Assessment of Key Model Parametric Uncertainties in Projections of Greenland Ice Sheet Behavior." *The Cryosphere* 6, No. 3 (2012): 589–606.

Appleman, Herbert S. *An Introduction to Weather Modification.* No. AWS-TR-177-REV. Air Weather Service, 1969.

Aquino, Marco. "Glacier Breaks in Peru, Causing Tsunami in Andes." *Reuters*, April 12, 2010. www.reuters.com/article/us-peru-glaciers/glacier-breaks-in-peru-causing-tsunami-in-andes-idUSTRE63B69Y20100412.

Archer, David. "Methane Hydrate Stability and Anthropogenic Climate Change." *Biogeosciences Discussions* 4, No. 2 (2007): 993–1057.

Arnell, Nigel W., Matthew J. L. Livermore, Sari Kovats, Peter E. Levy, Rob Nicholls, Martin L. Parry, and Stuart R. Gaffin. "Climate and Socio-economic Scenarios for Global-scale Climate Change Impacts Assessments: Characterising the SRES Storylines." *Global Environmental Change* 14, No. 1 (2004): 3–20.

Arsenault, Chris. "In Canada, Climate Change Could Open New Farmland to the Plow." *Reuters*, September 24, 2017. www.reuters.com/article/us-heatwave-canada-farming/in-canada-climate-change-could-open-new-farmland-to-the-plow-idUSKCN1BZ075.

Asian Development Bank and Asian Development Bank Institute. *Disaster Risk Management in Asia and the Pacific.* Tokyo: Asian Development Bank Institute, 2013.

Baard, Patrik, Henrik Carlsen, Karin Edvardsson Bjornberg, and Maria Vredin Johansson. "Scenarios and Sustainability: A Swedish Case Study of Adaptation." *Tools for Local Decision-Makers*, No. 124 (2011).

Baba, K., and Y. Yamada. "BSRs and Associated Reflections as an Indicator of Gas Hydrate and Free Gas Accumulation: An Example of Accretionary Prism and Forearc Basin System along the Nankai Trough, off Central Japan." *Resource Geology* 54 (2004): 11–24. doi:10.1111/j.1751-3928.2004.tb00183.x

Banerjee, Bidisha. "The Limitations of Geoengineering Governance in a World of Uncertainty." *Stanford Journal of Law, Science and Policy* 4, No. 1 (2011): 426.

Banerjee, Bidisha, George Collins, Sean Low, and Jason J. Blackstock. *Scenario Planning for Solar Radiation Management.* New Haven, CT: Yale Climate and Energy Institute, 2013.

Barley, Shanta. "Climategate: Russian Secret Service Blamed for Hack." *New Scientist*, December 7, 2009. www.newscientist.com/blogs/shortsharpscience/2009/12/since-over-1000-confidential-e.html.

Barnett, John. "Security and Climate Change." *Global Environmental Change* 13, No. 1 (2003): 7–17.

Bearman, Peter. "Just-So Stories: Vaccines, Autism, and the Single-bullet Disorder." *Social Psychology Quarterly* 73, No. 2 (2010): 112–15.

Belden, Thomas G. "Indications, Warning, and Crisis Operations." *International Studies Quarterly* 21, No. 1 (1977): 181–98.

Bergerut, Eric M. *Fire in the Sky: The Air War in the South Pacific.* Boulder, CO: Westview Press, 2000.

Betts, Richard K. "Analysis, War, and Decision: Why Intelligence Failures Are Inevitable." *World Politics* 31, No. 1 (1978): 61–89.

Blackstock, Jason J., and Jane C. S. Long. "The Politics of Geoengineering." *Science* 327, No. 5965 (2010): 527.

Blaikie, Piers, Terry Cannon, Ian Davis, and Ben Wisner. *At Risk: Natural Hazards, People's Vulnerability and Disasters.* New York: Routledge, 2004.

Blair, Bruce G. *The Logic of Accidental Nuclear War.* Washington, DC: Brookings Institution Press, 2011.

Boland, Rita. "Forces Take Pre-emptive Measures to Improve Response." AFCEA Signal, October 2008. www.afcea.org/content/?q=forces-take-pre-emptive-measures-improve-response.

Borenstein, Seth. "Jet Stream Seen as a Culprit in Alberta Floods and Path of Superstorm Sandy." *Global News*, June 25, 2013. https://globalnews.ca/news/671326/jet-stream-seen-as-a-culprit-in-alberta-floods-and-path-of-superstorm-sandy/.

Bosetti, Louise, Alexandra Ivanovic, and Menaal Munshey. "Fragility, Risk, and Resilience: A Review of Existing Frameworks." United Nations University Centre for Policy Research Background Paper, October 2016.

Boswell, Ray. "Resource Potential of Methane Hydrate Coming into Focus." *Journal of Petroleum Science and Engineering* 56, No. 1–3 (2007): 9–13.

Bowen-Williams, Katherine J. "Tensions over Hydroelectric Developments in Central Asia: Regional Interdependence and Energy Security." *Asia Pacific Perspectives* 10, No. 2 (2011): 133–60.

Boyarsky, Igor, and Amiram Shneiderman. "Natural and Hybrid Disasters – Causes, Effects, and Management." *Topics in Emergency Medicine* 24, No. 3 (2002): 1–25.

Bradfield, Ron, George Wright, George Burt, George Cairns, and Kees Van Der Heijden. "The Origins and Evolution of Scenario Techniques in Long Range Business Planning." *Futures* 37, No. 8 (2005): 795–812.

Bray, David A., Sean Costigan, Keith A. Daum, Helene Lavoix, Elizabeth L. Malone, and Chris Pallaris. "Perspective: Cultivating Strategic Foresight for Energy and Environmental Security." *Environmental Practice* 11, No. 3 (2009): 209–11.

Briggs, Chad M. "Abrupt Environmental Changes: Scenario Planning for Catastrophic Security Risks." In *Governing Disasters: The Challenge of Emergency Regulation – Beyond the European Volcanic Ash Crisis*, edited by Alberto Alemanno, 166–81. London: Edward Elgar, 2011.

"Climate Security, Risk Assessment and Military Planning." *International Affairs* 88, No. 5 (2012): 1049–64.

"Damming Science: Problems of Scientific Research in Environmental Administration." PhD diss., Carleton University, Ottawa, ON, 2001.

"Developing Strategic and Operational Environmental Intelligence Capabilities." *Intelligence and National Security* 27, No. 5 (2012): 653–68.

"The Emperor's Clothes: International Relations Theory beyond the Cold War." *Political and Economic Review* 1, No. 1 (1996): 1–13.

"Environmental Change, Strategic Foresight and Impacts on Military Powers." *Parameters* 40, No. 3 (2010): 1–15.

"Is Geoengineering a National Security Risk?" *Policy* 109 (2010): 85–96.

"Risk and Scenario Planning for Climate Security." *Environmental Change and Security Program Report* 14, No. 2 (2013): 49.

"Risk Assessment: Perchlorate as a National Security Threat." *IEEE Technology and Society Magazine* 27, No. 3 (2008): 19–24.

"Science and Environmental Risk: The Case of Perchlorate Contamination in California." *Environmental Politics* 15, No. 4 (2006): 532–49.

"Water Scarcity, Regional Security and Comprehensive Planning." Remarks as prepared for the Al Nahrain Center workshop Water, Food, Energy, and the Security of Iraq. Air University, USAF, 2012.

Briggs, Chad M., and Henrik Carlsen. "Environmental and Climate Security: Improving Scenario Methodologies for Science and Risk Assessment." American Geophysical Union, Fall Meeting, 2010.

Briggs, Chad M., Moneeza Walji, and Lucy Anderson. "Environmental Health Risks and Vulnerability in Postconflict Regions." *Medicine, Conflict and Survival* 25, No. 2 (2009): 122–33.

Briggs, Chad M., and Inka Weissbecker. "Salting the Earth: Environmental Health Challenges in Post-conflict Reconstruction." In *Assessing and Restoring Natural Resources in Post-conflict Peacebuilding*, edited by David Jensen and Steve Lonergan, 111–34. New York: Earthscan, 2012.

Briggs, David J., Clive E. Sabel, and Kayoung Lee. "Uncertainty in Epidemiology and Health Risk and Impact Assessment." *Environmental Geochemistry and Health* 31, No. 2 (2009): 189–203.

Britton, Neil R. "Constraint or Effectiveness in Disaster Management? The Bureaucratic Imperative versus Organizational Mission." In *Seminar on New Directions in Understanding Civil Disaster Management*. Sydney: University of Sydney, Department of Government and Public Administration, 1989.

Broniatowski, David A., Amelia M. Jamison, SiHua Qi, Lulwah AlKulaib, Tao Chen, Adrian Benton, Sandra C. Quinn, and Mark Dredze. "Weaponized Health Communication: Twitter Bots and Russian Trolls Amplify the Vaccine Debate." American Journal of Public Health, published online August 23, 2018. https://ajph .aphapublications.org/doi/10.2105/AJPH.2018.304567.

Brulle, Robert J. "Institutionalizing Delay: Foundation Funding and the Creation of US Climate Change Counter-movement Organizations." *Climatic Change* 122, No. 4 (2014): 681–94.

Brulle, Robert J., Jason Carmichael, and J. Craig Jenkins. "Shifting Public Opinion on Climate Change: An Empirical Assessment of Factors Influencing Concern over Climate Change in the US, 2002–2010." *Climatic Change* 114, No. 2 (2012): 169–88.

Buffett, Bruce, and David Archer. "Global Inventory of Methane Clathrate: Sensitivity to Changes in the Deep Ocean." *Earth and Planetary Science Letters* 227, No. 3–4 (2004): 185–99.

Bury, Jeffrey, Bryan G. Mark, Mark Carey, Kenneth R. Young, Jeffrey M. McKenzie, Michel Baraer, Adam French, and Molly H. Polk. "New Geographies of Water and Climate Change in Peru: Coupled Natural and Social Transformations in the Santa River Watershed." *Annals of the Association of American Geographers* 103, No. 2 (2013): 363–74.

Buzan, Barry. "New Patterns of Global Security in the Twenty-first Century." *International Affairs* 67, No. 3 (1991): 431–51.

"Rethinking Security after the Cold War." *Cooperation and Conflict* 32, No. 1 (1997): 5–28.

Caballero-Anthony, Mely, and Ralf Emmers. "The Dynamics of Securitization in Asia." In *Studying Non-traditional Security in Asia: Issues and Trends*, edited by Ralf Emmers, Mely Caballero-Anthony, and Amitav Acharya. Singapore: Marshall-Cavendish Academic, 2006.

Calzada, Joan, Susana Iranzo, and Alex Saenz. "Community Managed Water Systems: The Case of Peru." *Journal of Environment and Development* 26, No. 4 (2017): 400–428.

Campbell, Charlie. "The Tsunami's Wake." *Time*, December 25, 2014. http://time.com/tsunamis-wake/.

Canadian Hydropower Association. *Hydropower in Canada: Past, Present and Future.* Ottawa, ON: Canadian Hydropower Association, 2008.

Capra, Lucia. "Abrupt Climatic Changes as Triggering Mechanisms of Massive Volcanic Collapses." *Journal of Volcanology and Geothermal Research* 155, No. 3–4 (2006): 329–33.

Carlsen, Henrik E., Anders Eriksson, Karl Henrik Dreborg, Bengt Johansson, and Orjan Bodin. "Systematic Exploration of Scenario Spaces." *Foresight* 18, No. 1 (2016): 59–75.

Carlsen, Henrik E., Richard J. T. Klein, and Per Wikman-Svahn. "Transparent Scenario Development." Nature Climate Change 7, No. 9 (2017): 613.

Carney, Barbara, Thomas Feeley, and Andrea McNemar. "Water Requirements for Thermoelectric Generation." NETL UNESCO Conference paper, US DOE. www.netl.doe.gov/technologies/coalpower/ewr/water/pdfs/NETL%20Paper%20Unesco%20Conference.pdf.

Carrington, Damian. "Climate Change Will Stir 'Unimaginable' Refugee Crisis, Says Military." *The Guardian*, December 1, 2016. www.theguardian.com/environment/2016/dec/01/climate-change-trigger-unimaginable-refugee-crisis-senior-military.

Casey, Tina. "In First Test, U.S. Military's SPIDERS Microgrid Uses 90% Renewable Energy." *Clean Technica*, February 12, 2013. https://cleantechnica.com/2013/02/12/u-s-militarys-new-spiders-renewable-energy-microgrid/.

CBC. "2003: The Great North America Blackout." August 14, 2003. www.cbc.ca/archives/entry/2003-the-great-north-america-blackout.

"Here Are the Places in Canada – Yes, Canada – Vulnerable to Drought." *CBC News*, March 22, 2018. www.cbc.ca/news/technology/water-at-risk-canada-drought-1.4570333.

CBS News. "Impacts from Irene, State by State." August 29, 2011. www.cbsnews.com/news/impacts-from-irene-state-by-state/.

Chen, Zhongyuan, Zhanghua Wang, Brian Finlayson, Jing Chen, and Daowei Yin. "Implications of Flow Control by the Three Gorges Dam on Sediment and Channel Dynamics of the Middle Yangtze (Changjiang) River, China." *Geology* 38, No. 11 (2010): 1043–46.

Chermack, Thomas J., Susan A. Lynham, and Wendy E. A. Ruona. "A Review of Scenario Planning Literature." *Futures Research Quarterly* 17, No. 2 (2001): 7–32.

Chossudovsky, Michel. "The Ultimate Weapon of Mass Destruction: 'Owning the Weather' for Military Use." *Global Research*, September 9, 2017. www.globalre

search.ca/the-ultimate-weapon-of-mass-destruction-owning-the-weather-for-mili
tary-use-2/5306386.

Chung, Emily. "Shrinking Mountain Snowpack, Drier Summers Spell Trouble for
Vancouver Water Supply." *CBC News*, March 16, 2018. www.cbc.ca/news/technol
ogy/vancouver-water-shortage-climate-snowpack-conservation-1.4562900.

City News. "Ontario Fruit Crops Decimated by Frost." May 9, 2012. http://toronto
.citynews.ca/2012/05/09/ontario-fruit-crops-decimated-by-frost/.

Clarke, Richard A., and R. P. Eddy. *Warnings: Finding Cassandras to Stop
Catastrophes*. New York: HarperCollins, 2017.

CNA Corporation. *National Security and the Threat of Climate Change*. Alexandria,
VA: CNA Corporation, 2007.

Cockburn, Patrick. *Getting Russia Wrong: The End of Kremlinology*. New York: Verso
Books, 1989.

Cohen, Michael D., James G. March, and Johan P. Olsen. "A Garbage Can Model
of Organizational Choice." Administrative Science Quarterly 17, No. 1 (1972):
1–25.

Collet, Timothy S. "Natural Gas Hydrate as a Potential Energy Resource." In *Natural
Gas Hydrate in Oceanic and Permafrost Environments*, edited by Michael D. Max.
Dordrecht: Kluwer Academic, 2003.

Collins, Thomas H. "Change and Continuity: The US Coast Guard Today." *Naval War
College Review* 57, No. 2 (2004): 1–19.

Collomb, Jean-Daniel. "The Ideology of Climate Change Denial in the United States."
European Journal of American Studies 9, No. 9–1 (2014).

Collyns, Dan. "Climate Change Has Turned Peru's Glacial Lake into a Deadly Flood
Timebomb." *The Guardian*, June 29, 2018. www.theguardian.com/environment/
2018/jun/29/climate-change-has-turned-perus-glacial-lake-into-a-deadly-flood-
timebomb.

Coman, Julian. "On the Frontline of Europe's Forgotten War in Ukraine." *The
Guardian*, November 12, 2017. www.theguardian.com/world/2017/nov/12/
ukraine-on-the-front-line-of-europes-forgotten-war.

Conca, Ken, and Geoffrey D. Dabelko, eds. *Environmental Peacemaking*. Washington,
DC: Woodrow Wilson Center Press, 2002.

Corner, Adam, and Nick Pidgeon. "Geoengineering the Climate: The Social and Ethical
Implications." *Environment: Science and Policy for Sustainable Development* 52,
No. 1 (2010): 24–37.

Covello, Vincent T., Detlof von Winterfeldt, and Paul Slovic. "Communicating
Scientific Information about Health and Environmental Risks: Problems and
Opportunities from a Social and Behavioral Perspective." In *Uncertainty in Risk
Assessment, Risk Management, and Decision Making*, edited by Vincent T.
Covello, Lester B. Lave, A. Alan Moghissi, and V. R. R. Uppuluri, 221–39.
Boston: Springer, 1987.

Crisis and Risk Network. *Focal Report 2: Risk Analysis – Integrated Risk Management
and Societal Security*. Zurich: Center for Security Studies, 2009.

Cullen, Heidi, Peter B. Demenocal, Silke Hemming, G. Hemming, Francis H. Brown,
Tom Guilderson, and Frank Sirocko. "Climate Change and the Collapse of the
Akkadian Empire: Evidence from the Deep Sea." *Geology* 28, No. 4 (2000): 379–
82.

Cullen, Patrick. "Hybrid Threats as a New 'Wicked Problem' for Early Warning." *Hybrid COE Strategic Analysis*, May 25, 2018. www.hybridcoe.fi/wp-content/uploads/2018/06/Strategic-Analysis-2018-5-Cullen.pdf.

Dabelko, Geoffrey D., and David D. Dabelko. "Environmental Security: Issues of Conflict and Redefinition." *ECSP Report* 1 (1995): 3–13.

Dalby, Simon. *Environmental Security*. Vol. 20. Minneapolis, MN: University of Minnesota Press, 2002.

Daniels, Ronald J., Donald F. Kettl, and Howard Kunreuther. "Introduction." In *On Risk and Disaster. Lessons from Hurricane Katrina*, edited by Ronald J. Daniels, Donald F. Kettl, and Howard Kunreuther, 1–14. Philadelphia: University of Pennsylvania Press, 2006.

Danyk, Yuriy, Tamara Maliarchuk, and Chad Briggs, "Hybrid War: High-Tech, Information and Cyber Conflicts," *Connections* 16, No. 2 (2017): 5–24.

Darwall, Rupert. *The Age of Global Warming: A History*. London: Quartet Books, 2013.

Davis, Tom. "Select Bipartisan Committee to Investigate the Preparation for and Response to Hurricane Katrina." Final Report, US House of Representatives, February 15, 2006.

de Franco, Chiara, and Christoph Meyer, eds. *Forecasting, Warning and Responding to Transnational Risks*. New York: Palgrave Macmillan, 2011.

de Menocal, Peter. "Palaeoclimate: End of the African Humid Period." *Nature Geoscience* 8 (2015): 86–87.

Department of Foreign Affairs and International Trade. "Northern Dimension of Canada's Foreign Policy." 2000. www.dfait-maeci.gc.ca/circumpolar/pdf/ndcfp-en.pdf.

de Pryck, Kari, and François Gemenne. "The Denier-in-Chief: Climate Change, Science and the Election of Donald J. Trump." *Law and Critique* 28, No. 2 (2017): 119–26.

Deudney, Daniel. "Muddled Thinking." *Bulletin of the Atomic Scientists* 47, No. 3 (1991): 22–28.

Dewar, James A. "The Importance of 'Wild Card' Scenarios." Air University. www.au.af.mil/au/awc/awcgate/cia/nic2020/dewar_nov6.pdf.

Dickens, Gerald R. "A Methane Trigger for Rapid Warming?" *Science* 299, No. 5609 (2003): 1017.

Diplomat. "What Will the 2018 Cobra Gold Military Exercises in Thailand Look Like?" January 31, 2018. https://thediplomat.com/2018/01/what-will-the-2018-cobra-gold-military-exercises-in-thailand-look-like/.

Drye, Willie. "A Timeline of Hurricane Sandy's Path of Destruction." *National Geographic*, November 2, 2012. https://blog.nationalgeographic.org/2012/11/02/a-timeline-of-hurricane-sandys-path-of-destruction/.

Duggan, Patrick. "Strategic Development of Special Warfare in Cyberspace." *Joint Forces Quarterly* 79 (2015): 46–53.

Dumaine, Carol. "On a Global Foresight Commons." *SEED Magazine*, November 23, 2010. http://seedmagazine.com/content/article/on_a_global_foresight_commons/.

Dumaine, Carol, and Irving Mintzer. "Confronting Climate Change and Reframing Security." *SAIS Review of International Affairs* 35, No. 1 (2015): 5–16.

Dunlap, Riley E., Aaron M. McCright, and Jerrod H. Yarosh. "The Political Divide on Climate Change: Partisan Polarization Widens in the US." *Environment: Science and Policy for Sustainable Development* 58, No. 5 (2016): 4–23.

Dupont, Claire. "When Decarbonisation Meets Disinformation: EU-Russia Energy Relations." *IES Policy Brief*, No. 15 (June 2016).

Durance, Philippe, and Michel Godet. "Scenario Building: Uses and Abuses." *Technological Forecasting and Social Change* 77, No. 9 (2010): 1488–92.

Earth Observatory. "World of Change: Drought Cycles in Australia." NASA. https://earthobservatory.nasa.gov/WorldOfChange/AustraliaNDVI.

Ehrlich, Paul R. *The Population Bomb*. New York: Sierra Club/Ballantine Books, 1968.

Eiser, J. Richard, Ann Bostrom, Ian Burton, David M. Johnston, John McClure, Douglas Paton, Joop Van Der Pligt, and Mathew P. White. "Risk Interpretation and Action: A Conceptual Framework for Responses to Natural Hazards." *International Journal of Disaster Risk Reduction* 1 (2012): 5–16.

Eleftheriou, Krista. "World's Highest Glaciers, in Peruvian Andes, May Disappear within 40 Years." *ABC News*, November 5, 2015. www.abc.net.au/news/2015–11-05/perus-highest-disappearing-glaciers-climate-change/6915668.

Ellison, Katherine. "Why Climate Change Skeptics Are Backing Geoengineering." *Wired*, March 28, 2018. www.wired.com/story/why-climate-change-skeptics-are-backing-geoengineering/.

Environmental Leader. "Worst US Drought in 50 Years Drives Up Grain Prices, Ethanol under Pressure." August 13, 2012. www.environmentalleader.com/2012/08/13/worst-us-drought-in-50-years-drives-up-grain-prices-ethanol-under-pressure/.

Environmental News Service. "Unstable Siberian Arctic Shelf Leaking Greenhouse Gas Methane." March 8, 2010. www.ens-newswire.com/ens/mar2010/2010–03-08-03.html.

European Commission. "Risk Assessment and Mapping Guidelines for Disaster Management." Commission Staff Working Paper SEC, 2010.

Fackler, Martin. "U.S. Airmen Quietly Reopen Wrecked Airport in Japan." *New York Times*, April 13, 2011. hwww.nytimes.com/2011/04/14/world/asia/14sendai.html.

Fadeel, Bengt, Hanna L. Karlsson, and Kunal Bhattacharya. "Geoengineering: Perilous Particles." *Science* 340, No. 6132 (2013): 548–49.

Fagin, Dan. "Toxicology: The Learning Curve." *Nature* 490 (2012): 462–65.

Falasca, Mauro, Christopher W. Zobel, and Deborah Cook. "A Decision Support Framework to Assess Supply Chain Resilience." In Proceedings of the 5th International ISCRAM Conference, 596–605. Beijing: Information Systems for Crisis Response and Management, 2008.

Farjoun, Moshe. "Organizational Learning and Action in the Midst of Safety Drift: Revisiting the Space Shuttle Program's Recent History." In *Organization at the Limit: Lessons from the Columbia Disaster*, edited by William Starbuck and Moshe Farjoun, 60–80. London: Wiley-Blackwell, 2005.

Farrell, Justin. "Corporate Funding and Ideological Polarization about Climate Change." *Proceedings of the National Academy of Sciences* 113, No. 1 (2016): 92–97.

Fitzpatrick, Michael. "Japan to Drill for Controversial 'Fire Ice.'" *Guardian*, September 27, 2010. www.theguardian.com/business/2010/sep/27/energy-industry-energy.

Fleming, James Rodger. "The Pathological History of Weather and Climate Modification: Three Cycles of Promise and Hype." *Historical Studies in the Physical and Biological Sciences* 37, No. 1 (2006): 3–25.

Francis, Jennifer, and Natasa Skific. "Evidence Linking Rapid Arctic Warming to Mid-Latitude Weather Patterns." *Philosophical Transactions of the Royal Society of London, Series A* 373, No. 2045 (2015): 20140170.

Francis, Jennifer, and Stephen J. Vavrus. "Evidence Linking Arctic Amplification to Extreme Weather in Mid-Latitudes." *Geophysical Research Letters* 39, No. 6 (2012). https://agupubs.onlinelibrary.wiley.com/doi/10.1029/2012GL051000.

Francis, Matthew R. "When Carl Sagan Warned the World about Nuclear Winter." *Smithsonian Magazine*, November 15, 2017. www.smithsonianmag.com/science-nature/when-carl-sagan-warned-world-about-nuclear-winter-180967198/.

Frankel, Glenn. "Tourists Bring Home Tales of Nature's Random Horror." *Washington Post*, December 31, 2004. www.washingtonpost.com/wp-dyn/articles/A36930-2004Dec30.html?nav=rss_world/europe/westerneurope/sweden.

Freedman, Andrew. "Hawaii at Growing Risk of Hurricanes, Studies Show." *Climate Central*, May 8, 2013. www.climatecentral.org/news/hawaii-at-risk-for-more-hurricanes-studies-show-15966.

Freedman, Lawrence. "Ukraine and the Art of Limited War." *Survival* 56, No. 6 (2014): 7–38.

Frumhoff, Peter, Richard Heede, and Naomi Oreskes. "The Climate Responsibilities of Industrial Carbon Producers." *Climatic Change* 132, No. 2 (2015): 157–71.

Fuerth, Leon S., and Evan M. Faber. *Anticipatory Governance Practical Upgrades: Equipping the Executive Branch to Cope with Increasing Speed and Complexity of Major Challenges.* Fort McNair, DC: Institute for National Strategic Studies, 2012.

Fuller, Thomas. "Thailand Flooding Cripples Hard-Drive Suppliers." *New York Times*, November 5, 2011. www.nytimes.com/2011/11/07/business/global/07iht-floods07.html.

Gallaudet, Tim. *The US Navy's Task Force Climate Change & The Navy's Arctic Roadmap.* Washington, DC: Office of the Oceanographer of the Navy, 2011.

Gatehouse, Jonathon. "When science goes silent." *Maclean's* 126, No.18 (2013). www.macleans.ca/news/canada/when-science-goes-silent/.

Georges, Christian. "20th-Century Glacier Fluctuations in the Tropical Cordillera Blanca, Peru." *Arctic Antarctic and Alpine Research* 36, No. 1 (2004): 100–7.

Giles, Keir. "The Next Phase of Russian Information Warfare." NATO Strategic Communications Centre of Excellence, 2016. www.stratcomcoe.org/next-phase-russian-information-warfare-keir-giles.

Gillaspie, Timothy W. "Focused Logistics Wargame." *Air Force Journal of Logistics* 25, No. 2 (2001): 35.

Gislason, Sigudur R., Tue Hassenkam, Sorin Nedel, N. Bovet, Eydis S. Eiriksdottir, Helgi A. Alfredsson, Caroline P. Hem, Z. I. Balogh, K. Dideriksen, N. Oskarsson, B. Sigfusson, G. Larsen, and S. L. S. Stipp. "Characterization of Eyjafjallajökull Volcanic Ash Particles and a Protocol for Rapid Risk Assessment." *Proceedings of the National Academy of Sciences* 108, No. 18 (2011): 7307–12.

Gonzalez, Jennifer. "Abrupt Climate Change Scenarios and Security Foresight: Climate Change & Water in Peru." US Department of Energy Background Study, 2010.

Gorondi, Pablo. "Hungary's Orban: EU Leaders Don't Want to Stop the Migrants." Associated Press, February 29, 2016. www.samoaobserver.ws/en/29_02_2016/world/3091/Hungary's-Orban-EU-leaders-don't-want-to-stop-the-migrants.htm.

Green, Penny. "Disaster by Design: Corruption, Construction and Catastrophe." *British Journal of Criminology* 45, No. 4 (2005): 528–46.

Greenberg, Andy. "How an Entire Nation Became Russia's Test Lab for Cyberwar." *Wired*, June 20, 2017. www.wired.com/story/russian-hackers-attack-ukraine/.

Guardian. "Kosovo Cuts Pristina Water Supply over Alleged Isis Plot to Poison Reservoir." July 11, 2015. www.theguardian.com/world/2015/jul/11/kosovo-cuts-pristina-water-supply-over-alleged-isis-plot-to-poison-reservoir.

Hamblin, Jacob Darwin. "The Navy's 'Sophisticated' Pursuit of Science: Undersea Warfare, the Limits of Internationalism, and the Utility of Basic Research, 1945–1956." *Isis* 93, No. 1 (2002): 1–27.

Hameiri, Shahar, and Lee Jones. "The Politics and Governance of Non-traditional Security." *International Studies Quarterly* 1 (2012): 462–73.

Hammer, Joshua. "The Killers of Kiev: How Putin Created an Assassin's Metropolis." *GK*, March 6, 2018. www.gq.com/story/killers-of-kiev-putin-assassins.

Hancock, Graham. *Lords of Poverty: The Power, Prestige, and Corruption of the International Aid Business*. New York: Atlantic Monthly Press, 1992.

Hansen, James E. "Scientific Reticence and Sea Level Rise." *Environmental Research Letters* 2, No. 2 (2007): 024002.

Haraszti, Miklos. "Behind Viktor Orban's War on Refugees in Hungary." *New Perspectives Quarterly* 32, No. 4 (2015): 37–40.

Harmon, Michael. "The Responsible Actor as 'Tortured Soul': The Case of Horatio Hornblower." *Administration and Society* 21, No. 3 (1989): 283–312.

Harrop, Wayne, and Ashley Matteson. "Cyber Resilience: A Review of Critical National Infrastructure and Cyber Security Protection Measures Applied in the UK and USA." *Journal of Business Continuity and Emergency Planning* 7, No. 2 (2013): 149–62.

Hartmann, Betsy. "Converging on Disaster: Climate Security and the Malthusian Anticipatory Regime for Africa." *Geopolitics* 19, No. 4 (2014): 757–83.

"Population, Environment and Security: A New Trinity." *Environment and Urbanization* 10, No. 2 (1998): 113–28.

"Rethinking Climate Refugees and Climate Conflict: Rhetoric, Reality and the Politics of Policy Discourse." *Journal of International Development: The Journal of the Development Studies Association* 22, No. 2 (2010): 233–46.

Hawaii News Now. "Flash Floods Inundate East Honolulu." March 7, 2012. www.hawaiinewsnow.com/story/17097126/flash-floods-inundate-east-honolulu.

Hayashi, Masatsugu, and Larry Hughes. "The Policy Responses to the Fukushima Nuclear Accident and Their Effect on Japanese Energy Security." *Energy Policy* 59 (2013): 86–101.

Hayden, Michael. *Playing to the Edge: American Intelligence in the Age of Terror*. New York: Penguin, 2018.

Helmreich, Robert L. "Managing Human Error in Aviation." *Scientific American* 276, No. 5 (1997): 62–67.

Helston, Charlotte, and Andrew Farris. "Large Hydropower." Energy BC. http://energybc.ca/largehydro.html.

Hendrix, Cullen S., and Idean Salehyan. "Climate Change, Rainfall, and Social Conflict in Africa." *Journal of Peace Research* 49, No. 1 (2012): 35–50.

Herman, Gerald, and Winthrop Johnson. "The Sensitivity of the General Circulation to Arctic Sea Ice Boundaries: A Numerical Experiment." *Monthly Weather Review* 106 (1978): 1649–64.

Herring, Stephanie C., Martin P. Hoerling, James P. Kossin, Thomas C. Peterson, and Peter A. Stott. "Explaining Extreme Events of 2014 from a Climate Perspective." *Bulletin of the American Meteorological Society* 96, No. 12 (2015): S1–S172.

Herrmann, Victoria. "I Am an Arctic Researcher. Donald Trump Is Deleting My Citations." *Guardian*, March 28, 2017. www.theguardian.com/commentisfree/2017/mar/28/arctic-researcher-donald-trump-deleting-my-citations.

——— "Why Sustainability Is Important to Me: Victoria Herrmann '12." *The Goblet*, July 14, 2017. www.lehighgoblet.com/why-sustainability-is-important-to-me-victoria-herrmann/.

Hoffman, Lance J., Diana Burley, and Costis Toregas. "Thinking across Stovepipes: Using a Holistic Development Strategy to Build the Cybersecurity Workforce." *IEEE Security and Privacy* 1 (2011): 1–11.

Holmes, Philip, K., A. F. James, and Len S. Levy. "Is Low-Level Environmental Mercury Exposure of Concern to Human Health?" *Science of the Total Environment* 408, No. 2 (2009): 171–82.

Homer-Dixon, Thomas. "Environmental Scarcities and Violent Conflict." *International Security* 19, No. 1 (1994): 5–40.

——— "On the Threshold: Environmental Changes as Causes of Acute Conflict." *International Security* 16 (1991): 76–116.

Honolulu Star Advertiser. "Nearly 9 Million Gallons of Sewage Spilled in Windward Waters after Weekend Storms." May 23, 2018. www.staradvertiser.com/2018/02/22/breaking-news/sewage-brown-water-advisories-posted-for-windward-oahu-beaches/.

Hornbeck, Richard, and Pinar Keskin. "The Historically Evolving Impact of the Ogallala Aquifer: Agricultural Adaptation to Groundwater and Drought." *American Economic Journal: Applied Economics* 6, no. 1 (2014): 190–219.

Houser, Trevor, Solomon Hsiang, Robert Kopp, and Kate Larsen. *Economic Risks of Climate Change: An American Prospectus.* New York: Columbia University Press, 2015.

Hsu, Jeremy. "Bill Gates's Hidden Dreams of Geoengineering Revealed." *Popular Science*, January 27, 2010. www.popsci.com/science/article/2010-01/bill-gates-geoengineering-passion-revealed.

Hulbe, Christina. "Is Ice Sheet Collapse in West Antarctica Unstoppable?" *Science* 356, No. 6341 (2017): 910–11.

Hunter, David R. *Risk Perception and Risk Tolerance in Aircraft Pilots.* No. DOT/FAA/AM-02/17. Washington, DC: Federal Aviation Administration, Office of Aviation Medicine, 2002.

Ilcheva, Mariya. "Traveling along the Balkan Route One Year On." *Deutsche Welle*, August 26, 2016. www.dw.com/en/traveling-along-the-balkan-route-one-year-on/a-19506005.

Interfax-Ukraine. "Defense Ministry Says over 100,000 Military Volunteers Join Ukrainian Army." *Kyiv Post*, March 14, 2017. www.kyivpost.com/ukraine-politics/defense-ministry-says-100000-military-volunteers-join-ukrainian-army.html.

Ioris, Antonio A.R. "The Geography of Multiple Scarcities: Urban Development and Water Problems in Lima, Peru." *Geoforum* 43, No. 3 (2012): 612–22.

"Water Scarcity and the Exclusionary City: The Struggle for Water Justice in Lima, Peru." *Water International* 41, No. 1 (2016): 125–39.

Irfan, Umair. "'Climate Change' and 'Global Warming' Are Disappearing from Government Websites." *Vox*, January 11, 2018. www.vox.com/energy-and-envir onment/2017/11/9/16619120/trump-administration-removing-climate-change-epa-online-website.

Irvine, Peter J., Stefan Schafer, and Mark G. Lawrence. "Solar Radiation Management Could Be a Game Changer." *Nature Climate Change* 4, No. 10 (2014): 842.

Jabour, Julia. "China and the Rules of Engagement in Antarctica." *Maritime Issues*, April 25, 2017. www.maritimeissues.com/commentary/china-and-the-rules-of-engagement-in-antarctica.html.

Jayaram, Dhanasree. "The 'Three Geos': A New Approach to Study Environmental Security Scenarios in the Asia-Pacific." *International Affairs Forum* 5, No. 2 (2014): 106–17.

Jericho, Greg. "If You're Talking about Drought but Not Climate Change, You're Not Doing Your Job, PM." *Guardian*, August 29, 2018. www.theguardian.com/busi ness/grogonomics/2018/aug/30/if-youre-talking-about-drought-but-not-climate-change-youre-not-doing-your-job-pm.

Johnson, Eric J., and Amos Tversky. "Affect, Generalization, and the Perception of Risk." *Journal of Personality and Social Psychology* 45, No. 1 (1983): 20–31.

Johnston, Ian. "Officials in US Replace Science with Climate Change Denial Days after Donald Trump's Election Victory." *Independent*, January 3, 2017. www.indepen dent.co.uk/news/world/americas/climate-change-denial-us-officials-wisconsin-donald-trump-presidential-election-victory-global-a7506831.html.

Johnstone, Sarah, and Jeffrey Mazo. "Global Warming and the Arab Spring." *Survival: Global Politics and Strategy* 53, No. 2 (2011): 11–17.

Kahn, David. "The Intelligence Failure of Pearl Harbor." *Foreign Affairs* 70, No. 5 (1991): 138–52.

Kahneman, Daniel, and Amos Tversky. "On the Psychology of Prediction." *Psychological Review* 80, No. 4 (1973): 237–51.

Kam, Ephraim. *Surprise Attack: The Victim's Perspective*. Cambridge, MA: Harvard University Press, 1988.

Kaplan, Fred. *The Wizards of Armageddon*. Palo Alto, CA: Stanford University Press, 1991.

Keith, David W. "Geoengineering the Climate: History and Prospect." *Annual Review of Energy and the Environment* 25, No. 1 (2000): 245–84.

"Photophoretic Levitation of Engineered Aerosols for Geoengineering." *Proceedings of the National Academy of Sciences* 107, No. 38 (2010): 16428–31.

Kelman, Ilan. "Acting on Disaster Diplomacy." *Journal of International Affairs* 59, No. 2 (2006): 215–40.

"Hybrid Disasters or Usual Disasters?" *Disaster and Social Crisis Research Network Electronic Newsletter*, No. 41 (2010): 9.

Kennedy, Andrew B., Joannes J. Westerink, Jane M. Smith, Mark E. Hope, Michael Hartman, Alexandros A. Taflanidis, Seizo Tanaka, Hans Westerink, Kwok Fai Cheung, Tom Smith, Madeleine M. Hamann, Masashi Minamide, Aina Ota, and

Clint Dawson. "Tropical Cyclone Inundation Potential on the Hawaiian Islands of Oahu and Kauai." *Ocean Modelling* 52 (2012): 54–68.

Kennett, James P., Kevin G. Cannariato, Ingrid L. Hendy, and Richard J. Behl. "Methane Hydrates in Quaternary Climate Change: The Clathrate Gun Hypothesis." American Geophysical Union, 2003.

Kim, Karl, Pradip Pant, and Eric Yamashita. "Evacuation Planning for Plausible Worst Case Inundation Scenarios in Honolulu, Hawaii." *Journal of Emergency Management* 13, No. 2 (2015): 93–108.

Kimmel, Carole A. "Quantitative Approaches to Human Risk Assessment for Noncancer Health Effects." *Neurotoxicology* 11, No. 2 (1990): 189–98.

Klare, Michael. *Resource Wars: The New Landscape of Global Conflict*. New York: Henry Holt, 2002.

Klein, Roger. "Bradford, Ont. Declares State of Emergency over Flooded Farms." *CTV News*, June 12, 2013. https://barrie.ctvnews.ca/bradford-ont-declares-state-of-emergency-over-flooded-farms-1.1322798.

Kohnen, David. "The US Navy Won the Battle of Jutland." *Naval War College Review* 69, No. 4 (2016): 123–45.

Kolmes, Steven. "Climate Change: A Disinformation Campaign." *Environment: Science and Policy for Sustainable Development* 53, No. 4 (2011): 33–37.

Kondratyev, Kirill Ya., Alexei A. Grigoryev, and Costas A. Varotsos. *Environmental Disasters: Anthropogenic and Natural*. Chichester, UK: Springer-Praxis, 2002.

Konno, Yoshihiro, Tetsuya Fujii, Akihiko Sato, Koya Akamine, Motoyoshi Naiki, Yoshihiro Masuda, Koji Yamamoto, and Jiro Nagao. "Key Findings of the World's First Offshore Methane Hydrate Production Test off the Coast of Japan: Toward Future Commercial Production." *Energy and Fuels* 31, No. 3 (2017): 2607–16.

Konrad, Hannes, Andrew Shepherd, Lin Gilbert, Anna E. Hogg, Malcolm McMillan, Alan Muir, and Thomas Slater. "Net Retreat of Antarctic Glacier Grounding Lines." *Nature Geoscience* 11 (2018): 258–62.

Kousky, Carolyn. "Informing Climate Adaptation: A Review of the Economic Costs of Natural Disasters." *Energy Economics* 46 (2014): 576–92.

Kraft, Claudia, Wolf von Tumpling, and Dieter W. Zachmann. "The Effects of Mining in Northern Romania on the Heavy Metal Distribution in Sediments of the Rivers Szamos and Tisza (Hungary)." *CLEAN – Soil, Air, Water* 34, No. 3 (2006): 257–64.

Krause, Keith, and Michael C. Williams. *Critical Security Studies: Concepts and Strategies*. New York: Routledge, 2002.

Krepinevich, Andrew F., and Barry D. Watts. *The Last Warrior: Andrew Marshall and the Shaping of Modern American Defense Strategy*. New York: Basic Books, 2015.

Kroenig, Matthew. "Facing Reality: Getting NATO Ready for a New Cold War." *Survival* 57, No. 1 (2015): 49–70.

Lahneman, William J. "Outsourcing the IC's Stovepipes?" *International Journal of Intelligence and Counterintelligence* 16, No. 4 (2003): 573–93.

Larson, Christina. "China's Looming Conflict between Energy and Water." *Yale Environment 360*, April 10, 2012. http://e360.yale.edu/feature/chinas_looming_conflict_between_energy_and_water/2522/.

Larson, Dana, Cheryl Lee, Stacy Tellinghuisen, and Arturo Keller. "California's Energy-Water Nexus: Water Use in Electricity Generation." Southwest Water, 2007. www.swhydro.arizona.edu/archive/V6_N5/feature3.pdf.

Laverty, Gene. "Oil, Gas May Soar as Storm Shuts U.S. Gulf Production." *Bloomberg*, August 28, 2005.

Lazaroff, Cynthia. "Dawn of a New Armageddon." *Bulletin of the Atomic Scientists*, August 6, 2018. https://thebulletin.org/2018/08/dawn-of-a-new-armageddon/.

Lazer, David M. J., Matthew A. Baum, Yochai Benkler, Adam J. Berinsky, Kelly M. Greenhill, Filippo Menczer, Miriam J. Metzger, Brendan Nyhan, Gordon Pennycook, David Rothschild, Michael Schudson, Steven A. Sloman, Cass R. Sunstein, Emily A. Thorson, Duncan J. Watts, and Jonathan L. Zittrain. "The Science of Fake News." *Science* 359, No. 6380 (2018): 1094–96.

Leiserowitz, Anthony A., Edward W. Maibach, Connie Roser-Renouf, Nicholas Smith, and Erica Dawson. "Climategate, Public Opinion, and the Loss of Trust." *American Behavioral Scientist* 57, No. 6 (2013): 818–37.

Lenton, Timothy. "Arctic Climate Tipping Points." *Ambio* 41, No. 1 (2012): 10–22.

"Early Warning of Climate Tipping Points." *Nature Climate Change* 1, No. 4 (2011): 201–9.

Lenton, Timothy, and Juan-Carlos Ciscar. "Integrating Tipping Points into Climate Impact Assessments." *Climatic Change* 117, No. 3 (2013): 585–97.

Lenton, Timothy, Hermann Held, Elmar Kriegler, Jim W. Hall, Wolfgang Lucht, Stefan Rahmstorf, and Hans Joachim Schellnhuber. "Tipping Elements in the Earth's Climate System." *Proceedings of the National Academy of Sciences* 105, No. 6 (2008): 1786–93.

Letukas, Lynn. "Indian Ocean Tsunami (2004)." In *Encyclopedia of Disaster Relief*, edited by K. Bradley Penuel and Matt Statler. Thousand Oaks, CA: Sage, 2011.

Leveson, Nancy, Nicolas Dulac, Karen Marais, and John Carroll. "Moving beyond Normal Accidents and High Reliability Organizations: A Systems Approach to Safety in Complex Systems." *Organization Studies* 30, No. 2–3 (2009): 227–49.

Li, Xiao Lei, Huan Li, Min Gang Cheng, and Zhong Qi Fan. "Framework for Emergency Decision Exercise System of Urban Crisis Based on Wargaming." *Applied Mechanics and Materials* 373 (2013): 1139–43.

Lin, Ning, Kerry A. Emanuel, J. A. Smith, and E. Vanmarcke. "Risk Assessment of Hurricane Storm Surge for New York City." *Journal of Geophysical Research: Atmospheres* 115, No. D18 (2010): D013630.

Lippert, Tyler. "NATO, Climate Change, and International Security: A Risk Governance Approach." PhD diss., RAND, 2016.

Lipscy, Phillip Y., Kenji E. Kushida, and Trevor Incerti. "The Fukushima Disaster and Japan's Nuclear Plant Vulnerability in Comparative Perspective." *Environmental Science and Technology* 47, No. 12 (2013): 6082–88.

Liu, Jiping, Judith A. Curry, Huijun Wang, Mirong Song, and Radley M. Horton. "Impact of Declining Arctic Sea Ice on Winter Snowfall." *Proceedings of the National Academy of Sciences* 109 (2012).

Livi Bacci, Massimo. "Does Europe Need Mass Immigration?" *Journal of Economic Geography* 18, No. 4 (2017): 695–703.

Logel, Jon Scott. "100 Years of Learning: The Battle of Jutland at the Naval War College." US Naval War College. www.usnwcarchive.org/exhibits/show/nwc-bat tle-jutland/war-gaming-at-the-naval-war-co.

Looa, Yen Yi, Lawal Billab, and Ajit Singha. "Effect of Climate Change on Seasonal Monsoon in Asia and Its Impact on the Variability of Monsoon Rainfall in Southeast Asia." *Geoscience Frontiers* 6, No. 6 (2015): 817–23.

Lukacs, Martin. "Trump Presidency 'Opens Door' to Planet-Hacking Geoengineer Experiments." *Guardian*, March 27, 2017. www.theguardian.com/environment/ true-north/2017/mar/27/trump-presidency-opens-door-to-planet-hacking-geoengi neer-experiments.

Malaska, Pentti, and Ilkka Virtanen. "Theory of Futuribles." *Futura* 24 (2005): 2–3.

Mann, Michael E. "FiveThirtyEight: The Number of Things Nate Silver Gets Wrong about Climate Change." *Huffington Post*, September 24, 2012. www.huffington post.com/michael-e-mann/nate-silver-climate-change_b_1909482.html.

——— *The Hockey Stick and the Climate Wars: Dispatches from the Front Lines.* New York: Columbia University Press, 2013.

Martelli, Antonio. *Models of Scenario Building and Planning: Facing Uncertainty and Complexity.* New York: Palgrave Macmillan, 2014.

Martin, Adrian, Andy Blowers, and Jan Boersema. "Is Environmental Scarcity a Cause of Civil Wars?" *Environmental Sciences* 3, No. 1 (2006): 1–4.

Masuda, Yoshihiro, Koji Yamamoto, Shimada Tadaaki, Takao Ebinuma, and Sadao Nagakubo. "Japan's Methane Hydrate R&D Program Progresses to Phase 2." *Fire in the Ice* 9, No. 4 (2009). www.netl.doe.gov/File%20Library/Research/Oil-Gas/ methane%20hydrates/MHNewsFall09.pdf.

Matejova, Miriam, Stefan Parker, and Peter Dauvergne. "The Politics of Repressing Environmentalists as Agents of Foreign Influence." *Australian Journal of International Affairs* 72, No. 2 (2018): 1–18.

Matheny, Keith. "Canadian Trash Again Filling Michigan Landfills." *Detroit Free Press*, February 19, 2018. www.freep.com/story/news/local/michigan/2018/02/ 19/canadian-garbage-michigan-landfills-solid-waste/337837002/.

Mazzocchi, Mario, Francesca Hansstein, and Maddalena Ragona. "The 2010 Volcanic Ash Cloud and Its Financial Impact on the European Airline Industry." *CESifo Forum* 11, No. 2 (2010): 92–100.

McEntire, David A. "Triggering Agents, Vulnerabilities and Disaster Reduction: Towards a Holistic Paradigm." *Disaster Prevention and Management: An International Journal* 10, No. 3 (2001): 189–96.

McFate, Montgomery, and Andrea V. Jackson. *The Object beyond War: Counterinsurgency and the Four Tools of Political Competition.* Alexandria, VA: Institute for Defense Analysis, 2006.

McGurty, Eileen Maura. "From NIMBY to Civil Rights: The Origins of the Environmental Justice Movement." Environmental History 2, No. 3 (1997): 301–23.

McNally, Tony, Massimo Bonavita, and Jean-Noel Thepaut, "The Role of Satellite Data in the Forecasting of Hurricane Sandy." *Monthly Weather Review* 142, No. 2 (2014): 634–46.

Meadows, Donella H., Dennis L. Meadows, Jorgen Randers, and William W. Behrens. *The Limits to Growth.* New York: Potomac Associates, 1972.

Mears, David K., and Sarah McKearnan. "Rivers and Resilience: Lessons Learned from Tropical Storm Irene." *Vermont Journal of Environmental Law* 14 (2012): 177–210.

Mendonça, Sandro Miguel Pina e Cunha, Jari Kaivo-Oja, and Frank Ruff. "Wild Cards, Weak Signals and Organisational Improvisation." *Futures* 36, No. 2 (2004): 201–18.

Mercer, Jessica, Ilan Kelman, Lorin Taranis, and Sandie Suchet-Pearson. "Framework for Integrating Indigenous and Scientific Knowledge for Disaster Risk Reduction." *Disasters* 34, No. 1 (2010): 214–39.

Meyer, Robert J. "Why We Under-prepare for Hazards." In *On Risk and Disaster: Lessons from Hurricane Katrina*, edited by Ronald J. Daniels, Donald F. Kettl, and Howard Kunreuther, 153–74. Philadelphia: University of Pennsylvania Press, 2006.

Mienert, Jurgen, Maarten Vanneste, Stefan Bunz, Karin Andreassen, Haflidi Haflidason, and Hans Petter Sejrup. "Ocean Warming and Gas Hydrate Stability on the Mid-Norwegian Margin at the Storegga Slide." *Marine and Petroleum Geology* 22, No. 1–2 (2005): 233–44.

Mietzner, Dana, and Guido Reger. "Advantages and Disadvantages of Scenario Approaches for Strategic Foresight." *International Journal of Technology Intelligence and Planning* 1, No. 2 (2005): 220–39.

Miller, Gifford H., Aslaug Geirsdottir, Yafang Zhong, Darren J. Larsen, Bette L. Otto-Bliesner, Marika M. Holland, David A. Bailey, Kurt A. Refsnider, Scott J. Lehman, John R. Southon, Chance Anderson, Helgi Bjornsson, and Thorvaldur Thordarson. "Abrupt Onset of the Little Ice Age Triggered by Volcanism and Sustained by Sea-Ice/Ocean Feedbacks." *Geophysical Research Letters* 39, No. 2 (2012): L02708.

Millett, Stephen M. "The Future of Scenarios: Challenges and Opportunities." *Strategy and Leadership* 31, No. 2 (2003): 16–24.

Minnis, Patrick, Edwin F. Harrison, Larry L. Stowe, G. G. Gibson, Fred M. Denn, D. R. Doelling, and W. L. Smith. "Radiative Climate Forcing by the Mount Pinatubo Eruption." *Science* 259, No. 5100 (1993): 1411–15.

Minoura, Koji, Fumihiko Imamura, D. Sugawara, Y. Kono, and T. Iwashita. "The 869 Jogan Tsunami Deposit and Recurrence Interval of Large Scale Tsunami on the Pacific Coast of Northeastern Japan." *Journal of Natural Disaster Science* 23 (2011): 83–88.

Minoura, Koji, and S. Nakaya. "Traces of Tsunami Preserved in the Inter-Tidal Lacustrine and Marsh Deposits: Some Example from Northeast Japan." *Journal of Geology* 99, No. 2 (1991): 265–87.

Minville, Marie, François Brissette, Stephane Krau, and Robert Leconte. "Adaptation to Climate Change in the Management of a Canadian Water-Resources System Exploited for Hydropower." *Water Resources Management* 23, No. 14 (2009): 2965–86.

Mitchell, Shannon K. "Death, Disability, Displaced Persons and Development: The Case of Landmines in Bosnia and Herzegovina." *World Development* 32, No. 12 (2004): 2105–20.

Moore, James S. *The US Military's Reliance on Bottled Water during Military Operations*. Norfolk, VA: National Defense University, 2011.

Mori, Nobuhito, Tomoyuki Takahashi, and 2011 Tohoku Earthquake Tsunami Joint Survey Group. "Nationwide Post Event Survey and Analysis of the 2011 Tohoku Earthquake Tsunami." *Coastal Engineering Journal* 54, No. 1 (2012): 1250001.

Mosher, David E., Beth E. Lachman, Michael D. Greenberg, Tiffany Nichols, Brian Rosen, and Henry H. Willis. *Green Warriors: Environmental Considerations for Army Contingency Operations from Planning through Post-conflict.* Santa Monica, CA: RAND Corporation, 2008.

Munson, Robert. "Do We Want to 'Kill People and Break Things' in Africa?" *ASPJ Africa and Francophonie*, 4th Quarter (2009). www.airuniversity.af.mil/Portals/ 10/ASPJ_French/journals_E/Volume-01_Issue-1/Munson_e.pdf.

Munz, Philip, Ioan Hudea, Joe Imad, and Robert J. Smith. "When Zombies Attack! Mathematical Modelling of an Outbreak of Zombie Infection." *Infectious Disease Modelling Research Progress* 4 (2009): 133–50.

Murakami, Hiroyuki, Gabriel A. Vecchi, Thomas L. Delworth, Karen Paffendorf, Liwei Jia, Richard Gudgel, and Fanrong Zeng. "Investigating the Influence of Anthropogenic Forcing and Natural Variability on the 2014 Hawaiian Hurricane Season." *Bulletin of the American Meteorological Society* 96, No. 12 (2015): S115–19.

Murakami, Hiroyuki, Gabriel A. Vecchi, Thomas L. Delworth, Andrew T. Wittenberg, Seth Underwood, Richard Gudgel, Xiaosong Yang, Liwei Jia, Fanrong Zeng, Karen Paffendorf, and Wei Zhang. "Dominant Role of Subtropical Pacific Warming in Extreme Eastern Pacific Hurricane Seasons: 2015 and the Future." *Journal of Climate* 30, No. 1 (2017): 243–64.

Muur, Kristiina, Holger Molder, Vladimir Sazonov, and Pille Pruulmann-Vengerfeldt. "Russian Information Operations against the Ukrainian State and Defence Forces: April-December 2014 in Online News." *Journal on Baltic Security* 2, No. 1 (2016): 28–71.

Myers, Candice A., Tim Slack, and Joachim Singelmann. "Social Vulnerability and Migration in the Wake of Disaster: The Case of Hurricanes Katrina and Rita." *Population and Environment* 29, No. 6 (2008): 271–91.

Nagarajan, Chitra, Benjamin Pohl, Lukas Ruttinger, Florence Sylvestre, Janani Vivekananda, Martin Wall, and Susanne Wolfmaier. *Climate-Fragility Profile: Lake Chad Basin.* Berlin: Adelphi Research, 2018.

Nagl, John A. *Learning to Eat Soup with a Knife: Counterinsurgency Lessons from Malaya and Vietnam.* Chicago: University of Chicago Press, 2009.

Nagl, John A., James F. Amos, Sarah Sewall, and David H. Petraeus. *The US Army/ Marine Corps Counterinsurgency Field Manual.* Chicago: University of Chicago Press, 2008.

National. "Pakistan Flood Victims Face Food Shortages." August 4, 2010. www.thena tional.ae/world/asia/pakistan-flood-victims-face-food-shortages-1.535351.

National Energy Board. "2015 Electricity Exports and Imports Summary." www.neb-one.gc.ca/nrg/sttstc/lctrct/stt/lctrctysmmr/2015/smmry2015-eng.html.

National Weather Service. "The Great New England Hurricane of 1938." www.weather .gov/okx/1938HurricaneHome.

News.LK. "'Tempest Express – 24' Concludes." www.news.lk/news/sri-lanka/item/ 297-tempest-express-24-concludes.

Nguyen, Dung T., Yilin Shen, and My T. Thai. "Detecting Critical Nodes in Interdependent Power Networks for Vulnerability Assessment." *IEEE Transactions on Smart Grid* 4, No. 1 (2013): 151–59.

Nichols, Tom. *The Death of Expertise: The Campaign against Established Knowledge and Why It Matters.* New York: Oxford University Press, 2017.

Noegerath, Johannis, Robert J. Geller, and Viacheslav K. Gusiakov. "Fukushima: The Myth of Safety, the Reality of Geoscience." *Bulletin of the Atomic Scientists* 67, No. 5 (2011): 37–46.

Office of the Director of National Intelligence. "National Intelligence Council – Global Trends." www.dni.gov/index.php/who-we-are/organizations/nic/nic-related-menus/nic-related-content/global-trends.

Ogilvy, Jay. "Scenario Planning, Art or Science?" *World Futures* 61, No. 5 (2005): 331–46.

Olive, Andrea. *Canadian Environment in Political Context.* Toronto: University of Toronto Press, 2016.

Olsen, Lise. "Record Reservoir Flood Predictions Kept Secret before Hurricane Harvey Hit Houston." *Houston Chronicle*, February 22, 2018. www.chron.com/news/houston-weather/hurricaneharvey/article/Record-reservoir-flood-predictions-kept-secret-12633506.php.

Oppenheimer, Clive. "Climatic, Environmental and Human Consequences of the Largest Known Historic Eruption: Tambora Volcano (Indonesia) 1815." *Progress in Physical Geography* 27, No. 2 (2003): 230–59.

Oreskes, Naomi. *Merchants of Doubt: How a Handful of Scientists Have Obscured the Truth on Issues from Tobacco Smoke to Climate Change.* London: Bloomsbury Press, 2015.

Oreskes, Naomi, and Erik M. Conway. "Defeating the Merchants of Doubt." *Nature* 465, No. 7299 (2010): 686–87.

Ostrom, Lee T., and Cheryl A. Wilhemsen. *Risk Assessment: Tools, Techniques and Their Application.* Hoboken, NJ: John Wiley, 2012.

Pacific Disaster Center. "Modeling Dam Failure Scenarios for the Hawaiian Islands." www.pdc.org/about/projects/hawaii-dam-failure-modeling/.

Paehlke, Robert. "Environmentalism in One Country: Canadian Environmental Policy in an Era of Globalization." *Policy Studies Journal* 28, No. 1 (2000): 160–75.

Paris, Roland. "Human Security: Paradigm Shift or Hot Air?" *International Security* 26, No. 2 (2001): 87–102.

Parker, Charles F., Eric K. Stern, Eric Paglia, and Christer Brown. "Preventable Catastrophe? The Hurricane Katrina Disaster Revisited." *Journal of Contingencies and Crisis Management* 17, No. 4 (2009): 206–20.

Paskal, Cleo. *Global Warring: How Environmental, Economic, and Political Crises Will Redraw the World Map.* New York: St. Martin's Press, 2010.

―――. *The Vulnerability of Energy Infrastructure to Environmental Change.* London: Chatham House, 2009.

PBS. "The Father of Soil Conservation." www.pbs.org/wgbh/americanexperience/features/surviving-the-dust-bowl-biography-hugh-hammond-bennett/.

Perla, Peter P. *The Art of Wargaming: A Guide for Professionals and Hobbyists.* Annapolis, MD: Naval Institute Press, 1990.

Perla, Peter P., and E. D. McGrady. "Why Wargaming Works." *Naval War College Review* 64, No. 3 (2011): 1–20.

Perovich, Donald K., Bonnie Light, Hajo Eicken, Kathleen F. Jones, Kay Runciman, and Son V. Nghiem. "Increasing Solar Heating of the Arctic Ocean and Adjacent Seas, 1979–2005: Attribution and Role in the Ice-Albedo Feedback." *Geophysical Research Letters* 34, No. 19 (2007): L19505.

Peruvian Private Investment Promotion Agency. "Electricity Sector Data." 2017. www.investinperu.pe/modulos/JER/PlantillaStandard.aspx?are=1&prf=0&jer=59 40&sec=50.

Peruvian Times. "Aird Lima among Most Wasteful Cities for Water Consumption." September 21, 2010. www.peruviantimes.com/21/arid-lima-among-most-waste ful-cities-for-water-consumption/9195/.

Peterson, Jon. *Playing at the World: A History of Simulating Wars, People and Fantastic Adventures, from Chess to Role-Playing Games.* San Diego, CA: Unreason Press, 2012.

Peterson, Nolan. "In Ukraine, Russia Weaponizes Fake News to Fight a Real War." *Daily Signal,* March 30, 2017. www.dailysignal.com/2017/03/30/in-ukraine-rus sia-weaponizes-fake-news-to-fight-a-real-war/.

Petts, Judith, ed. *Handbook of Environmental Impact Assessment: Vol. 2. Impact and Limitations.* London: John Wiley, 2009.

Pidd, Helen. "India Blackouts Leave 700 Million without Power." *Guardian,* July 31, 2012. www.theguardian.com/world/2012/jul/31/india-blackout-electricity-power-cuts.

Pidgeon, Nick, Roger E. Kasperson, and Paul Slovic, eds. *The Social Amplification of Risk.* Cambridge: Cambridge University Press, 2003.

Planetary Security Initiative. "The Hague Declaration on Planetary Security." www .planetarysecurityinitiative.org/declaration.

Powers, Thomas. *Heisenberg's War: The Secret History of the German Bomb.* New York: Alfred A. Knopf, 1993.

Price-Smith, Andrew. *Contagion and Chaos: Disease, Ecology, and National Security in the Era of Globalization.* Cambridge, MA: MIT Press, 2009.

Racoviteanu, Adina E., Yves Arnaud, Mark W. Williams, and Julio Ordonez. "Decadal Changes in Glacier Parameters in the Cordillera Blanca, Peru, Derived from Remote Sensing." *Journal of Glaciology* 54, No. 186 (2008): 499–510.

Ratcliffe, John. "Scenario Building: A Suitable Method for Strategic Property Planning?" *Property Management* 18, No. 2 (2000): 127–44.

Ray, Rebecca, K., P. Gallagher, Andres Lopez, and Cynthia Sanborn. "China in Latin America: Lessons for South-South Cooperation and Sustainable Development." In *China and Sustainable Development in Latin America,* edited by Rebecca Ray, K. P. Gallagher, Andres Lopez, and Cynthia Sanborn. New York: Anthem Press, 2015.

Read, Mark R. "Planning through Complexity: Employing Scenario Analysis to Facilitate Climate Change Adaptation in Fragile States." *Climate Change and Fragile States: Rethinking Adaptation* 16 (2012): 110–14.

Reed, Christina. "Floods Fail in War, Win as Weapon against Sea Level Rise." *Earth and Space Science News,* June 29, 2015. https://eos.org/articles/floods-fail-in-war-win-as-weapon-against-sea-level-rise.

Research Center for Disaster Reduction Systems. "Tsunamis in Indonesia." www.drs
.dpri.kyoto-u.ac.jp/eqtap/report/indonesia/tsunamis_in_indonesia/tsunamis_in_in
donesia.htm.

Rice, Doyle. "Remembering the Catastrophic 2005 Hurricane Season." *USA Today*,
August 24, 2015. www.usatoday.com/story/weather/2015/08/24/2005-hurricane-
season-katrina/32269245/.

Robinson, David. "Energy Security Revisited." *Oxford Energy Forum*, No. 100 (2015):
39–42.

Rossel, Pierre. "Early Detection, Warnings, Weak Signals and Seeds of Change: A
Turbulent Domain of Futures Studies." *Futures* 44, No. 3 (2012): 229–39.

Rouse, Richard, and Steve Illustrator-Ogden. *Game Design Theory and Practice*.
Sudbury, MA: Wordware, 2000.

Ruhle, Michael, and Julijus Grubliauskas. "Energy as a Tool of Hybrid Warfare." NATO
Research Paper, No. 113 (2015).

Salas, Eduardo, Jennifer E. Fowlkes, Renee J. Stout, Dana M. Milanovich, and Carolyn
Prince. "Does CRM Training Improve Teamwork Skills in the Cockpit? Two
Evaluation Studies." *Human Factors* 41, No. 2 (1999): 326–43.

Salehyana, Idean, and Cullen S. Hendrix. "Climate Shocks and Political Violence."
Global Environmental Change 28 (2014): 239–50.

Sanders, Linley. "'Geostorm' Hurricane Conspiracy Theory Claims the U.S.
Government Controls Weather." *Newsweek*, October 24, 2017. www.news
week.com/government-not-controlling-hurricanes-despite-conspiracy-theory-
692252.

Scheffer, Marten, Stephen R. Carpenter, Timothy M. Lenton, Jordi Bascompte, William
Brock, Vasilis Dakos, Johan Van de Koppel, Ingrid A. van de Leemput, Simon A.
Levin, Egbert H. van Nes, Mercedes Pascual, and John Vandermeer. "Anticipating
Critical Transitions." Science 338, No. 6105 (2012): 344–48.

Schiermeier, Quirin. "Dumping Iron at Sea Does Sink Carbon." *Nature*, July 18, 2012.
www.nature.com/news/dumping-iron-at-sea-does-sink-carbon-1.11028.

Schmidt, Charles W. "Unfair Trade e-Waste in Africa." *Environmental Health
Perspectives* 114, No. 4 (2006): A232–35.

Schneider, Mark, and Roscoe Bartlett. *The Emerging EMP Threat to the United States*.
Fairfax, VA: National Institute Press, 2007.

Schoemaker, Paul J. H. "Forecasting and Scenario Planning: The Challenges of
Uncertainty and Complexity." In *Blackwell Handbook of Judgment and Decision
Making*, edited by Derek J. Koehler and Nigel Harvey, 274–96. Oxford: Blackwell,
2004.

Schoemaker, Paul J. H., George S. Day, and Scott A. Snyder. "Integrating
Organizational Networks, Weak Signals, Strategic Radars and Scenario
Planning." *Technological Forecasting and Social Change* 80, No. 4 (2013): 815–
24.

Schultz, Teri. "Russia Is Hacking and Harassing NATO Soldiers, Report Says." *DW*,
October 6, 2017. www.dw.com/en/russia-is-hacking-and-harassing-nato-soldiers-
report-says/a-40827197.

Schuur, Edward, A. D. McGuire, Christina Schadel, Guido Grosse, J. W. Harden, D. J.
Hayes, Gustaf Hugelius, Charles D. Koven, P. Kuhry, David Lawrence, Sue Natali,
David Olefeldt, Vladimir E. Romanovsky, Kevin Schaefer, M. R. Turetsky, Claire

C. Treat, and Jorien E. Vonk. "Climate Change and the Permafrost Carbon Feedback." *Nature* 520, No. 7546 (2015): 171–79.

Schwartz, Peter, and Tony Randall. *An Abrupt Climate Change Scenario and Its Implications for United States National Security.* Pasadena, CA: California Institute of Technology, Pasadena Jet Propulsion Lab, 2003.

Science Daily. "Climate Change Poses Serious Threat to U.S. National Security." Press release, April 17, 2007. www.sciencedaily.com/releases/2007/04/070417092232.htm.

Scott, James. *Seeing Like a State.* New Haven, CT: Yale University Press, 2002.

Scott, Michon. "Heavy Rains and Dry Lands Don't Mix: Reflections on the 2010 Pakistan Flood." Earth Observatory, NASA, April 6, 2011. https://earthobservatory.nasa.gov/Features/PakistanFloods.

Seddon, Alistair W. R., Marc Macias-Fauria, Peter R. Long, David Benz, and Kathy J. Willis. "Sensitivity of Global Terrestrial Ecosystems to Climate Variability." *Nature* 531, No. 7593 (2016): 229–32.

Shackelford, Scott. "Estonia Three Years Later: A Progress Report on Combating Cyber Attacks." Journal of Internet Law 13, No. 8 (2010): 22–29.

Shah, Abhishek. "List of World's Largest Hydroelectricity Plants and Countries – China Leading in Building Hydroelectric Stations." Green World Investor, March 29, 2011. www.greenworldinvestor.com/2011/03/29/list-of-worlds-largest-hydroelectricity-plants-and-countries-china-leading-in-building-hydroelectric-stations/

Shakarian, Paulo. "The 2008 Russian Cyber Campaign against Georgia." *Military Review* 91, No. 6 (2011): 63–68.

Shakhova, Natalia, Igor Semiletov, Anatoly Salyuk, and Denis Kosmach, "Anomalies of Methane in the Atmosphere over the East Siberian Shelf: Is There Any Sign of Methane Leakage from Shallow Shelf Hydrates?" *Geophysical Research Abstracts* 10 (2008): EGU2008-A-01526.

Shakhova, Natalia, Igor Semiletov, Anatoly Salyuk, Vladimir Yusupov, Denis Kosmach, and Orjan Gustafsson. "Extensive Methane Venting to the Atmosphere from Sediments of the East Siberian Arctic Shelf." *Science* 327, No. 5970 (2010): 1246–50.

Sharifi, Arash, Ali Pourmand, Elizabeth Canuel, Erin Ferer-Tyler, Larry C. Peterson, Bernhard Aichner, Sarah J. Feakins, Touraj Daryaee, Morteza Djamali, Abdolmajid Naderi Beni, Hamid Lahijani, and Peter Schwart. "Abrupt Climate Variability since the Last Deglaciation Based on a High-Resolution, Multi-proxy Peat Record from NW Iran: The Hand That Rocked the Cradle of Civilization?" *Quaternary Science Reviews* 123 (2015): 215–30.

Shirreff, Richard. *War with Russia.* London: Coronet, 2017.

Shrader-Frechette, Kristin. "Comparative Risk Assessment and the Naturalistic Fallacy." *Trends in Ecology and Evolution* 10, No. 1 (1995): 50

"The Conceptual Risks of Risk Assessment." *IEEE Technology and Society Magazine* 5, No. 2 (1986): 4–11.

"Methodological Rules for Four Classes of Scientific Uncertainty." In *Scientific Uncertainty and Environmental Problem Solving*, edited by John Lemons, 12–39. Cambridge, MA: Blackwell Scientific, 1996.

Nuclear Power and Public Policy: The Social and Ethical Problems of Fission Technology. Dordrecht, Netherlands: D. Reidel, 1980.

Risk Analysis and Scientific Method: Methodological and Ethical Problems with Evaluating Societal Hazards. Dordrecht, Netherlands: Springer Science and Business Media, 2012.

Silver, Nate. *The Signal and the Noise: Why So Many Predictions Fail – but Some Don't.* New York: Penguin Press, 2012.

Simon, Herbert A. "Prediction and Prescription in Systems Modeling." *Operations Research* 38, No. 1 (1990): 7–14.

"Theories of Bounded Rationality." *Decision and Organization* 1, No. 1 (1972): 161–76.

Singer, P. W. "Stuxnet and Its Hidden Lessons on the Ethics of Cyberweapons." *Case Western Reserve Journal of International Law* 47 (2015): 79–86.

Slovic, Paul, and Ellen Peters. "Risk Perception and Affect." *Current Directions in Psychological Science* 15, No. 6 (2006): 322–25.

Smith, John N., Robin M. Brown, William J. Williams, Marie Robert, Richard Nelson, and S. Bradley Moran. "Arrival of the Fukushima Radioactivity Plume in North American Continental Waters." *Proceedings of the National Academy of Sciences* 112, No. 5 (2015): 1310–15.

Smith, Perry M., and Daniel M. Gerstein. *Assignment: Pentagon: How to Excel in a Bureaucracy.* Washington, DC: Potomac Books, 2007.

Smith, Roger. "The Long History of Gaming in Military Training." *Simulation and Gaming* 41, No. 1 (2010): 6–19.

Soldatov, Andrei, and Irina Borogan. *Red Web: The Struggle between Russia's Digital Dictators and the New Online Revolutionaries.* New York: Public Affairs, 2015.

Solomon, Susan, Dahe Qin, Martin Manning, Zhenlin Chen, Melinda Marquis, K. B. Averyt, Melinda Tignor, and H. L. Miller, eds. *IPCC, 2007: Climate Change 2007: The Physical Science Basis. Contribution of Working Group I to the Fourth Assessment Report of the Intergovernmental Panel on Climate Change.* Cambridge: Cambridge University Press, 2007.

Spence, Alexa, Wouter Poortinga, and Nick Pidgeon. "The Psychological Distance of Climate Change." *Risk Analysis: An International Journal* 32, No. 6 (2012): 957–72.

Srinivas, Hari, and Yuko Nakagawa. "Environmental Implications for Disaster Preparedness." *Journal of Environmental Management* 89 (2008): 4–13.

Stack, Liam. "Food Crisis: A Daily Quest for Bread in Cairo." *Christian Science Monitor*, June 6, 2008. www.csmonitor.com/World/Middle-East/2008/0606/p04s05-wome.html.

State Ministry for National Development Planning. "National Action Plan for Disaster Risk Reduction 2010–2012." www.bnpb.go.id/uploads/pubs/451.pdf.

Stevenson, David. *Cataclysm: The First World War as Political Tragedy.* New York: Basic Books, 2004.

Stewart, Scott. "The Dirty Work of Russian Assassins." *Stratfor Worldview*, September 14, 2017. https://worldview.stratfor.com/article/dirty-work-russian-assassins.

Suhrke, Astri. "Human Security and the Interests of States." *Security Dialogue* 30, No. 3 (1999): 265–76.

Suskind, Ron. *One Percent Doctrine: Deep Inside America's Pursuit of Its Enemies since 9/11.* New York: Simon and Schuster, 2006.

The Way of the World: A Story of Truth and Hope in an Age of Extremism. New York: HarperCollins, 2008.

Tagliabue, John. "Europe Decides Air-Conditioning Is Not So Evil." *New York Times*, August 13, 2003. www.nytimes.com/2003/08/13/business/europe-decides-air-con ditioning-is-not-so-evil.html.

Takeda, Margaret B., and Marilyn M. Helms. "'Bureaucracy, Meet Catastrophe.' Analysis of Hurricane Katrina Relief Efforts and Their Implications for Emergency Response Governance." *International Journal of Public Sector Management* 19, No. 4 (2006): 397–411.

Taleb, Nassim Nicholas. *The Black Swan*. New York: Random House, 2007.

Telegraph. "Volcanic Ash: Ryanair Boss Michael O'Leary in Withering Attack on Met Office." June 1, 2010. www.telegraph.co.uk/travel/travelnews/7794331/Volcanic-ash-Ryanair-boss-Michael-OLeary-in-withering-attack-on-Met-Office.html.

Tilly, Charles. "War Making and State Making as Organized Crime." In *Bringing the State Back In*, edited by Peter Evans, Dietrich Rueschemeyer, and Theda Skocpol, 169–91. Cambridge: Cambridge University Press, 1985.

Toumey, Chris. "Science Policy in the Days of Trump." *Nature Nanotechnology* 12, No. 10 (2017): 934–35.

Trenberth, Kevin E., Lijing Cheng, Peter Jacobs, Yongxin Zhang, and John Fasullo. "Hurricane Harvey Links to Ocean Heat Content and Climate Change Adaptation." *Earth's Future*, May 9, 2018). https://agupubs.onlinelibrary.wiley.com/doi/10.1029/2018EF000825.

Trenberth, Kevin E., John T. Fasullo, and Jeffrey Kiehl. "Earth's Global Energy Budget." American Meteorological Society (March 2009).

Tretkoff, Ernie. "Legislation Seeks to Protect Power Grid from Space Weather." *Space Weather* 8, No. 5 (2010): Article 589.

Trevithick, Joseph. "Firestorm: Forest Fires as a Weapon in Vietnam." *Armchair General*, June 13, 2012. http://armchairgeneral.com/firestorm-forest-fires-as-a-weapon-in-vietnam.htm.

Tullock, Gordon. *The Politics of Bureaucracy*. New York: Public Affairs Press, 1965.

Turco, Richard P., Owen B. Toon, Thomas P. Ackerman, James B. Pollack, and Carl Sagan. "Nuclear Winter: Global Consequences of Multiple Nuclear Explosions." *Science* 222, No. 4630 (1983): 1283–92.

Turner, Graham M. "A Comparison of the Limits to Growth with 30 Years of Reality." *Global Environmental Change* 18, No. 3 (2008): 397–411.

Tversky, Amos, and Daniel Kahneman. "The Framing of Decisions and the Psychology of Choice." *Science* 211, No. 4481 (1981): 453–58.

Udall, Bradley, and Jonathan Overpeck. "The Twenty-First Century Colorado River Hot Drought and Implications for the Future." *Water Resources Research* 53, No. 3 (2017): 2404–18.

UK Ministry of Defence. *Adaptability and Partnership: Issues for the Strategic Defence Review*. London: MOD, 2010.

Ullman, Richard. "Redefining Security." *International Security* 8, No. 1 (1983): 129–53.

Uscinski, Joseph, Casey Klofstad, and Matthew D. Atkinson. "What Drives Conspiratorial Beliefs? The Role of Informational Cues and Predispositions." *Political Research Quarterly* 69, No. 1 (2016): 57–71.

US Department of Defense. "National Security Implications of Climate-Related Risks and a Changing Climate." OSD report to the Senate Appropriations Committee, July 23, 2015. www.defense.gov/pubs/150724-Congressional-Report-on-National-Implications-of-Climate-Change.pdf.

US Department of Homeland Security. "The Strategic National Risk Assessment in Support of PPD 8: A Comprehensive Risk-Based Approach toward a Secure and Resilient Nation." December 2011. www.dhs.gov/xlibrary/assets/rma-strategic-national-risk-assessment-ppd8.pdf.

US House of Representatives Committee on Science, Space, and Technology. "Russian Attempts to Influence US Domestic Energy Markets by Exploiting Social Media." March 1, 2018. https://science.house.gov/sites/republicans.science.house.gov/files/documents/SST%20Staff%20Report%20-%20Russian%20Attempts%20to%20Influence%20U.S.%20Domestic%20Energy%20Markets%20by%20Exploiting%20Social%20Media%2003.01.18.pdf.

US International Trade Administration. "Peru Country Commercial Guide: Agricultural Sectors." September 22, 2017. www.export.gov/article?id=Peru-Agricultural-Sectors.

US NOAA. "Extremely Active 2017 Atlantic Hurricane Season Finally Ends." November 30, 2017. www.noaa.gov/media-release/extremely-active-2017-atlantic-hurricane-season-finally-ends.

US Pacific Command. "PH, US Concluded Participation in Tempest Express-27 Multinational Staff Planning Workshop." PACOM press release, August 5, 2015. www.pacom.mil/Media/News/Article/612322/ph-us-concluded-participation-in-tempest-express-27-multinational-staff-plannin/.

Valdes, Paul. "Built for Stability." *Nature Geoscience* 4 (2011): 414–16.

Varum, Celeste Amorim, and Carla Melo. "Directions in Scenario Planning Literature – A Review of the Past Decades." *Futures* 42, No. 4 (2010): 355–69.

Verchick, Robert R. M. "Risk, Fairness, and the Geography of Disaster." *Issues in Legal Scholarship* 6, No. 3 (2007).

Vivekananda, Janani. "How Are Climate Change and Human Security Interrelated?" In *Implications of Climate Change and Disasters on Military Activities*, edited by Orlin Nikolov and Swathi Veeravalli, 87–90. Dordrecht, Netherlands: Springer, 2017.

Volkle, Hansruedi. "A Brief History of Nuclear Disasters: Prevention, Consequences and Re-coverage." *Planet@Risk* 2, No. 3 (2015): 1–4.

Vuille, Mathias, Bernard Francou, Patrick Wagnon, Irmgard Juen, Georg Kaser, Bryan G. Mark, and Raymond S. Bradley. "Climate Change and Tropical Andean Glaciers: Past, Present and Future." *Earth-Science Reviews* 89, No. 3–4 (2008): 79–96.

Wachinger, Gisela, Ortwin Renn, Chloe Begg, and Christian Kuhlicke. "The Risk Perception Paradox – Implications for Governance and Communication of Natural Hazards." *Risk Analysis* 33, No. 6 (2013): 1049–65.

Wack, Pierre. "Scenarios: 'Shooting the Rapids.'" *Harvard Business Review* 63, No. 6 (1985): 139–50.

"Scenarios: Uncharted Waters Ahead." Harvard Business Review 63, No. 5 (1985): 73–89.

Wagner, T., M. Themeßl, A. Schuppel, H. Gobiet, H. Stigler, and S. Birk. "Impacts of Climate Change on Stream Flow and Hydro Power Generation in the Alpine Region." *Environmental Earth Sciences* 76, No. 4 (2017): 1–22.

Walt, Stephen M. "The Renaissance of Security Studies." *International Studies Quarterly* 35, No. 2 (1991): 211–39.

Walter, Katey M., S. A. Zimov, J. P. Chanton, David Verbyla, and F. Stuart Chapin III. "Methane Bubbling from Siberian Thaw Lakes as a Positive Feedback to Climate Warming." *Nature* 443, No. 7107 (2006): 71–75.

Ward, Thomas. "Victory by Duress: Civilian Infrastructure as a Target in Air Campaigns." *Security Studies* 15, No. 1 (2006): 1–33.

Watson, Scott. "The 'Human' as Referent Object? Humanitarianism as Securitization." *Security Dialogue* 42, No. 1 (2011): 3–20.

Watts, Jonathan. "Underwater Melting of Antarctic Ice Far Greater than Thought, Study Finds." *Guardian*, April 2, 2018. www.theguardian.com/environment/2018/apr/02/underwater-melting-of-antarctic-ice-far-greater-than-thought-study-finds.

Weart, Spencer R. *The Discovery of Global Warming*. Cambridge, MA: Harvard University Press, 2008.

Weather Network. "Canada in 2030: Frequent, More Intense Wildfires a Reality." August 11, 2018. www.theweathernetwork.com/news/articles/canada-in-2030-alberta-british-columbia-wildfires-heatwave-drought-lightning-climate-change/108193.

Weber, Bodo. "The EU-Turkey Refugee Deal and the Not Quite Closed Balkan Route." Friedrich Ebert Stiftung, Dialogue Southeast Europe, June 2017.

Week. "The Military's $20 Billion Air Conditioning Bill: By the Numbers." June 18, 2011. http://theweek.com/articles/483608/militarys-20-billion-air-conditioning-bill-by-numbers.

Weinstein, Adam, and William M. Arkin. "The U.S. Is Going to War Tomorrow at This Fancy Pacific Beach Resort." *Gawker*, April 1, 2015. http://phasezero.gawker.com/the-u-s-is-going-to-war-tomorrow-at-this-fancy-pacific-1691769286.

Weiss, Harvey. "Late Third Millennium Abrupt Climate Change and Social Collapse in West Asia and Egypt." In *Third Millennium BC Climate Change and Old World Collapse*, edited by H. Nuzhet Dalfes, George Kukla, and Harvey Weiss, 711–23. Berlin: Springer, 1997.

Wertheim Tuchman, Barbara. *The Guns of August*. New York: Ballantine Books, 1962.

Whyte, Chelsea. "Ancient Andes Glaciers Have Lost Half Their Ice in Just 40 Years." *New Scientist*, October 10, 2016. www.newscientist.com/article/2108455-ancient-andes-glaciers-have-lost-half-their-ice-in-just-40-years/.

Wilkie, Robert. "Hybrid Warfare Something Old, Not Something New." *Air and Space Power Journal* 23, No. 4 (2009): 13–18.

Wilson, Ian. "From Scenario Thinking to Strategic Action." *Technological Forecasting and Social Change* 65, No. 1 (2000): 23–29.

Wintjes, Jorit. "Europe's Earliest Kriegsspiel? Book Seven of Reinhard Graf zu Solms' Kriegsregierung and the 'Prehistory' of Professional War Gaming." *British Journal for Military History* 2, No. 1 (2015): 15–33.

Winton, Michael. "Amplified Arctic Climate Change: What Does Surface Albedo Feedback Have to Do with It?" *Geophysical Research Letters* 33, No. 3 (2006): L03701.

Winzer, Christian. "Conceptualizing Energy Security." *Energy Policy* 46 (2012): 36–48.

Wither, James K. "Making Sense of Hybrid Warfare." *Connections* 15, No. 2 (2016): 73–87.

Wolfberg, Adrian. "Full-Spectrum Analysis: A New Way of Thinking for a New World." *Military Review* 86, No. 4 (2006): 35–42.

Wong, Alia. "Pandemonium and Rage in Hawaii: A False Alert of an Impending Missile Attack Highlights Just How Unprepared the Country Is for Nuclear Disaster." *Atlantic*, January 14, 2018. www.theatlantic.com/international/archive/2018/01/pandemonium-and-rage-in-hawaii/550529/.

Woodhouse, Tom. "The Gentle Hand of Peace? British Peacekeeping and Conflict Resolution in Complex Political Emergencies." *International Peacekeeping* 6, No. 2 (1999): 24–37.

Yale Environment 360. "Trump Removes Climate Change as Threat to US in New Security Strategy." *Yale School of Forestry and Environmental Studies* 18 (December 2017). https://e360.yale.edu/digest/trump-removes-climate-change-as-threat-to-u-s-in-new-security-strategy.

Yang, Shilun L., Jianbo Zhang, and X. J. Xu. "Influence of the Three Gorges Dam on Downstream Delivery of Sediment and Its Environmental Implications, Yangtze River." *Geophysical Research Letters* 34, No. 10 (2007): L10401.

Yergin, Daniel. "Ensuring Energy Security." *Foreign Affairs* 85, No. 2 (2006): 69–82.

Zanchettin, Davide, Oliver Bothe, Hans F. Graf, Stephan J. Lorenz, Juerg Luterbacher, Claudia Timmreck, and Johann H. Jungclaus. "Background Conditions Influence the Decadal Climate Response to Strong Volcanic Eruptions." *Journal of Geophysical Research: Atmospheres* 118, No. 10 (2013): 4090–106.

Zehr, Stephen C. "Public Representations of Scientific Uncertainty about Global Climate Change." *Public Understanding of Science* 9, No. 2 (2016): 85–103.

Zetter, Kim. "Inside the Cunning, Unprecedented Hack of Ukraine's Power Grid." *Wired*, March 3, 2016. www.wired.com/2016/03/inside-cunning-unprecedented-hack-ukraines-power-grid/.

Zhang, Sarah. "Looking Back at Canada's Political Fight over Science." *Atlantic*, January 26, 2017. www.theatlantic.com/science/archive/2017/01/canada-war-on-science/514322/.

Index